BETTING THE LINE

BETTING
THE LINE

Sports Wagering in American Life

Richard O. Davies AND *Richard G. Abram*

THE OHIO STATE UNIVERSITY PRESS
Columbus

Library of Congress Cataloging-in-Publication Data

Davies, Richard O., 1937–
Betting the line : sports wagering in American life / Richard O. Davies
and Richard G. Abram
p.   cm.
Includes bibliographical references (p.   ) and index.
ISBN 0-8142-0880-0 (alk. paper) — ISBN 0-8142-5078-5 (pbk. : alk. paper)
1. Sports betting—United States—History.   2. Sports—Corrupt
practices—United States—History   I. Abram, Richard G.   II. Title.
GV717 .D38   2001
796—dc21
2001000771

Text and jacket design by Gary Gore.
Type set in Electra by BookComp, Inc.
Printed by Thomson-Shore, Inc.

Sports gambling is a vast commercialized and heavily capitalized outlaw business.

—Christian Century, 1930

One thing I do for entertainment is gamble a little. Win or lose, a bet steps up my pulse and I like it. There is nothing morally wrong with gambling and everybody ought to have the right to bet.

—Jimmy Breslin, 1963

Sports gambling is a crime, a crime with victims. It also potentially affects the integrity of the game.

—William Saum, 1999

Betting on games is fun. It's challenging and entertaining. And there's no reason to be defensive about something that brings enjoyment to so many.

—Mort Olshan, 1999

People bet for a lot of different reasons. Some of them are trying to predict and influence the future. Some of them are trying to show that they're smarter than everybody else. Gambling is the ultimate ego trip. People very rarely bet just to win money.

—anonymous bookie, 1977

Contents

Acknowledgments

This book has benefited from the assistance of the University of Nevada Foundation which provided funding for research assistance through its University Foundation Professorship program. We have benefited greatly from the research assistance of Dee Kille, a doctoral student in American History, and Lori Anderson, an honors student in English education. Without their assistance this book would not have been completed on schedule. The quality of the final product was substantially improved by the diligent and perceptive editing of the manuscript by Ruth Melville, managing editor of the Ohio State University Press. We also express our deep appreciation to our wives, Sharon Davies and Fran Abram, for their understanding and support as we worked through the time-consuming stages of researching and writing this book.

Introduction

The historian John Findlay got it right when he identified Americans as a "people of chance." "From the seventeenth century through the twentieth," he writes, "both gambling and [the westward movement] thrived on high expectations, risk taking, opportunism, and movement, and both activities helped to shape a distinctive culture."[1] Despite the dim views taken of gambling within certain religious and social reform circles, it has been an integral and often unappreciated force in the development of American life and popular culture. American capitalism thrived on speculation, risk taking, and shrewd calculations of an investment's potential, but when these same traits were displayed at the racetrack or card table, many moralists were quick to condemn gamblers as slick thieves whose success made a mockery of such important values as the work ethic, thrift, and caution. As the historian Ann Fabian explains, a profound "moral confusion has plagued the whole long history of gambling in the United States."[2]

Although ambiguity about its role remains in some sectors of American society, gambling has overcome its once sinister image and the staunch opposition of antigambling organizations to become an integral part of the popular culture. By the end of the twentieth century major forms of gambling existed in forty-eight of the fifty states; only Hawaii and Utah did not offer some form of legally sanctioned gambling. Gambling is undoubtedly the biggest single industry in the United States, in terms of both revenues generated and the number of customers/participants. In the year 2000 an estimated 125 million Americans gambled at least once, putting some $2 trillion dollars into play. In 1999 even the resolute majority of social conservatives on the congressionally mandated National Gambling Impact Study Commission understood that prohibition or repeal of mainstream gambling was no longer politically feasible. They recognized that they had to content themselves with nibbling around the margins. "Once exotic, gambling has quickly taken its place in mainstream culture," the commission explained. "Televised megabucks drawings; senior citizens day trips to nearby casinos; and the transformation of Las Vegas into family friendly theme resorts, in which gambling is but one of a menu of attractions, have become familiar backdrops to daily life."[3]

Although gambling has become an accepted part of everyday American life, the "moral confusion" that Fabian describes nonetheless remains, and it is especially evident in the continuing and contentious debate over the issue of sports betting. No one knows for certain how many Americans bet on sports, but it is estimated that about 25 percent of adult Americans make at least one bet on a sporting event each year—often by participating in modest office pools on the NCAA basketball tournament or the Super Bowl—while an estimated 15 million persons bet regularly and often heavily on football, baseball, basketball, prizefights, and horse races. Legal horse racing exists in thirty states, but other sports wagering is illegal in forty-nine of the fifty states.[4] In the year 2000 only the maverick state of Nevada offered a full range of legal gambling opportunities on sporting events.

Horse racing, long a popular part of state tax collectors' portfolios, remains an important but slowly declining pastime for an aging group of dedicated horse players. Wagering on human sports, however, has become the primary focus of a new generation of sports gamblers, and it is the primary focus of this book. Although sports wagering has grown from an estimated $20 billion wagered in 1975 to an estimated $80 billion in 1990, and upward to $200 billion in the year 2000, lawmakers in state capitals have been exceedingly reluctant to cut themselves in for a piece of the sports gambling action, although they have not hesitated to do so with pari-mutuel horse racing, million-dollar lotteries, bingo parlors, card rooms, and riverboat casinos.

The reasons for this anomaly are deeply embedded in the nation's past. Sports wagering has long existed in the subterranean corridors of American life— illegal, condemned by reformers and concerned sports officials, but popular with substantial segments of the male population. Bookmakers have plied their illegal trade in urban places since the middle of the nineteenth century, making their peace with law enforcement and political bosses through a wide range of creative financial incentives. Although from time to time zealous reformers instigated crackdowns, the reform impulse would inevitably fade, and the bookmakers and their faithful clients would resume business as usual. By the late twentieth century, sports gambling had become so much a part of American life that it was generally ignored by law enforcement authorities. Sports gambling is and will undoubtedly remain for the foreseeable future one of the largest untapped sources of potential tax revenue in the nation.

Wagering is an important part of—some would say the driving force be-hind—the enormous popularity of sports in contemporary American society.

It comes in many and often seemingly innocent forms: the five-dollar office pool on the NCAA basketball tournament or the World Series, a two-dollar Nassau bet among friends on the golf course, the weekly meeting of the Fantasy Football League, a casual day at the aging county fairgrounds watching the pacers and trotters go around the timeless oval, putting ten bucks down on a six-team college football parlay card with the bartender at the neighborhood tavern, or even making a twenty-dollar futures bet on the distant Super Bowl while visiting family-friendly Las Vegas during summer vacation.

Despite its central role in the growth of sports in twentieth-century America, gambling has been treated casually, if not with downright indifference, by most sports historians. The reluctance of historians to delve into the complex topic of sports gambling—and sports history more generally—is readily understandable. For one thing, sports are often looked down upon by university faculty members as unnecessary and even corrupt appendages to the American system of higher education. Not interested themselves in team sports, and perhaps engaging in a bit of academic snobbery, they certainly do not want to make sports a part of their professional work. We find it intriguing that social historians, who have so often proclaimed their appreciation of the lives led by average citizens— the noble "common people"—have so overwhelmingly refused to examine the significance of sports history. No society has ever evidenced such a level of interest in sports as the United States. Certainly, there is no society in the history of mankind in which sports have generated larger amounts of revenue. Yet, with a few exceptions, social historians have refused to incorporate into their classes and writings a subject in which ordinary Americans are deeply involved. It is our contention that, beyond the rather narrow realm of sports history, gambling on athletic contests holds much broader significance for the student of American history and popular culture, providing powerful insights into such larger issues as gender roles, class structure, ethnicity, modernization, local and national politics, and economic enterprise. At the very least, the subject deserves a larger place in the discourse of the rapidly increasing number of academic historians of sports.

This is essentially an exploratory work that seeks to focus attention on the role of sports gambling in American life. Although we examine the formative years of the phenomenon, our emphasis is on the period of rapid growth that began with the "golden age" of spectator sports during the 1920s and accelerated during the second half of the century. John Findlay's pioneering study of gambling in the United States emphasized the formative role of the frontier and the American West. Although some forms of sports gambling can be traced to the colonial era and to the western frontier of the nineteenth century, the roots of modern

sports gambling are to be found largely in the industrial cities of the post–
Civil War period. Sports wagering in the United States has been and remains
essentially an urban phenomenon. It is our contention, however, that sports
wagering took on a distinctly new form in the years immediately following the
Second World War. Like many other aspects of American life—such as civil
rights, the economy, feminism, suburban life, communications, public education, mass entertainment—the structure of organized sports was fundamentally
transformed by the powerful and galvanizing forces unleashed by the Second
World War. Not only did organized sports in America grow exponentially in size
and scope in the postwar era, but they were also fundamentally altered by new
social and economic forces, including increased leisure time, a large increase in
disposable income, changing demographic patterns that extended professional
leagues to all points of the national compass, and fundamental changes in public
values that came to view commercialized gaming as an acceptable form of
leisure activity.

Television, however, was the primary force propelling sports wagering into
a multibillion dollar industry during the latter half of the twentieth century.
During the 1950s, network television programming created a much larger sports-
viewing audience, generating high ratings for its coverage of baseball, football,
basketball, and boxing. Television became, in a very real sense, an electronic
form of *The Racing Form*, providing gamblers with enormous amounts of
information regarding future wagers. Many sports fans discovered that if they
had a bet down on a game being shown on television their viewing pleasure was
intensified.[5] The rapid expansion of cable television in the early 1980s produced
a seemingly insatiable demand for sports programming, which in turn stimulated
additional interest in sports betting.

The growth of organized sports during the age of television has been stag-
gering. Major League Baseball, constricted to the northeastern quadrant of the
nation and just eleven cities in 1950, grew to thirty teams by century's end. The
National Hockey League is no longer the small private bailiwick of a handful
of Canadian and northern American cities; the league now has franchises in
such unlikely sunbelt cities as Miami, Dallas, Tampa–St. Petersburg, Nashville,
Charlotte, Phoenix, and Los Angeles. But the greatest professional sports success
story has been the National Football League, growing from a struggling eight-
team league in 1945 to the thirty-two franchise multibillion dollar dynamo of
today. In terms of fan interest and television ratings, it is now the unrivaled
American game.

The NFL has become the intense focus of a new and more sophisticated
generation of sports gamblers who for six months of the year closely follow

the ebb and flow of computer-generated national betting lines published in daily newspapers, tune into an endless parade of radio talk shows that seek to provide a "bettor's edge" on upcoming games, watch cable television shows devoted exclusively to football handicapping, and subscribe to Internet tout services that sell their "releases" to an estimated two million subscribers each week. Nonetheless, professional football authorities will never publicly admit the obvious: that one of the most powerful forces propelling their product to the heights of fan popularity is that professional football offers an ideal format for sports wagering.

College sports also benefited financially from this technological and commercial revolution. Where college football teams played nine-game seasons in 1950 with only a lucky handful of teams being invited to New Year's Day bowl games, by the year 2000 Division I-A teams routinely played eleven-game schedules—and sometimes an extra twelfth game thanks to preseason kickoff games, postseason conference playoffs, and trips to Hawaii—and twenty-five postseason bowl games. Division I-A college teams now play seasons that begin in early August with three weeks of preseason practice and do not end until five months later. Incredibly, the college football season starts weeks before the fall semester begins and ends after final exams are completed. Nearly all of these games are televised, either by one of several competing networks or by local stations, and thanks to the efforts of Nevada sports books, the national media, and an estimated 250,000 hustling illegal bookies in the other forty-nine states, they are the vehicle whereby untold hundreds of millions of dollars change hands between gamblers and bookmakers each week. College football coaches, a beleaguered if well-paid group of professionals, are often given to lamenting that, because of the popularity of betting by alumni and boosters, they are expected not only to win games but to beat the point spread in the process.

College basketball has been similarly influenced by television and the intense interest of gamblers. The introduction of the point spread idea at the end of the Second World War fundamentally changed the way in which gamblers bet on college basketball games: instead of taking odds on one team, they now bet on the number of points separating the two teams at the final buzzer. Introduction of the point spread in the mid-1940s had the effect of making every game a handicapping challenge to the gambler; it also created major problems for college officials. Some players, eager to earn spending money, became vulnerable to gamblers who, seeking a sure thing, offered them a modest payoff in return for winning a game by a margin less than the betting point spread. Because a basketball game, with only five players per team and a more unstructured form of play, is much less complex than football, it became the game of choice for unscrupulous gamblers/fixers during the postwar era. The point spread idea greatly increased the potential for fixed games.

The most famous fix of all occurred in 1919 when eight members of the Chicago White Sox lost the World Series to the underdog Cincinnati Reds for a payoff of about $10,000 each. However, athletes on the take had been a significant, if largely ignored, part of the American sports scene long before the Black Sox Scandal, and they haven't disappeared yet. For the next eighty years gambling became the bane of professional and college sports officials as nasty headlines repeatedly proclaimed the latest scandal. Although many antigambling safeguards have been put in place, it seems that unscrupulous gamblers seeking the sure thing have found ways to circumvent the best of preventative measures.

Fear of such misdeeds has caused sports gambling, of all the gambling venues, to be singled out for special treatment. In 2000 sports gambling was theoretically legal in four states—Nevada, South Dakota, New Jersey, and Oregon—but in reality it existed only in Nevada. Although it has been legal in the Silver State since 1931, sports wagering didn't become an important part of the Nevada casino scene until the 1980s, as a result of changed federal tax laws and the increased popularity of college and professional sports. In 1999 the National Gambling Impact Study Commission, a nine-person federal commission created in response to strong antigambling pressure from the socially conservative political establishment, disappointed its fervent supporters by submitting a bland and relatively benign final report that essentially suggested there were both good and bad features to the recently developed national gambling culture of state lotteries, Indian casinos, state-licensed casinos, riverboat casinos, and the proliferation of video poker and slot machines in several states. Only one form of gambling was singled out by the commission for criticism: legalized sports gambling in the state of Nevada. The commission's recommendation to make wagering on college games illegal nationwide was in part a response to the lobbying efforts of the National Collegiate Athletic Association, but in a broader context it was based upon a widespread uneasiness among the general public regarding sports gambling. The irony of this development is that sports wagering in Nevada's legal books is the only casino gaming venue in which management does not have a built-in statistical advantage over the customer. Sports books can and do lose money, although the general ignorance of the betting public and the vagaries of Lady Luck have given the Nevada books a reasonable 4 percent take (before overhead) for the last twenty years. In 1999 the state's seventy-five sports books cleared a profit of about $100 million out of $2.5 billion wagered—small potatoes in the larger scheme of things for the bottom line–conscious corporate casino establishment that now controls Nevada's casinos.

As we were conducting research for this book it became increasingly evident that the topic poses serious and often frustrating challenges. There is little in the published academic historical literature that explores the major topics presented in the pages that follow, although many writers have nibbled around the edges of the subject. One traditional form of historical documentation is missing from our bibliography: the private papers of participants. For obvious reasons, bookies operating outside the law have been reluctant to keep records and files of their business transactions beyond the weekly settlement day, for fear that they might fall into the hands of law enforcement officials. We know of no bookie or professional gambler who has deposited his collected papers in a historical society's manuscript collection. Even sophisticated professional sports gamblers in Nevada—the so-called wise guys—are reluctant to consent to interviews for fear of somehow being exposed to the Internal Revenue Service or other federal authorities; many old-timers harbor deep resentments about treatment they've received from the authorities in other states. Although we were fortunate to obtain the cooperation of several prominent handicappers, we were also refused by many others. For whatever reason, most professional gamblers prefer their anonymity. Consequently, our research has had to rely on other sources. Although there is a dearth of scholarly treatment of sports gambling issues, there is a seemingly inexhaustible amount of information scattered throughout newspapers, magazines, memoirs, books, government documents, and how-to-beat-the-bookies manuals. Our major problem has been to sift through this enormous body of eclectic material to cull the information essential to the writing of a serious study.

Finally, we make this observation to those optimistic folk who look upon sports gambling as an easy and painless way to increase their personal wealth: although there are individuals who make money betting on sports over the long haul, they are relatively few in number. Even the most successful of professional sports gamblers will affirm that they can seldom win 60 percent of their sports wagers over a full season, and that they often lose money when their luck turns sour. Because the standard bet with any modern bookmaker, whether in a Nevada book or on a New York City street corner, requires the wagering of $11 to win $10, the bettor has to win 52.38 percent on all monies bet simply to break even. This seemingly small percentage—which one of the most famous and most successful of sports handicappers, Lem Banker, calls "the implacable reality of eleven-to-ten"—is what does in many an overconfident gambler.[6]

The prospective gambler needs to appreciate that the great majority of successful professionals in the field are the ones on the favorable side of eleven-to-ten: the ones setting odds and booking bets, not making them. Our research, especially our interviews with successful professionals, confirms that the goal of consistently outsmarting the modern computer-assisted handicappers who set professional betting lines is an almost impossible task for the amateur. Las Vegas Stardust sports book manager Scotty Schettler matter-of-factly told a journalist in 1986 that, given the opportunity, "We will get your money. Gamblers always find a way to screw it up. That's the way they are."[7] Picking more winners than losers is often too great a challenge even for the most talented and experienced of handicappers. As Lem Banker, reflecting on a half century spent attempting to beat the line, put it, "You have a better chance of becoming a rock star than becoming a [successful] professional gambler."[8] Thus, the most persuasive argument we have come up with against the practice of sports gambling—which for some reason is seldom mentioned by its determined opponents—is simply this: the great majority of players regularly and consistently lose money.

1

A People of Chance

Gambling was an important part of everyday life in colonial America. There was even gambling in seventeenth-century Massachusetts and its less populated neighboring colonies, although it was generally restricted within fairly narrow boundaries thanks to the powerful influence of Puritanism, which viewed such activity as dangerous to the participant and even more damaging to the public weal. Further to the south, however, a different culture emerged in which leisure activities, including gambling, flourished. In fact, the Virginia Company was funded in part by an English lottery, and its frontier environment proved conducive to dice and card games.[1]

The Puritan ethic never established a dominant presence in the colonies from Maryland southward. Rather, a more tolerant culture developed there that held up as the social ideal the life of the English country gentry. Especially in Virginia, where a prevailing leisure ethic placed high social importance upon strenuous dedication to the good life, gambling flourished from the outset, with wagering on horse races, cockfights, and bare-knuckle prizefights commonplace by the end of the seventeenth century. These pastimes were invariably accompanied by the consumption of alcoholic beverages. Serious card and dice games were routine among all classes. Although organized sports as we know them today were not a part of colonial American society, the practice of making a friendly (or sometimes not so friendly) wager was widespread. In Virginia, but also in the heartland of Puritanism, colonial and local governments—even churches—regularly raised funds through lotteries. Thus when thirty-seven states instituted lotteries in the latter part of the twentieth century as a means of increasing revenue without raising taxes, they were (most likely unbeknownst to their political sponsors), in a real sense, returning to America's historical roots.[2]

In general the English colonists, with the notable exception of the Puritans, attempted to replicate the life they had known in Merry England. Gambling had been widespread there for centuries, and although many colonists came to America from other northwest European countries, it was a transplanted English culture that constituted the dominant social force. The English, especially the rural gentry, had made sports an important part of their lifestyle. Lawn bowling, tennis, quoits, and a primitive form of cricket were common throughout Elizabethan England. Life in the countryside, especially among the landed aristocracy, revolved around the horse. Leading citizens of rural England enjoyed racing their best horses against those put forward by their neighbors. Like racing, hunting on horseback, including riding to the hounds in quest of the wary fox, became much more than a mere hunt—it was the basis for social interaction, including extravagant parties and receptions. The aristocratic classes also enjoyed cockfights, bearbaiting, dog fighting, and, with the spread of firearms, fowling and other forms of hunting. These activities were accompanied by extensive wagering.[3]

The common folk of England were encouraged to enliven their tedious and hardworking existences by the playing of games. Such sports as a crude (and often dangerous) form of football, human races, wrestling, and cudgeling were popular. The rules of these contests were subject to innumerable local variations, and their enforcement led to many an argument, perhaps culminating in a raucous brawl. This was especially true of the game of hurling (similar to modern lacrosse, played with a small ball with each player armed with a broad-blade wooden stick). Hurling amounted to little more than organized mayhem, sometimes with the young males of entire towns being pitted against those of a nearby rival community. The goal was to advance a ball across the opposition's line by any manner of stealth or force; in the nineteenth century hurling evolved into the English game of rugby. Such games, often played on holidays or the Sabbath, involved entire communities and were usually followed by a large feast (if not a donnybrook), washed down with plenty of beer, rum, and other spirits. Naturally, wagers were an integral part of the day's events.[4]

During the first half of the seventeenth century, the English Crown encouraged such games. For one thing, the manly and often violent sports of hurling and wrestling were viewed as giving community expression to the masculine ideal of self-defense, strength, and dominance. These sports may have led to broken bones, concussions, and even deaths, but they were also viewed as a way to train Englishmen for battle. The close relationship of violent games, the cult of masculinity, and national defense was well understood. Similarly, for the upper classes, games involving horses were understood to be proper training for military service. The Crown under James I (1603–25) also saw these activities as a means of warding off the growing influence of his major political rivals—the Puritans. This expanding group of serious-minded middle-class Englishmen was appalled by the licentiousness and bawdiness that accompanied the games. The Puritans viewed wild sporting events, often intensified by the heavy consumption of alcohol, as a desecration of God's Kingdom, especially if played on the Sabbath. Sundays, they believed, should be reserved for prayer, contemplation, and church attendance. Beyond question, the playing of games—inevitably accompanied by drunkenness and gambling—detracted from the solemnity of the Sabbath. They also saw wasting time on games as impeding their building of a modern capitalist economy.[5]

Although the Puritans did not oppose all games, they did seek to enforce a rigid adherence to the sanctity of the Sabbath. (This emphasis on the solemn observance of the Sabbath would be part of the debate over organized sports in the United States well into the twentieth century.) England's Puritan leaders also believed that the playing of vigorous games tended to lead the working classes away from a life of hard work and piety and into violent and bawdy pastimes. To the rising group of urban businessmen flocking to the Puritan banner, such games as hurling, cockfighting, and horse racing were visible signs of the licentiousness and sinfulness that they wanted to extirpate from English life. Although the divisions within English society were complex, this struggle often boiled down to one between the carefree country gentry and the determined rising business classes concentrated in the urban areas.[6]

The large group of Puritans who descended upon the shores of New England after 1630 brought these values and tensions with them. Throughout the seventeenth century the theocracy they sought to establish took a dim view of any form of unbridled recreation that stimulated excessive drinking, gambling, and sexual activities. But although the leaders of the Puritan theocracy viewed most games as an unhealthy diversion from work, there never was a complete ban on sporting events. Properly conducted, the theocratic leaders conceded, sporting events and games could provide a form of tonic to restore the energy of a worker so that he could return to his fields or shop reinvigorated. Hence the Puritans encouraged such social events as quilting and husking bees, hunting and fishing, and for the youngsters the game of rounders (an English game played with a stick and ball, an early precursor of baseball). And the elders showed a surprising tolerance toward such games as skittles, billiards, and shuttlecock if played within the home and not in public places. Even dancing and cardplaying, if properly conducted beyond public view and not taken to excess, were acceptable forms of behavior.[7]

"All things in moderation" is perhaps the best way to describe the attitude of the Puritans toward games. Drinking was acceptable if it did not lead to idleness and drunkenness; wrestling matches, human races, and even fencing were acceptable if they did not produce violence and were conducted by the rules of fair play. However, if such pastimes led to a violation of the sanctity of the Sabbath or religious holidays, or to antisocial behavior, then the violators were subject to severe punishment. Even some forms of gambling were acceptable if not done in excess. However, if an individual should become obsessed with gambling and view it, rather than honest work, as a means of earning money, then it was considered a sin. Puritan governments and churches themselves conducted lotteries as a means of raising revenues. The holding of lotteries to fund schools or special community projects was especially encouraged.[8]

But in general the Puritans viewed gambling as a potential pitfall into which a wavering citizen might plunge. If gambling—the playing of cards or backgammon, or wagering on a horse race—led to a diminution of the work ethic, then it was rife with potential dangers. The Puritan view of gambling took firm root in colonial America, and the values expressed in seventeenth- and eighteenth-century New England would enjoy great longevity. The arguments employed against gambling in twentieth-century America by various religious and reform organizations were surprisingly similar to those of the colonial Puritans.[9]

In the southern colony of Virginia, however, no holds were barred when it came to the vigorous pursuit of pleasure. The lower classes could play games and gamble at the many taverns that dotted the rural landscape. A frustrated clergyman complained in 1751 that taverns had become the places of "rendezvous of the very dregs of the people . . . where not only time and money are vainly and unprofitably squandered away, but (and is yet worse) where prohibited and unlawful games, sports, and pastimes are used, followed and practiced, almost without intermission, namely cards, dice, horse-racing, and cock-fighting, together with vices and enormities of every other kind."[10]

It was the upper classes in colonial Virginia, however, that gave public sanction to the importance of sports and wagering. Affluent town merchants and the slave-owning plantation aristocrats vigorously sought to emulate the life of the English country gentry, building lavish homes and entertaining extensively. Substantial sums changed hands over games of dice and cards or after races between prize quarter horses owned by prominent gentlemen. Such races provided justification not only for a day of drinking and feasting but also for the making of serious bets. The southern aristocracy worked hard at playing and gambling; lawn bowling, boat racing, and a primitive form of cricket were popular, and rumors about the exchange of large sums of money over cards and dice were commonplace.[11]

Among the most affluent a passion for thoroughbred horses spread in the latter years of the eighteenth century. Across Virginia, Maryland, and the Carolinas new oval tracks replaced the quarter-mile dash down a dusty country road. The thoroughbreds raced for distances of a mile or more, and the oval tracks gave all spectators a good view of the race, not just those few who congregated at the finish line of a road race. As social historians have noted, the social lines and distinctions in the South were carefully drawn: gentlemen owned horses and bet on races, the lower classes flocked to bare-knuckle prizefights, cockfights, and dog baitings.[12]

After the American Revolutionary era, the popularity of horse racing continued to grow. Throughout the nineteenth century it became more organized and enjoyed enormous popularity among all social classes. Southerners seemed to be most inclined to the sport, and historians have observed that the papers of such famous figures as Thomas Jefferson and George Washington contain references to bets won and lost at local horse races. Perhaps one of the most committed southern horse players was Andrew Jackson, who during his tumultuous years in Tennessee as a land speculator, high stakes cardplayer, attorney, backwoods judge, and part-time soldier, also found plenty of time to own, race, and bet heavily on horses. His biographer Marquis James relates that Jackson's passion led to high-stakes bets, especially on one horse, Truxton, that Jackson had acquired by foreclosing on the former owner's debts. In one of Jackson's most famous duels, he killed a man named Charles Dickinson. The disagreement between the two men involved many charges and denials, public insults and arguments, but it apparently originated in a dispute over a horse race wager.[13]

In 1845 the attention of the nation turned to a classic showdown at the Union Race Course on Long Island that was billed by the *New York Herald* as "The Great Contest between the North and the South." It was but one in a long series of highly publicized races between northern and southern horses that had its origins in 1823. A *Herald* reporter noted that an enormous crowd, estimated to exceed 50,000, created a scene of "tumult, disorder, and confusion." The "Pride of the South," a filly named Peytona, was matched against the northern champion, Fashion. "In addition to the sectional feeling and the strong rivalry of sportsmen, and in one sense partisans—the vast sums of money pending on the race, attached a degree of absorbing interest to the result," the *Herald* reported. Peytona won both four-mile heats by narrow margins amid boisterous cheering from a predominantly male crowd of "race-going blades" that also included a motley collection of "indescribable camp followers, sutlers, loungers, rowdies, gamblers, and twenty other species" whose attention was drawn to the many "dramshops" they passed en route to the track.[14]

After the Civil War, horse racing became much more organized, and standardized gambling formats became widely accepted. The construction of an oval track at the resort town of Saratoga Springs, New York, by a former champion prizefighter named John "Old Smoke" Morrissey, proved to be a pivotal development. Morrissey had immigrated from Ireland with his parents at the age of three and had grown up in the small city of Troy, New York. As a young man he amassed a considerable financial stake from his winnings as a bare-knuckle fighter in New York City (including collecting high-stakes bets he placed on himself). In 1853 he won the equivalent of the world's heavyweight championship in a thirty-seven-round bloody bout with Yankee Sullivan. A shrewd and convivial Irishman, Morrissey became heavily involved in the Democratic Party's Tammany Hall organization. He wisely invested his prizefight and gambling winnings in a fancy gambling parlor that became the most popular in the city. He soon held majority interests in five such enterprises, and in 1861 he moved to Saratoga Springs, where he operated a plush hotel and restaurant that also provided his wealthy clientele with opportunities to test their luck at high-stakes table games. In 1863 Morrissey constructed a racetrack with a wooden grandstand, and thousands of well-heeled gamblers and their ladies, flush with large profits generated from Civil War enterprises, flocked to his hotel-casino and racetrack.[15]

Morrissey, now a close friend and confidant of the railroad magnate Cornelius Vanderbilt, courted the blue bloods of American society. He joined forces with wealthy stockbroker William R. Travers, sportsman John Hunter, and the wealthy New York City yachtsman and attorney Leonard Jerome to form a racing association. They rounded up twenty-six horses and held an initial four-day meet at Saratoga; it was widely proclaimed a social and financial success. One observer noted that the event rivaled the social scene at Ascot in England, "where the elegance and superb costumes of the ladies vie with the blood and beauty of the running horses and the neat but splendid appointments of the various riders."[16]

By the last quarter of the nineteenth century horse racing had become deeply entrenched in the American sporting scene. At its heart lay the wagering instincts of the American people. In the wake of "Old Smoke" Morrissey's success at Saratoga Springs, a spate of new tracks were opened in the East and Midwest. Jerome Park in New York City, operating under the aegis of the elite American Jockey Club, opened in 1866; notable among its initial membership were such business tycoons as August Belmont II and William C. Whitney, and Tammany Hall machine politicians of dubious reputation like Richard Croker and Tim

Sullivan. Soon thereafter Brooklyn's Sheepshead Bay and the luxurious New York City Belmont Park were opened. In New Jersey two tracks—Guttenberg (located across the Hudson River from New York City) and Gloucester (located near Philadelphia) became infamous for the many questionable races run for the benefit of gamblers in on a fix; they also set a new trend by running races throughout the year, come rain or snow, freezing temperatures or the searing heat of summer. Owing to the many controversies over fixed races, progressive reformers ultimately closed these two tracks in the 1890s, and New Jersey did not permit another track to open until 1940.[17]

Beyond the Appalachian Mountains, Churchill Downs in Louisville held the first Kentucky Derby in May of 1875, and Chicago's stylish Washington Park attracted large crowds, although antigambling reformers forced its closure for five years during the last decade of the century. By the 1920s more than three hundred racetracks—large and small—operated across the United States. Some racing fans were attracted by their love of horses, others by the pageantry and colorful crowds that thronged to the tracks. However, horse racing was almost completely dependent upon gambling for its survival.[18]

During the late nineteenth century, most track managements sold space to bookmakers who conducted "auction pools." The bookmaker would form a "pool" for a race and auction off each of the horses to the highest bidder; a bookmaker might create several such pools for a popular race. After the race the bookmaker would take his commission—usually about 10 percent—and distribute the remaining dollars in the pool to the individual who had won that horse in the prerace auction.

By the 1880s the auction system had lost out to one where the bookmaker would post his own odds on all horses entered in a race, raking off his commission before distributing the winnings to the lucky holders of the right tickets. This enabled more than one bettor to have a stake in a particular horse. The prerace scenes under this system were often tumultuous as eager bettors negotiated odds with the bookmaker. Bookmaking in this environment was, most assuredly, a perilous profession, the action often giving the impression of organized chaos as bettors and bookmakers came to agreement on wagers within a closed area where shouting and shoving were the order of the day. This system required of the bookmaker an agile mind capable of executing crucial mental calculations while negotiating with an excited cluster of clients. As the bookmaker began to take bets on a race, using the initial odds that he had set on each horse, he would have to adjust the odds by instinct as the monies flowed in order to keep his books in balance. When the money bet on one horse became an obvious risk, an astute bookmaker would encourage bettors to move to different horses by changing the odds. Today's racetracks use computers to accomplish the same balancing act.[19]

On occasion, however, even the best of bookmakers would be caught short and suffer a disastrous loss when a heavily bet favorite came home the winner. Those who could not balance their books with regularity, of course, had to find another line of work. Despite many calls for the abolition of trackside betting, state legislatures and local governments recognized that wagering was essential if the sport was to survive. Thus from the early days of organized racing, hypocrisy reigned supreme: While trackside betting was perfectly legal and even encouraged by tax-hungry state governments, legislators did not want to permit those working folk or the poor, unable to afford a visit to the racetracks, to ruin their moral character by betting with offtrack street bookies. State and local governments routinely legislated against the offtrack betting halls, popularly known as "poolrooms," found in many large cities. These parlors were connected by telegraph lines to racetracks around the country. It was here that less affluent bettors could place their bets without having to pay admission and transportation fees.[20]

A popular magazine reported that about two thousand such poolrooms existed in New York City early in the twentieth century. The author described a large basement room patrolled by several large goons who carefully screened each person who approached the door. Inside, the patron encountered a crowded room, heavily laden with cigar smoke, in which an estimated two hundred men and fifty women wrote out their bets on printed slips of paper—a minimum wager of five dollars was required—before shoving the paper and their money through a caged window to a clerk. These poolrooms were operated, the reporter for *Cosmopolitan* emphasized, by a "syndicate—a close combination with police attachment." In New York City, several syndicates operated simultaneously, but all did so with the approval of one man—"Big Tim" Sullivan, the boss of Tammany Hall. The reporter found a similar poolroom situation in Chicago, where "its political machinations and its police attachments are of the same character." The rapid growth in popularity of these new betting venues, the reporter concluded, was the result of "the horse-racing madness" that had broken out across America. Wherever this investigative reporter went, there was one constant: "The type of the big pool-room man—the man higher up—is about the same. He is either a politician or the friend of politicians. To be precise, he is 'in right.' "[21]

Although many such places were closed down by well-publicized police raids, the underlying fact was that local law enforcement officials were often on the take and padded their pocketbooks with bribes from those operating these establishments. As the famed Chicago defense lawyer Clarence Darrow once explained to an inquiring journalist: "Gambling is deeply inbred in the Republic because of police and law corruption. . . . To be honest is to be a fool in an imperfect world. Police take payoffs, judges do favors, politicians often split the loot with big-city bosses. The underworld crime boss exists only because it pays off. And the best lawyers mostly don't work for the people. They protect the big gambler, the gambling hoodlums who own casinos, the bookie wires, the numbers games. Look always for the evil side of gambling as being protected by our lawmakers and law enforcers. Cynical? No. Go to the records."[22]

That these enterprises had to share their profits with local crime bosses was widely accepted as the price of doing business. It was the criminal syndicates themselves that often operated the offtrack parlors, using their thugs to collect debts from those reluctant to settle their accounts, and relying on their political connections and judiciously placed campaign contributions, plus a discrete percentage of the take, to keep district attorneys and the police at a safe distance.[23]

Sports gambling thus became an integral part of the post–Civil War urban environment. The industrial and commercial cities of the North attracted large numbers of young males who were in turn attracted to the saloons. Here sports took on a central role in the conversations and arguments that naturally flowed along with the beer and hard spirits. Saloon keepers often served the dual role of bookmaker, and some of the more prominent urban drinking establishments even sponsored on-site bare-knuckle prizefights (or the more gruesome cockfights and rat baitings), all venues for placing a wager. Despite earnest efforts by Victorian reformers, the gambling halls found ways to deal with the reformers and the local authorities. As Steven Riess explains in his study of late nineteenth-century New York City, "Poolroom operators learned to adapt and stay in business" despite antigambling legislation. "Occasional raids were instigated by reformers like Anthony Comstock of the Society for the Suppression of Vice, but the poolrooms usually operated with impunity. The poolroom operators were well protected by Mayor Hugh Grant and other Tammany officials . . . [b]y payoffs to police and local political powers."[24]

2

The National Pastime Imperiled

As the twentieth century began, sports gambling in the United States remained heavily focused on horse racing, but gamblers had discovered that the popular game of baseball also provided a venue for serious wagering. With the establishment of professional baseball during the 1870s, urban citizens found a new outlet for wagering beyond bare-knuckle prizefights and horse races. The new game proved to be a bonanza for gamblers because its complexity and myriad strategic possibilities created intriguing handicapping challenges for knowledgeable fans interested in betting on the games. Unfortunately, the game was seriously threatened by gamblers seeking a sure return on their bets by bribing key players to throw games.

Although occasional episodes of fixes surfaced, it was not until the 1919 World Series, won by the Cincinnati Reds over the favored Chicago White Sox five games to three, and the subsequent scandal that the seriousness of the practice was widely recognized. The allegations that came to light the following year rocked organized baseball to its foundations. The resulting "Black Sox Scandal" served to illuminate the shadowy world of sports gambling that had come into existence with the growing popularity of organized professional sports.

The roots of baseball betting are to be found in the early days of the sport. Baseball was formally organized in the 1840s as a game for young gentlemen in New York City, and friendly wagers were a natural part of the socialization process. The close association with cardplaying was evident in the initial names for parts of the game: a score was not a "run" but rather an "ace"; a team's half-inning at bat was referred to as a "hand." In the immediate post–Civil War era the game spread rapidly as both Confederate and Union veterans, who had played baseball in camp to relieve boredom, took the game home with them to every community, large and small, across the land. To gamblers, the local nine had several advantages over horse racing as a new source of action. "It was more intriguing than a horse race," Eliot Asinof writes, "more civilized than a boxing match or a cock fight. It afforded a pleasant, even exciting afternoon in the sunlight, an event to which a gentleman could take his lady—and bet."[1]

Although casual fans did not make the connection between baseball and gambling as they had with horse racing—a sport that probably would not have existed were it not for gambling—betting on baseball was an integral part of the game, especially in cities, since the inception of organized professional leagues in the 1870s. Baseball team owners were active gamblers who apparently bet heavily on their own teams. Fans who attended games in the nineteenth century knew full well the antics of gamblers at games: Betting occurred routinely in sections of the grandstands where those looking for action tended to congregate. Often the gamblers would blatantly assemble under a sign proclaiming "No Gambling." Patrons could bet not only on the outcome of the game but on such things as the fate of a batter or whether the next pitch would be a ball or a strike. Their raucous behavior was one of the many reasons stiff-lipped Victorians viewed baseball with considerable skepticism. This activity at games apparently lasted until at least the Second World War in several cities. Sonny Reizner, a prominent Las Vegas line maker during the 1970s and 1980s, recounted that he began his career as a professional sports gambler as a teenager sitting among a flock of enthusiastic gamblers in the right-field bleachers of Boston's Fenway Park during the late 1930s; others recall similar activity as a constant at Chicago's Wrigley Field.[2]

From the 1870s, on the streets of America's cities odds were offered by local bookmakers on professional baseball games. In anticipation of the college football parlay cards that gained great popularity during the 1930s, baseball pool cards were peddled on street corners and in taverns by enterprising bookmakers and their agents. Similar to lotteries, they provided gamblers a series of options over a week's schedule of games. Tickets were sold for as little as ten cents and permitted fans to bet on such variables as which teams would win the most games, strike out the most opposing batters, score the most runs, or hit the most home runs. Newspapers even ran game odds and kept "standings" on the items that were included in the weekly pool betting cards. During the 1890s, one such pool, The Keystone, operated in New York City and other eastern cities and sold an estimated 165,000 tickets a week through an army of fifty field directors and three hundred agents. Even after deducting the weekly $17,000 payoff to the police, The Keystone made a profit estimated at $50,000.[3]

As the historian Benjamin Rader has observed, "Patrons of the Victorian underworld found in baseball a sport to satisfy the widespread hunger for gambling." He notes that in the bigger cities, bookmakers conducted their business in "poolrooms," where they established odds, recorded bets, operated betting pools on games and races, and authorized payments to winners. Their goal was to keep the monies sufficiently balanced so as to collect a healthy commission. As described above, the more aggressive bookmakers even offered their services at local ballparks.

In 1871 the first truly professional league, the National Association of Baseball Players, played its first season; in 1876 it was replaced by a new eight-team organization (soon to be temporarily reduced to six in 1877), the National League. No longer just a game played for fun and comradeship by courtly gentlemen or raw-boned farm boys, at its highest levels baseball now took on a professional mien; grown men, nearly all of them representative of the recent immigrant groups that had swelled the population of the industrial cities, now worked at playing a game. Within this context gamblers asserted themselves even further, and as Asinof notes, "baseball became corrupted with almost incredible rapidity."[4] A member of the early Cincinnati Reds, A. G. Spalding, later a baseball executive and sporting goods manufacturer, recalled of this era: "Things were rotten. Gambling in all its features of pool-selling and side-betting was still openly engaged in. A few players, too, had become so corrupt that nobody could be certain as to whether the issue of any game in which these players participated would be determined on its merits. The occasional throwing of games was practiced by some, and no punishment was meted out to the offenders."[5]

In 1877 baseball's first major gambling scandal hit the front pages when it was revealed that four prominent members of the Louisville Grays had accepted bribes as low as $150 from a New York gambler to throw late-season games the previous year so that their team would lose the pennant. When these four players made inexplicable mental mistakes and innumerable errors in a crucial six-game September series with an inept team from Hartford, Connecticut, it prompted Louisville club president Charles Chase to investigate. He soon uncovered the conspiracy and informed league president William Hulbert, who banished the players from the league for life. What Chase did not publicly reveal was that the players had accepted the bribes at least in part because the club had failed to pay their salaries.[6]

Thus was the early history of baseball rife with gambling-induced corruption. Bribery of players became commonplace, with pitchers being the most common target of fixers. In 1878, in commenting on the dilemma in which baseball found itself, a St. Louis newspaper lamented, "Baseball, as a professional pastime, has seen its best days in St. Louis. The amount of crooked work is indeed startling, and the game will undoubtedly meet the same fate elsewhere unless some extra strong means are taken to prevent it."[7]

These problems, however, were kept under wraps, and as the twentieth century dawned baseball had become absorbed into the mainstream of American popular culture as its special "pastime." Americans now referred to it proudly as "Our Game," a term coined by the poet Walt Whitman. By this time baseball had successfully moved beyond its early sleazy reputation as a game played by hustlers and thugs who were under the thumb of gamblers, in large part because of the leadership of such innovative and politically astute men as Ban Johnson, the founder and longtime president of the American League. But as Charles Alexander, baseball's premier historian, notes, there were several episodes that should have sent warning signals to organized baseball's leadership.[8] Another pioneering historian of baseball, Harold Seymour, accurately summarized baseball's vulnerability to conniving gamblers: "The evidence is abundantly clear, without considering every hint, rumor, and veiled accusation, that the groundwork for the crooked 1919 World Series, like most striking events in history, was long prepared. The scandal," he concludes, "was not an aberration brought about solely by a handful of villainous players. It was a culmination of corruption and attempts at corruption that reached back nearly twenty years."[9]

A major turning point in the ascendancy of baseball wagering occurred in 1917 when the federal government shut down horse racing for the duration of the Great War. Professional gamblers and bookmakers, long dependent upon horse racing as the primary source of their livelihoods, quickly shifted their operations to baseball. Inevitably, high-stakes gamblers sought to influence the outcome of games, employing a wide range of tactics to obtain the cooperation of key players: alcohol, women, money, even the threat of physical violence. By 1919 gamblers were talking openly of players they controlled, but on the field it was impossible to ascertain if a player was truly "throwing" a game. Errors and strikeouts in clutch situations are, of course, an integral part of the game. So too are occasional streaks of wildness or ineffectiveness by a star pitcher, as well as mistakes in judgment in running the base paths or throwing to the wrong base. Detecting a player on the take was not an easy task and therefore not one that even the most impeccable of baseball men opted to pursue.[10]

Nonetheless, given the widespread rumors about fixed games floating on the streets, the most surprising aspect of the 1919 World Series was that such practices did not come to public attention much earlier. Naive fans had merely assumed that all games were played on the up-and-up, but as Charles Alexander observes, big-time gamblers had always been an integral part of the national pastime to a much greater extent than casual fans recognized. In his authoritative history of professional baseball, he describes a series of highly suspicious events that occurred between 1905 and 1919. League officials and team owners had been made aware of all too many games that had attracted large bets; they had been told by honest players of alleged bribery attempts but chose to overlook them; newspapermen came across rumors of efforts to bribe umpires and players but chose not to publish their findings. Apparently those in control of organized baseball were willing to tolerate a certain amount of corruption as the price of keeping the issue out of the newspapers.[11]

Certainly the open collusion with gamblers by the talented first baseman Hal Chase should have prompted decisive action. Throughout his long career Chase publicly associated with known gamblers and made no secret of placing big bets on baseball, including games he was playing in. He once offered a bribe to a young relief pitcher as he ambled in from the bull pen: "I've got some money bet on this game, kid. There's something in it for you if you lose." Chase entered the American League in 1906 with the New York Highlanders and was thereafter periodically accused of throwing games by frustrated managers. He played under the high-minded manager Christy Mathewson in Cincinnati in 1916. When the star pitcher-turned-manager learned that Chase and a teammate had both bet $500 against the Reds in a game with the Boston Braves, Mathewson suspended him. Chase appealed and, despite a strong statement by Mathewson, was reinstated by an intimidated league president. In 1919, now a member of the New York Giants of the National League, Chase continued to attempt to bribe teammates, prompting manager John McGraw to use the not-so-subtle device of forcing him to leave the team by offering a ridiculously low salary for the next season. "Undoubtedly the readiness of the Chicago White Sox players to collude with gamblers in the 1919 World Series," Alexander writes, "had much to do with official baseball's longtime toleration of Chase and others of his ilk."[12]

By ignoring the warnings of such dedicated baseball men as Mathewson and McGraw, the leaders of organized baseball virtually invited major trouble. The journalist Hugh Fullerton, whose investigative work forced the revelations of the Black Sox, lamented that "during the season of 1919 gamblers openly boasted that they or others controlled ball players on a number of clubs. The former racetrack gamblers, who disliked baseball save as a means of mulcting the public, sneeringly asserted that the game was more crooked than horseracing ever was."[13]

This is not to say that some leaders of organized baseball were not concerned, but they lacked support from many of the owners and players. American League President Ban Johnson, for one, had for years sought to combat gambling, even going to such lengths as hiring private detectives to work at ballparks where gamblers were known to operate and to collect evidence that was turned over to local officials. Yet he was brusquely rebuffed by the owner of the Boston Red Sox, Harry Frazee, when he attempted to crack down on the betting brazenly going on in the right-field pavilion of Fenway Park. Johnson was frustrated that most of his league team owners blithely assumed that all was well. Besides, Johnson's efforts at a crackdown had failed to catch any big-time gamblers. On at least two occasions Johnson's plan produced indictments of small-time gamblers but with no discernible impact. Whenever there was a crackdown, any brief hiatus that resulted would inevitably be followed by a return of the gamblers.[14]

The saga of the Black Sox scandal is extraordinarily complex. Certainly the complete story will never be known. Suffice it to say that the case is filled with surprising contradictions, replete with shocking revelations, and surrounded by enough examples of duplicity, outright corruption, clever deceptions, and broken trust to fill many a book—as it has indeed done. The essential story is simple enough. Two White Sox players, the first baseman Charles "Chick" Gandil and the right-handed pitching ace thirty-five-year-old Ed Cicotte, angered by what they considered to be the low salaries and meager benefits paid by the notoriously parsimonious White Sox owner, the "Old Roman" Charles Comiskey, but also apparently eager to secure their own post-baseball financial futures, obtained the cooperation of six other disgruntled teammates in their plan. They supposedly approached the notorious New York gambler Arnold Rothstein through intermediaries with a scheme to throw the World Series in return for payments of $10,000 to each player. Actually, as Alexander makes clear, the players' salaries were not all that different from those of baseball players of comparable skills on other teams; the domineering Comiskey simply had the ability to let his players know that he was rich and they were not and that, armed with organized baseball's Reserve Clause, he could force them to play for him for as long as he wished. "If they don't play for me, they can't play for anyone," he once told the press. Arrogant and brash, Comiskey loved to let his complaining players know who was in control.[15]

Rothstein had multiple interests that had made him a very rich man for his time. Some of his investments were legal, some not. Yet today the word *probably* is attached to cautious historians' accounts of his role in the scandal. His biographer, the journalist Leo Katcher, argues that Rothstein knew about the fix, that he accordingly placed large bets on Cincinnati, but that he also placed a few highly publicized bets on the White Sox to cover his tracks. Katcher suggests that Rothstein did not actually authorize the bribes but rather permitted the scam to take place through one of his associates, a champion featherweight boxer from

Philadelphia by the name of Abe Attell. Rothstein profited handsomely from his bets on the Reds, but there is no hard evidence that proves with certainty that he was the man behind the fix. His agile testimony before a Chicago grand jury in the fall of 1920 helped prevent his indictment (although seven of his associates were indicted). His attorney released to the press Rothstein's testimony behind locked doors to the grand jury:

> The whole thing started when [Abe] Attell and some other cheap gamblers decided to frame the Series and make a killing. The world knows I was asked in on the deal and my friends know how I turned it down flat. I don't doubt that Attell used my name to put it over. That's been done by smarter men than Abe. But I wasn't in on it, wouldn't have gone into it under any circumstances and didn't bet a cent on the Series after I found out what was under way. My idea was that whatever way things turned out, it would be a crooked Series anyhow and that only a sucker would bet on it.[16]

Rothstein's close proximity to those who were in direct communication with the players, however, indicates that he was fully aware of the tortured negotiations that occurred before the first game of the series. Beyond doubt, the fingerprints of New York City's premier gambler were all over the case, even if he managed to outwit his plodding associates (whom he let take the legal hit) and the inept, if not corrupt, Chicago district attorney's office.

Rothstein had long been known as a big-time horse, cards, and dice player, becoming heavily involved in high-stakes gambling as early as the age of fifteen. Over the years he became closely associated with the power brokers of his native New York City—Tammany Hall politicos, prominent Broadway figures, oil magnates, newspaper executives, investment bankers, and prominent gamblers. Between 1910 and his premature death in 1928 (he was shot by an unknown assailant, apparently the result of a card game turned sour), Rothstein profited handsomely from his heavy involvement in many forms of racketeering, including his operation of a string of gambling clubs and offtrack betting parlors. He died of a .38 caliber gunshot wound to the stomach on election day 1928; had he lived he would have been $500,000 richer on a series of bets he had made on the margin of presidential candidate Herbert Hoover's victory over Al Smith.[17] In the most authoritative study of the World Series scandal, journalist Eliot Asinof estimates that Rothstein won $270,000. Biographer Katcher sets his take at a more lofty $350,000. In either case, the man known as "The Big Bankroll" walked away with quite a large sum of money.[18]

From its clumsy inception, many persons were privy to the World Series conspiracy. The notorious Hal Chase apparently knew of the plan even before Rothstein became involved; he placed his own bets and allegedly collected $40,000 in winnings. Several other players from teams in both leagues also cashed in on their inside knowledge, and Ed Cicotte apparently bet heavily through agents on the Reds. Even before the series began, it had become, as Charles Alexander observes, "a remarkably open secret."[19]

The Reds eventually won the Series five games to three, but some of the major conspirators played very well in certain games, leading scholars to suggest that some but not all the games were fixed. The winning Reds made twice the number of errors as the White Sox. Shoeless Joe Jackson fielded flawlessly and batted .375 but nonetheless later admitted to taking $5,000 for his role in the plot, a confession he later recanted. "Chick" Gandil made seven hits including a clutch double that won a game for the Sox, and Cicotte pitched brilliantly to win game seven. On the other hand, White Sox pitcher Claude "Lefty" Williams pitched horribly and took three losses. In any event, Gandil, the originator of the plot, reportedly received $30,000, and the other seven collected between $5,000 and $10,000 each, amounts that equalled or exceeded most of their salaries.[20]

Rumors about the fix floated across the baseball world the following winter, fueled by a series of articles in the *New York World* by the respected Chicago sportswriter Hugh Fullerton. (His employer, the *Chicago Herald and Examiner*, had refused to publish his allegations.) Before the series, Fullerton had gone on record predicting, based upon his close analysis of the strengths and weaknesses of the two teams, a decisive White Sox victory. During the series, which he watched with incredulity, Fullerton picked up several rumors about a possible fix, but then he also heard contradicting rumors that key members of the Cincinnati club had also been touched by gamblers. He consulted with the famed pitcher-manager Christy Mathewson, who was covering the series for the *New York World*. Together they charted the games, underlining in their game notes suspicious developments that occurred on the field. Baseball's leaders loudly condemned Fullerton's speculations, charging that he was merely embarrassed because of his wrong prediction on the outcome of the series. Comiskey, who had learned of the scandal in October but elected to keep it quiet for fear of destroying his investment in his team, ostentatiously offered a reward of $20,000 (later reduced to $10,000) for anyone who could provide solid evidence supporting Fullerton's allegations.[21]

As the 1920 season unfolded, the White Sox were involved in several other suspicious games. In addition, the cancer had evidently spread across the major leagues; the president of the Chicago Cubs ordered pitcher Claude Hendrix benched when he learned that his pitcher had been offered a bribe to throw a game against the Philadelphia Phillies. This news was leaked to the press on the heels of a civil trial involving another member of the Chicago Cubs during which testimony revealed some of Hal Chase's gambling associations and activities. Consequently, the Illinois district attorney in Chicago had no choice but to launch a grand jury probe of allegations regarding conspiracies to fix baseball games. His primary witness was a small-time Philadelphia gambler, Billy Maharg, who had been an intermediary between the White Sox players and Rothstein and Attell. But on September 28, 1920, star pitcher Ed Cicotte and the much adored power-hitting left fielder "Shoeless" Joe Jackson confessed to having participated in the scam and implicated six other players.[22]

The resulting trial in the summer of 1921 made a mockery of the justice system—not an unusual development to those who closely followed the twists and turns of Cook County jurisprudence. Eight players and seven gamblers were indicted by the grand jury, but Arnold Rothstein had managed to convince the jurors that he was not implicated. By the time the case reached a jury another fix was obviously in place. Most of the indicted gamblers—Rothstein's intermediaries— had simply disappeared on long-term vacations to Mexico and Europe courtesy of Rothstein's large bankroll. The key witness, boxer Abe Attell, who had apparently been the payoff man, fled to Canada and successfully fought extradition. The prosecution's key piece of evidence—signed confessions by Cicotte and Jackson—mysteriously disappeared from the state attorney's secured files. Cicotte and Jackson immediately issued denials that they had confessed; meanwhile other witnesses had contracted what seemed to be a collective case of serious amnesia. Eventually, the presiding judge issued such a narrow set of instructions to the jury that a verdict of innocent on all counts was virtually inevitable.[23]

By this time the shaken owners of baseball, facing a major loss of public confidence in their product, had hired the irascible federal district judge Kenesaw Mountain Landis as their new commissioner. Desperate to obtain Landis's reputation for honesty to help them survive their darkest hour, they reluctantly granted his demand that he be given complete and absolute power to make any decision he deemed necessary for "the good of baseball." They certainly did not want to grant him, or anyone, unlimited authority, but they feared for their investment's future if Landis should turn down their generous offer (a whopping salary of $50,000 as compared to just $7,500 for a federal judge). Their trust in this arbitrary and self-assured judge was quickly confirmed. Even before the players had recovered from their night of celebration after the innocent verdicts had been handed down, Landis issued a decree that all eight were banished from organized baseball for life.[24]

His shocking decision let the world know that he believed that the trial had been fixed by underworld gambling figures. The courts of the land were on one level; Landis soared above them: "Regardless of the verdict of juries, no player who throws a ball game, no player that undertakes or promises to throw a ballgame, no player that sits in conference with a bunch of crooked players and gamblers where the ways and means of throwing a game are discussed and does not promptly tell his club about it, will ever play professional baseball." One of the eight banished players was George "Buck" Weaver. The star third baseman had played spectacularly during the series; he had originally agreed to participate but had changed his mind before the series began. His crime was that he knew of the fix but out of loyalty to his teammates did not report it to authorities. Landis refused to reinstate him, tersely informing the press, "Birds of a feather flock together. Men associating with gamblers and crooks should expect no leniency."[25]

In an ironic twist of events, three years later, when Shoeless Joe Jackson brought suit against owner Charles Comiskey in a Milwaukee court for alleged breach of contract, the missing affidavits he and Cicotte had signed before the prosecuting attorney suddenly reappeared and were used to exonerate Comiskey. Although it cannot be proved, most students of this bizarre case believe that Rothstein had paid a hefty price to ensure their disappearance and now had arranged through Comiskey's attorney, Alfred Austrian, for their timely reappearance to damage Jackson's case. Nonetheless, the jury awarded Jackson $17,000, but the judge overturned their verdict and Jackson landed in organized baseball's version of purgatory, playing semipro baseball for a time and operating a small liquor store in his native Greenville, South Carolina, until his death at age sixty-three of cardiac arrest.[26] In 1996 the aging Ted Williams, one of the best pure hitters in the history of baseball and an admirer of a batter he believed to be almost his equal, launched an effort to have Jackson's name cleared and for him to be elected into the Hall of Fame. The issue seemingly has a life of its own, refusing to go away.

"Say it ain't so, Joe," a disbelieving boy cried out to Jackson outside the Chicago federal courthouse. "Say it ain't so." "Kid, I'm afraid it is," the legendary hitter told his young fan.[27] Although doomsayers feared the worst for "our game" following the sensational trial in 1921, baseball fans quickly moved on, convinced that the stern Judge Landis would restore credibility to the national pastime. And indeed he did, in part by instituting rigid rules regarding gambling that have remained a fundamental part of organized baseball's policies to this day. All of which he did with a flurry of press releases, putting the proper spin on his every move to cleanse the game. However, it was the soaring home runs that leaped off the bat of Babe Ruth during the 1920s that did more to bring the fans back to the game than the leadership of the dictatorial commissioner.

The respected baseball historian Bill James argues that the problem was far greater than Landis's shrewd public relations moves led a gullible public to believe. "Few oversimplifications of memory are as bizarre as the notion that the Black Sox scandal hit baseball out of the blue, that there was just this one blight on an otherwise faultless record of integrity. In fact, of course, the Black Sox scandal was merely the largest and ugliest wart of a disease that had infested baseball at least a dozen years earlier and grown, unchecked, to ravage the features of a generation."[28]

No matter the legal disposition of the Black Sox scandal, the truth was out: just beyond the field of play, gamblers were also major players in the world of American sports. As a leading opinion journal commented as the scandal was unfolding,

> Whoever it may have been that "fixed" the series, it was someone who ran a modest risk and carried off an enormous swag. . . . Whoever it was that took the bribe, it was men who got pitifully little for it in the way of actual money but who jeopardized their reputations and careers, tricked their fellows on the team, deceived the public at large, and besmirched the credit of the game for a dozen years. . . . To find out that famous players have been corrupted is more than to lose faith in them personally; it is to begin to doubt the whole system. All may be fair in love and war, but in sport nothing is fair but the rules.[29]

3

Moses Annenberg and His Wire Empire

The stain of the Black Sox fiasco ultimately did nothing to deter the public's growing zest for sports wagering. During the two decades between the world wars, betting on sports continued to grow. In fact, by focusing attention on the phenomenon, baseball's greatest scandal seemed to intensify interest in sports betting among the American people. The number of gamblers and the estimates of amounts wagered grew steadily, despite strong opposition from politicians, journalists, religious spokespeople, and assorted other reformers. Despite various efforts to curtail gambling of all types, observers concluded that millions of new Americans were now getting down their bets with their local bookies. Americans were obviously not only betting more but doing so on a much wider spectrum of sporting events.

Despite the attention drawn to baseball by the Black Sox episode, the sport of choice for most bettors remained horse racing. It can be argued that as the "sport of kings" took on increasing economic importance, horse racing no longer even remained a sport. One of the prominent myths put forward by horse racing buffs was that racing encouraged the improvement of the breed through scientific breeding and advanced training regimens, but as the prominent gambling expert John Scarne observed, by 1940 horse racing had "degenerated into a purely commercial operation. Track owners, horse owners and state officials [were] far more interested in the dollar than in developing the breed."[1]

The growing popularity of horse racing resulted from several interrelated factors. First and foremost, more and more state governments were embracing gambling as a new, and politically appealing, means of generating state income without having to raise state taxes, always an unpleasant task for elected officials. By legalizing racing seasons to be operated under the pari-mutuel system, state governments essentially broke with long-standing Puritan tradition and

sanctioned sports gambling as a legitimate form of popular leisure entertainment. Thus the millions who flocked to the racetrack during the 1920s reflected
a distinct change in the socioeconomic composition of race fans: no longer was
it primarily a "sport of kings" or reserved for the upper classes, the members
of high society that the summer meets at Saratoga catered to. Track managers
were encouraged to attract the middle and working classes to the track to help
fill state coffers. State regulatory committees increased the length of seasons
and welcomed new establishments. The action by state governments during the
1920s to tap horse racing as a new revenue stream not only gave wagering on
horses a new legitimacy but by implication suggested that wagering on human
sports (still illegal in all states) might also be acceptable. By 1930, with half the
states now permitting horse racing in one form or another, traditional moral
arguments against betting were decisively undercut.

The horse racing phenomenon was also attributable to advances in communication offered by the telegraph and telephone. Recognizing a strong demand,
entrepreneurs established elaborate nationwide communications networks to
service the growing number of horse wire rooms that enabled dedicated players
a chance to bet on major races held hundreds, if not thousands, of miles away.
These illegal operations became a continuing source of controversy and, because
of their popularity, an important part of the mythology surrounding the rise of
organized crime.

The acceptance that horse racing enjoyed in the 1920s and after was a major
change in public attitude and public policy. Throughout the latter half of the
nineteenth century and up until the end of the First World War, most state
legislatures—feeling the heat of self-righteous Victorians and later progressive
reformers—refused to authorize trackside betting. Even in states that did allow
it, the practice was often susceptible to wild swings in public sentiment. For
example, in 1908 a resurgence of antigambling sentiment, part of a crusading
progressive reform impulse, prompted the New York State Legislature to enact
legislation that declared all wagering on horse races illegal. By 1911, following
several court test cases, all New York tracks had shut down; spectators had no
interest in watching horse races unless they could place a wager on the outcome.
But the hiatus in New York lasted for only a few years. The legislature—torn
between its gambling and its reform constituencies—got off the hook in 1913
when a New York State court ruled that the new law prohibited only written bets,
not those made orally. This legal technicality provided the opening gamblers

desperately sought, and everyone connected with horse racing—track operators, law enforcement officials, racehorse owners, state officials, bookies, and the media—readily concurred in the essential truth that all bets made at racetracks were in fact transacted orally, printed tickets and receipts notwithstanding. When racing reappeared after the federal ban against all horse racing during the First World War, New York once again led the nation as the state with the most racetracks, the largest attendance, and, of course, the largest betting handle.[2]

As horse race fever spread across America during the 1920s, twenty-nine nationally recognized major tracks attracted record crowds and betting handles. In an important development, the popularity of the horses filtered down to millions of citizens who seldom, if ever, attended a race in person. These were the bettors who placed their bets away from the tracks with an estimated 30,000 illegal bookies operating in cities large and small. The large-scale offtrack betting operations derived their information from telegraph wire services. By the 1940s use of telegraph lines in many eastern and midwestern cities had been supplanted by telephone lines, but the term "wire service" remained in vogue. In 1940 the fifth largest customer of the American Telephone and Telegraph Corporation was the nation's leading horse wire service; communications giant Western Union also received a substantial piece of the action. For a weekly fee of several hundred dollars, bookies received up-to-the-minute reports from the tracks. The wire services hired several "spotters" who flashed information from within the racetracks via complex visual signals to associates located nearby, who then sent the news speeding across the nation to their subscribers. Such a system was needed because, in an attempt to discourage the wire services, which siphoned off potential trackside bettors, most racetrack operators had prohibited public telephones on their premises.[3]

Many small-time bookies making book on distant horse races ran their businesses out of their homes, from a booth in the back of a bar, across the counter of their newsstand or candy store, or in a room adjacent to a billiards parlor. But in medium-sized and large cities the most popular location for horseplayers to congregate was at a "horse parlor" or "wire room." Because only a few tracks were in season at any given time, and because millions of gamblers lived great distances from any track, the wire rooms became havens for dedicated horseplayers. Here they could swap information with friends while making wagers on races being held simultaneously at several tracks located around the country, and bettors found that the smoky atmosphere of these gambling emporiums provided a level of excitement even greater than being at the track. The wire services provided current race information—entries, jockey assignments, scratches, changing odds, the position of the horses at the quarter posts, and, most important, the official race results and payoffs. In a wire room bettors could scan the boards listing the entries and odds at several racetracks, belly up to a bar well fortified with bootleg liquor (until repeal of Prohibition in 1933), bet on top races from New York to California, and listen to an announcer, blessed with a vivid imagination and captivating voice, re-create the trackside drama from the telegraph tape; this narrative included a prerace summary of the odds on each entry, a dramatic description of the running of the race, and a summary of payoffs on the horses finishing in the money.[4]

The vast popularity of horse racing in the United States coincided with the rapid spread of horse wire rooms across the nation during the 1920s and 1930s. It was an illegal business that encouraged one of many close relationships between local crime organizations and law enforcement. The record of those associations is, of course, unclear, and no reliable documentary track has been left for inquiring historians. But the essential facts are that law enforcement knew the location of the rooms and permitted them to operate in return for a substantial payoff. Law enforcement officials not only looked upon the wire rooms as a means of supplementing their mediocre salaries but also felt they were committing a victimless crime. They knew the players and the managers and understood that the gamblers were willing participants; as with their de facto approach to prostitution, urban police departments and prosecuting attorneys considered gambling a more or less harmless form of entertainment that did not threaten the public safety.

Wire services had been introduced during the late nineteenth century, with Western Union providing most transcontinental wires. For a time the company had even placed its own employees at the tracks to speed racing information to subscribers across the nation. In 1905, however, Western Union ceased using its own agents at the tracks in response to antigambling political pressures. Several rival enterprises jumped in to provide similar service, albeit in a fragmented and unsophisticated fashion. Among the leading services during the early years of the twentieth century was the Metropolitan News Company of Louisville, Kentucky, whose midwestern wire network earned hefty annual profits estimated at $1 million. A rival company, the Payne Telegraph Service, located in Cincinnati, Ohio, provided a similar service. In 1910, one of Chicago's leading gambling figures, Mont Tennes, who had profitable ties to the Chicago underworld through his North Side bookmaking syndicate, acquired the Payne Service and reorganized it into the highly profitable General News Bureau. Although several competitors challenged Tennes's dominant position, he remained the leader of the wire service business until he sold the General News Bureau in 1927 to an aggressive businessman with substantial newspaper managerial expertise, Moses L.

Annenberg. In the early 1930s the Department of Justice estimated that the wire services provided information to more than 15,000 bookmaking customers.[5]

By the time Moe Annenberg entered the wire service business, he had already lived a Horatio Alger–type existence. Born into poverty in the desolate East Prussian farming village of Kalwichen in 1878, he had emigrated at age four to the United States. His parents were part of the large exodus of Jews fleeing the pogroms creating havoc for Jews living in Russia and eastern Europe. In 1885 his father settled in Chicago, where he supported his family by peddling secondhand goods on the streets of the growing city. Moe dropped out of school at age twelve to become a messenger runner for Western Union. By his late teens, this aggressive young man had learned the ways of the city streets and moved on to the dangerous business of newspaper agency sales. He joined his older brother Max—a husky young man with a reputation as a brawler—in the notorious Chicago "newspaper wars" of the early 1900s. They became key participants in many a spirited South Side battle over circulation between their employer, the established *Chicago Tribune*, and its upstart rival, the *Examiner*, owned by William Randolph Hearst.[6]

After using their muscle on behalf of the *Tribune*, the youthful Annenbergs switched sides to accept a more lucrative offer from the determined Hearst organization. They often became involved in bloody fights with rival agents as they sought to secure control of the best street corners. Moe supervised a small army of newspaper boys, devoting his energies to expanding the *Examiner*'s circulation throughout the city and its suburbs. Violence was commonplace in Chicago's ongoing newspaper wars, and during these tempestuous times it was not unusual for delivery trucks to be hijacked or bundles of newspapers tossed into a river by rivals. Broken bones and worse were commonplace. Many of the thugs who participated in the newspaper wars later became major players in Chicago's bloody battles between rival bootlegging gangs during the 1920s. According to his biographer John Cooney, Moe Annenberg was not nearly as prone to violence as his brother, but he never hesitated to defend his turf. By the time Chicago's newspaper wars ended in 1913, twenty-seven newsdealers had been killed, and an unknown number of heads bashed.[7]

Moe Annenberg, however, left Chicago before the level of violence had peaked. In 1907, apparently following a disagreement with his brother, he moved to Milwaukee. By this time he had already demonstrated a considerable flair for making money. In the Beer City, he established a profitable newspaper circulation agency that would fuel his rise to the ranks of the city's most wealthy. Using his news agency as a foundation, he was soon heavily invested in a myriad of businesses—drugstores, insurance agencies, dry cleaning, bowling alleys, rental property. In 1917 he became publisher of Hearst's Milwaukee venture, the *Wisconsin News*, increasing circulation from 25,000 to 80,000 in just a few years. Business acumen such as this naturally came to the attention of Hearst, who made Annenberg a major lieutenant in charge of circulation for his growing national newspaper chain. At the age of forty Annenberg, already a millionaire several times over, relocated to New York City.[8]

Despite his accomplishments, Annenberg's thirst for new ventures, more power, an ever larger income was never satiated. Although he made money in a wide range of business investments, he remained at heart a newspaperman. It was this combination of motivations that led him to the horse racing business, although previously Annenberg had never shown any interest in horse racing, rarely attending a race or placing a bet. In fact, he had an aversion to betting on horses because, unlike cards, he had no control over the outcome. But in 1922 he purchased the *Daily Racing Form*, a publication that provided millions of bettors across the United States with a vast array of information about every horse running at every major racetrack in the country. It was the essential source for the mountains of minutiae that horseplayers live for; without the *Daily Racing Form* they would have no basis for making their betting decisions. Founded in 1894 by Frank Brunell, it had fallen on tough times under the aging founder's erratic leadership. Always alert to attractive investment opportunities, Annenberg purchased the foundering business for $400,000 and delivered the full amount to Brunell in cash, appropriately wrapped in newsprint. For unknown reasons, he brought in four equal partners to help him run the business even though they personally invested little or nothing in the enterprise. In his first year of ownership, the *Daily Racing Form* earned more than Annenberg's total investment.[9]

Under his direction the *Daily Racing Form* set a new standard for accuracy in reporting an incredible amount of detail on each race run at licensed tracks — temperature, wind, precipitation, track conditions, jockey, jockeys' weights, time for each eighth of a mile, place of each horse at each eighth-mile post, and so on. He turned his new acquisition into a highly profitable business and in 1927 bought out his four partners for $2.25 million. The price provided his four partners with an enormous profit, of course, but it proved to be an even better long-term investment for Annenberg and his heirs. Under his demanding management style, the *Daily Racing Form* became universally recognized as the nation's best racing sheet. He also published tip and scratch sheets and other materials needed by horseplayers. In establishing his publication as the national racing authority, he bought or forced out his competitors, sometimes employing some of the rough-and-tumble tactics he had learned on the streets of Chicago.

One favorite ploy was to force news agencies that handled Hearst's newspapers and magazines to sell only the *Daily Racing Form* and not competing local publications; if agency owners refused, he would cut them off from access to Hearst's profitable publications. As John Cooney writes, "Few of Moses' rivals had the nerve to step forward and accuse him of driving them out of business, and most of them sold out rather than fight the consequences."[10]

The *Daily Racing Form* proved so successful that Annenberg left Hearst's employ and never looked back. The *Daily Racing Form* became the basis of what would become one the nation's most profitable publishing conglomerates which ultimately included several magazines and newspapers (e.g., the *Milwaukee Journal, Philadelphia Inquirer,* and *Miami Tribune*), and one of the most profitable publications in American history, *TV Guide.*[11]

In 1927 Annenberg expanded his horse race information business when he purchased one-half of Mont Tennes's General News Bureau—by now the nation's dominant racing wire service. Tennes was under pressure from Chicago mobster Al Capone on several fronts; aging and tired, he wanted out of the wire business, and Annenberg seemed a logical successor. Before making this major step, Annenberg consulted with several attorneys to verify Tennes's assertion that the business was legal. As his son Walter later stated, "They told him racing results were news and that he would be collecting and disseminating news. Providing news was not different, in their opinion, than manufacturing playing cards. If people use the cards to gamble or the wire to gamble, that's not your business, that's their problem. He wasn't gambling. Race results are news. After all the Associated Press and others were getting the results, too."[12]

Although he and his associates knew they essentially had a monopoly in the lucrative horse race news business, they nonetheless devoted enormous energy to expansion. Using his usual guile and power, Annenberg acquired his major wire service rival, the Nationwide News Service, and became the dominant figure in the business. Annenberg was an aggressive operator whose tactics often pushed the outer limits of the law. For example, in 1927 a rival racing sheet publisher, Sol King, sued Annenberg in a New York court for operating a monopoly, even alleging that Annenberg's goons had slashed the tires of his delivery trucks and sabotaged his printing presses. King could not prove his allegations in court, but according to biographer John Cooney, Annenberg's "reputation as a brutal circulation mogul who would stop at nothing" was forever established.[13]

Annenberg had no qualms about the nature of his new business. He had routinely dealt with corrupt city bosses, underworld potentates, and gamblers of all types throughout his career, so this was business as usual as far as he was concerned. His top associates were often connected to acts of violence in shutting down competitors. He never conceded that by providing gamblers with an essential service he was engaged in unethical behavior. When challenged, he emphasized that his wire service was a legitimate business—as it was—and played down the fact that it served an estimated 15,000 bookies who were in fact breaking state and local laws on a daily basis with each bet they accepted. After all, his attorneys had assured him that his was a news business, not a gambling enterprise. Of course, without a reliable horse wire, the level of illegal gambling nationwide would have been severely diminished overnight. Because offtrack gambling was illegal in all forty-eight states (forty-seven after Nevada legalized gambling in 1931), his company dealt on a daily basis with men whose livelihoods were predicated upon breaking the law.

Although Annenberg walked on the edge of a slippery legal precipice, he was in turn rewarded with enormous profits. In the jargon of Wall Street, he operated a multifaceted vertically integrated business by encouraging individual bettors with the *Daily Racing Form* and by providing bookies with information essential to operating their enterprises. In the words of his biographer Christopher Ogden, however, he operated "a criminal tool" for his own benefit, although it should be noted that Annenberg operated at a time when American capitalism was a ruthless entity that often rewarded industrial buccaneers with fame and fortune. "Even by the standards of the time, however," Ogden writes, "the racing wire was notorious. . . . Owning it would tar him again with dark, unsavory associations and give his enemies, who began to multiply in number and influence, powerful ammunition to use against him."[14]

Annenberg rationalized his involvement in horse race betting by saying it provided the nation's "little guy" with recreation and economic opportunity. He contended that he performed a distinct social service by making it possible for the hard-working stiffs of America, who were unable to attend a race in person, to get rich by placing a lucky bet. "It isn't right to deprive the little people of a chance to be lucky," he once told his concerned son Walter. "If people can wager at a racetrack why should they be deprived of the right to do so away from a track? How many people can take time off from their jobs to go to a racetrack?"[15]

Once in control of the General News Bureau, Annenberg moved quickly to eliminate his many competitors and consolidate his control of the lucrative racing business. Operating out of a small office at 431 Dearborn Street in Chicago, a cadre of dedicated subordinates coordinated Annenberg's many investments in nationwide gambling, while Annenberg carefully insulated himself from implication in the corrupt and frequently violent aspects of this enterprise with a complex array of confusing corporate organizations and multiple levels of administration. His muscular emissaries intimidated bookies who used competing wire services: Reluctant subscribers were subjected to threatening telephone calls or had their places of business trashed. Others found themselves arrested, their wire rooms shut down by the local district attorney and police, who were repaying Annenberg for his contributions to their welfare from his "widows and orphans" fund—the euphemistic name for his bribery operations. Annenberg recognized the importance of making strategic contributions to local politicians and law enforcement officials so that illegal gambling could operate on the nation's streets with little fear of legal hassles. According to Cooney, his "widows and orphans" fund distributed an estimated $150,000 a year during the 1930s.[16]

By the mid-1930s Annenberg had defeated his enemies and outfoxed his trusting partners; his new agency, the Nationwide News Service, was now unchallenged, electronically serving the daily needs of bookies and bettors from coast to coast and into Canada, Mexico, and the Caribbean. Each year it returned to its owner in excess of $2 millon. The print side of the operation, the *Daily Racing Form*, produced a similar profit. The rapid rise in popularity of horse racing during the 1920s and 1930s was in no small way the result of the determined entrepreneurship of Moses L. Annenberg.

Annenberg's extraordinary success, however, eventually ended in his downfall. Ever aggressive in finding new investment opportunities, and ruthless and unrelenting when thrust into a competitive situation, Annenberg overextended himself when he purchased the staid and complacent *Philadelphia Inquirer* and engaged in a series of conflicts with rival New Jersey and Pennsylvania newspapers. He quickly found himself caught up in the murky labyrinth of Pennsylvania politics, supporting in 1938 a Republican candidate for governor. During the acrimonious campaign he published strident editorial attacks on President Franklin Roosevelt and his reform administration, whom he linked with the rival Democratic gubernatorial candidate.[17]

He was done in by a combination of complex factors. These included a seamy reputation derived from his close association with gambling interests and his take-no-prisoners approach to business competition and politics. His reputation as a brawling business man, his Jewish heritage, and his obvious close connections with corrupt city bosses and illegal gambling interests also made him someone whom the Philadelphia social and economic elite did not welcome into their traditional conservative circles. All of this, coupled with his unrelenting criticism of Roosevelt and the New Dealers, contributed to his indictment and conviction for evading federal income taxes in 1940. One of the telling pieces of evidence at the highly publicized Philadelphia trial—other than the discovery of a secret set of books that revealed major discrepancies in his income tax returns—was a letter written in 1936 to a friend that noted that his investments in the wire service and *Daily Racing Form* had evolved into a virtual monopoly: "We in the racing field own three-quarters of the world and manage the balance. In other words, the few little nations that are left have to pay us tribute to continue. Now, why isn't that the most beautiful and most satisfactory position to be in, which ought to satisfy even me?"[18]

Annenberg was hit with a stiff $8 million fine and a four-year prison sentence, of which he served two years in the federal prison at Lewisburg, Pennsylvania, before being released following the discovery of an inoperable brain tumor. He died in November 1942 at the age of sixty-four, and his son Walter—destined to become a major player and financial donor in Republican politics for the next four decades—took over his father's empire. The racing wire, soon to be rendered obsolete by television and new forms of communication, was already no longer a part of the Annenberg enterprises; Walter's father had divested himself of the Nationwide News Service in 1939 when he began to feel the heat of the federal investigation into his complex finances. But after the war Walter turned the *Daily Racing Form* into a "technological marvel" by incorporating new computer and high-speed communications technology in order to publish daily up to thirty-five separate versions to appeal to bettors interested in local races. The *Daily Racing Form* remained a highly profitable publication over the years, returning an estimated $10 million profit in 1988, when Walter sold it, along with other publications, to Rupert Murdoch for an estimated $3 billion; still profitable, and selling for $3.50 as a daily newspaper, it was estimated to be worth between $350 and $400 million at the time of the sale.[19]

As the United States entered the era of the Second World War, horse racing remained the most popular form of sports wagering. In urban places across the nation, bookies, dependent on the services of Moses Annenberg's Nationwide News Service, could be found plying their trade. In St. Louis, for example, a news magazine reporter readily found 250 "handbook shops," which he reported was "twice the number of movie houses" in the city. Most were located in small grimy stores "where windows are obscured with tobacco ads" as an "obvious blind of the racing paraphernalia in the back room—radios and direct telegraph connections with the tracks."[20]

Unlike during the First World War, the federal government permitted the tracks to operate during the Second World War. Postwar prosperity stimulated a healthy growth in betting handles. In 1949 the Continental News Service, established in 1940 by Cleveland businessman and gambler Mickey McBride to fill the void left by Annenberg's departure from the field, provided service from Canada to Mexico City, using 23,000 miles of lines leased from Western Union to supply 20,000 bookies with essential racing data. A handful of smaller competitors provided service to another 10,000 bookie customers. Because the weekly service fee ranged from $150 to $500, many smaller book operators joined forces in a so-called horse room where they shared wire service. Across the United States by 1950, gambling expert John Scarne estimated, there were some 270,000 bookies and their employees whose livelihood depended on the racing wires.[21]

Although offtrack betting had contributed to the general public's zeal for gambling, attendance at the tracks continued to grow throughout the middle part of the twentieth century, reaching its peak during the 1970s. By 1950 there were 150 tracks offering thoroughbred and harness racing in thirty states. About 100 of these venues were considered to be "major" tracks. These were indeed big businesses with hundreds of millions of dollars invested in the land and facilities, in breeding farms and horses. Operations costs also were astronomical, including the salaries and wages that were paid to track officials and employees, state oversight officials, jockeys, trainers, harness cart drivers, breeders, veterinarians, oddsmakers, grooms, and stable boys.

The investments required were more than justified by the public response. In 1960, 47 million persons paid admission to attend a day at the track; in 1972, about the time when attendance peaked, 74 million persons attended the races. Those 74 million persons bet $6.3 billion dollars, two-thirds of it on the thoroughbred races, one-third on the trotters and pacers. The tracks also paid out $305 million in purses.[22] As a point of comparison, attendance at all major league baseball games that year was just 50 percent of that at the tracks. The pari-mutuel wagering figures for 1972, however, only begin to tell the story. In that year John Scarne conducted an intensive study of illegal offtrack betting by asking a sample of 3,000 horseplayers at several representative major tracks if they ever bet illegally offtrack with a bookie; the response was that they did so often, betting $7 illegally with bookies for every $1 they bet at the track, leading him to conclude that at a minimum $42 billion was bet that year illegally! These same players also provided Scarne with data on the bookies with whom they bet; his conclusion was staggering, indicating that some 200,000 bookies operated across the United States employing 800,000 persons as runners and couriers.[23]

Despite the many professions by the horse race crowd of their love for horses and for the spirit and enthusiasm generated at the track, the bottom line was simply the essential human instinct of greed. They played the horses because they wanted to make money, and they enjoyed the thrill of having their money at risk in a race. "The great majority of race fans know nothing about horses and care less," Scarne concluded. "Elephant races would draw the same crowds if they offered the same opportunity of getting a bet down."[24]

4

Bootleggers and Bookies

Essential to the growth of gambling during the years between the world wars was the upsurge in the number of illegal bookies. Although these individuals were frequently mentioned in the news, little documentation about them and their enterprises exists today. Practices and customs varied from city to city, but it is possible to advance some generalizations. Many of the leading gambling figures who dominated the field from the 1930s to the 1960s got their start in bootlegging during the Prohibition era of the 1920s. They were often descendants of the large influx of immigrants from eastern and central Europe between 1880 and 1914. Although popular stereotypes suggest that the great majority were of Italian ancestry, the evidence is that at least as many gambling leaders were, like Moses Annenberg, of eastern European Jewish ancestry. These men, the sons of immigrants, had grown up in tough Jewish immigrant enclaves in large northeastern and midwestern cities. The historian Alan Balboni concludes that the Eighteenth Amendment struck these men, raised in a culture where moderate use of alcohol was a normal part of daily life, as "absurd." Not impressed by the antialcohol moralism of Protestant reformers, they moved without qualms to take advantage of the economic opportunity presented them. In their circles, Balboni concludes, "A young man who made or distributed liquor had a chance not only to get rich quickly but also to gain respect in his community."[1]

It was also natural for many of these men to establish themselves in gambling circles. Apparently, their lucrative bootlegging operations provided the capital reserves necessary to open sports books, and they were already well connected in their urban neighborhoods through a complex web of social and economic relationships—some legal, some illegal. They tended to enjoy close personal relationships with local politicians, law enforcement officials, gangsters, racing wire representatives, and racetrack operators. They were often sports fans and

41

regular bettors themselves, so when they opted to operate a sports book they already had an established network of connections upon which to build their business. Thus these gamblers/businessmen brought to their sports books substantial managerial expertise, including a solid grasp of the important skills of statistics and bookkeeping. In some instances, successful bootleggers merely invested in sports books operated by associates; other times, they established and operated them themselves. In either case, from the 1920s until the 1950s, the biggest operators in sports gambling had established themselves in their urban environment as respected businessmen who provided a product much in demand: beer and liquor at a time when the federal government sought to eliminate their consumption.[2]

Those who booked sports bets often operated policy or numbers operations, sometimes both, as well. Policy and numbers appealed to poor urban residents eager to cash in on a large payoff from small bets that ranged from as little as ten cents to a few dollars; urbanized African Americans were particularly prominent on the lists of regular policy/numbers clients. Policy, the older of the two games, was the forerunner to the current popular casino game of Keno. It was a complex game in which the bettor selected four numbers ranging from 1 to 78; if those four numbers were among the twelve drawn, he or she would win a large payoff. Numbers offered even lesser odds—requiring the winner to select one number ranging from 1 to 999; the winning number was commonly determined by the last three digits of the total number of stocks traded on the New York Stock Exchange, sometimes by the numbers carried by three winning horses at a designated track. Although the chance of winning at numbers was 1 in 999, payoffs usually ranged from 450 to 1 to 600 to 1.

These gambling bosses required a small army of agents—usually called "runners"—who blanketed the neighborhoods of the urban underclasses, often booking both numbers and sports wagers. The documentation about this era indicates that runners were men who seldom had a high school diploma and who often worked full-time at another job. Many runners were small-time operators who, in addition to their regular jobs as bartenders, barbers, billiards room operators, candy store owners, or streetcorner newspaper vendors, supplemented their income by serving the wagering needs of a neighborhood. They served a relatively small clientele, usually ranging from twenty to a hundred regulars. In large cities where sports gambling flourished, such as Detroit, Chicago, Cleveland, Philadelphia, and New York City, the great percentage of sports betting was operated, in one way or another, within the purview of local crime bosses, who possessed both political connections and ample resources to hire skilled lines makers and bookkeepers. They either ran the show themselves or extracted a tribute from independent bookies.

Whatever his location on the local status scale, the successful bookie had to rely on his good name to attract business—especially to maintain the long-term loyalty of repeat customers. In order to encourage a steady flow of bets, the bookie often extended credit and reaped a supplemental income from steep interest charges. A successful bookie paid off on winners without hesitation, usually on a weekly basis; if a bettor was ever stiffed by his bookie, he would naturally take his business elsewhere, but he would also inform all his friends of the bookie's treachery. A close working relationship between bookies and local law enforcement was also essential. Within any neighborhood it was no secret who made book. Policemen routinely looked the other way, often encouraged to do so by a regular gratuity provided by an appreciative bookie. After all, given the many criminal activities the cop on the beat routinely encountered, it was not unreasonable that he tended to view gambling as a nonviolent enterprise, a benign "victimless" form of criminal activity. Having considerably more serious issues to deal with, he was inclined to consider sports gambling merely as a popular form of urban recreation.[3]

Although condemned by antigambling spokesmen, and occasionally targeted by police when the spirit of reform reached high places in city government, bookies were usually respected in their neighborhoods. They were viewed as businessmen providing a wanted service. Bookies and their clients upon occasion even took on the image in popular literature of lovable rogues. The bookie/gambler was only one of a host of "thugs and mugs" whose ways of life on the streets of New York City were highlighted in the writings of newspaper columnist Damon Runyon from the First World War until his death in 1946. In his widely read columns in William Randolph Hearst's *New York American,* and in his popular short stories that appeared in such national magazines as *Colliers, Cosmopolitan,* and the *Saturday Evening Post,* Runyon described with affection and good humor the lives of the "Guys and Dolls" who made Broadway and its environs a special place. He romanticized the lives and careers of gangsters, hustlers, gamblers, bartenders, and show people. He gave his gambling characters such monikers as Dave the Dude, Lone Louie, Sleepout Sam, the Sinking Sailor, and Harry the Horse, and treated their antics and lifestyles with humorous and sympathetic detachment. His stories were usually located on a streetcorner, in a booth at Mindy's bar and grill, or at the racetrack. His delicious descriptions of the highs and lows of Nicholas Dandalos—"Nick the Greek"—turned the immigrant from Crete into a famous national figure.[4]

At various times the owner of a stable of club boxers ("who toppled over at the slightest suggestion of a breeze") and of five race horses (who collectively "achieved various levels of distinction ranging from very little to none"), Runyon found in sports wagering a metaphor for the modern American condition.[5] He

bet regularly on horses, prizefights, golf matches, and baseball games, seldom
with much success. In his columns and short stories, Runyon re-created—with
ample doses of exaggeration and sweetening—the lives of those he knew from
the racetrack, at ringside, at the ballpark, and at his favorite midtown restaurants
and watering holes.

Runyon painted an image of his gambling associates that only the most
hard-shelled Puritan could dislike. As he described the antics of "Bookie Bob"
or "Willie the Worrier," he did much to romanticize the world of sports betting.
Such conniving rogues as his magic typewriter produced—the hustlers, the
tinhorn gamblers, the touts, the promoters, the high rollers, the ticket scalpers—
were hardly the evil and corrupt criminals that antigambling forces routinely
described. A reading of such classic Runyon short stories as "All Horseplayers
Die Broke," "The Lemon Drop Kid,"[6] "Money from Home," "Pick the Winner,"
and "The Snatching of Bookie Bob" reveals the essential traits that Runyon's
gamblers shared—they wagered on sports to associate with other people like
themselves and for the rush of adrenalin that comes from scoring big time on a
long shot. What stands out clearly about Runyon's gamblers was that they knew
how to be graceful losers.[7]

Like his characters, Runyon himself would go to desperate lengths to find
a system to predict winners: in a column in the *American* entitled "No Justice,"
he complained, "I bet on favorites and long shots win, and I bet on long shots
and favorites win. All the time I get caught in switches. I got four photo finishes
last week. I went down and looked at the pictures and I don't see how the judges
could split them out, they were so close. They could have called them either way.
I don't know about that camera. It could be wrong." He never tired of telling his
readers about his latest "can't lose" system for picking winners. In one column,
he cheerfully noted, "A fellow has come up with a system for beating the races
based upon dreams. You dream about something and the next morning you look
up the subject of the dream in this guy's book."[8]

In recounting the adventures of his colorful collection of gambling acquaintances, Damon Runyon contributed greatly to the mythology underpinning the
Gambler's Dream—the eternal quest for the secret infallible system, for hitting
the long shot, for filling the inside straight. Witness his confession to his readers
about one of his many legendary Kentucky Derby fizzles:

> Getting back to the subject of systems for playing the races, I once
> made my selection of the probable winner of the Kentucky Derby by
> the simple device of closing my eyes and stabbing a pin into a list of the
> entries and choosing the steed whose name was impaled. I got the idea

from a lady player who always picked the horse she played in the race by using the same method in her program.

The list I employed was in a newspaper, and the name I pinned was Scapa Flow, and what happened to Scapa Flow in the Derby should not have happened to a poodle. I showed Major Bill Corum [a major official of the Kentucky Derby] the newspaper list and the way I had daggered it after the race, deploring my foolishness in adopting such a method, but after examining the paper, the Major said, "Your system was 100 per cent right only you forgot to notice the other side of the paper. Your pin also pierced an advertisement for a bank on the next page, and look at the line it went through." The Major held up the paper so I could see the line which read, "Save your Money."[9]

The inclusion of gamblers among the characters with whom Damon Runyon entertained three generations of Americans did much to help sports betting move into the realm of acceptable social behavior. It was difficult to dislike his "Guys and Dolls" even though they lived beyond the limits of the law and accepted standards of behavior. By the time Runyon died in 1946, bookies still lived on the edge between legitimacy and outlawry, between social acceptance and ostracism, but they had become substantially more respectable. Undoubtedly, Runyon overly romanticized their trade, which was in reality decidedly unromantic, a daily grind in search of the 5 percent vigorish. Perhaps Neil Isaacs and Gerald Strine best summarized the calling of the bookie in their book describing systems for winning at betting on football:

Contrary to popular belief, bookies are neither the colorful folk figures of Damon Runyon's mythology nor shadowy underworld types looking for dishonest opportunities for betting coups. They are businessmen trying to make an honest living despite the pesky encumbrance that their business is illegal in most parts of this country. A bookmaker's stock in trade is his own integrity; it has to be, since most of his business is built on credit, trust and faith. And his business relies absolutely on the integrity of the sporting event itself.[10]

The number of bookies expanded in the two decades between the world wars. Interest in sports and in betting on them generated a steadily expanding clientele for the street bookmaker. Although horse racing dominated the sports betting world before the Second World War, wagering on professional baseball and, especially, college football was increasing, a result of the hefty growth of public interest in those sports due to expanded coverage by newspapers, radio, and motion pictures. The 1920s were dubbed the "Golden Age" of sports because of increased spectator interest and a new era of national movie and radio audiences.

Boxing came out of the shadows when several states emulated New York's decision to legalize the sport in 1920. College football gained millions of new fans, overcoming substantial faculty opposition and public criticism of its several ethical problems. Out from under the World Series scandal of 1919, professional baseball enjoyed banner years, although attendance for most teams seldom exceeded 750,000 a season during the 1920s and fell precipitously during the Great Depression. The first generation of professional sportswriters, which came to prominence during the 1920s, played a major role in increasing public interest. The leader of this new group of journalists, Grantland Rice, emphasized the heroic aspects of sports, often turning average players into superhuman stars. Rice set the standard for this "gee whiz" school of sportswriters, and he had a small army of emulators. The first generation of sports radio broadcasters, led by Graham McNamee, joined in this deification of athletes.[11]

By the end of the decade the American people had a new type of hero—the exceptional athlete whose exploits quickly became the stuff of legend, thanks to star-struck sportswriters who covered up their human weaknesses and exaggerated their athletic achievements. During the 1920s such stars as baseball's Babe Ruth, Grover Cleveland Alexander, Rogers Hornsby, and John McGraw, tennis's Bill Tilden, college football's running back Red Grange and Notre Dame coach Knute Rockne, swimmer Gertrude Ederle, golfer Bobby Jones, and boxers Jack Dempsey and Gene Tunney—and many others—became larger-than-life figures to millions of American sports fans. Their exploits were written about in hyperventilated prose that emphasized only the positive aspects of their lives and sports exploits; the negative was seldom even alluded to, let alone addressed forthrightly.[12]

Increased public interest in the sports stars and the games they played naturally stimulated wagering. Bookies who once had devoted all of their attention to horses now had to accommodate customers who wanted to bet on prizefights, major league baseball games, and college football. If they set a line that provided the "wise guy" bettor a major advantage, they stood to lose big. The need for a good "line" that would keep bookies from getting blindsided led to the establishment in Minneapolis in the mid-1930s of a professional line-setting firm that brought a new level of sophistication to odds making. This company quickly developed a loyal national clientele of bookies whose substantial operations required a new level of professionalism in oddsmaking.

In addition to an upsurge in betting on individual games, there was a rapid growth in popularity of the baseball pool card. First introduced in New York City before the turn of the century, the first pools enabled fans to bet on the major league team they believed would score the most runs in a week; other forms of pools required the participant to guess the total number of runs to be scored by all major league teams during a seven-day period—or variations on that essential theme. The baseball pool card, which could be played for as little as ten cents, provided baseball fans with an alternative to the numbers or policy rackets being operated by many urban crime syndicates.[13]

The profitability of baseball pool cards led to the emergence of football pool cards during the early 1930s. The football pool was attractive to the thinking gambler because it offered a much more realistic form of gambling compared with having to pick the total number of runs scored by a team—a wildly fluctuating goal impossible to handicap in any rational, systematic manner. The football pool required that the bettor pick a minimum of five winning teams without a single loser from a list of nine games compiled by the bookie. Any tied game was scored as a loss for the bettor, greatly skewing the odds in the bookmaker's favor. Naturally, the card distributor selected the nine most competitive games, thereby compounding the players' difficulty in selecting a winning parlay. The football cards were aimed at the small-time gambler, since most bookies accepted a wager as small as twenty-five cents. Gullible participants never understood that the football cards posed almost impossible odds of successfully winning over a period of time: picking multiple winners was difficult enough in an amateur sport where upsets were not infrequent, but to compound the disadvantage confronted by the bettor, the established payoffs were about one-third what they should have been, given the actual odds.[14]

Nonetheless, the football cards proved to be extremely popular, and their use spread across the country from New York City and Chicago, where they originated. Agents found an especially lucrative market on college campuses and in working-class neighborhoods in cities large and small. By the eve of the Second World War the football pool cards had become, by one serious estimate, a $5-million-a-year business. One journalist, W. Thorton Martin, writing in the *Saturday Evening Post* in 1936, suggested grandly that "the football pool is America's fastest growing industry," with the bookies' profits being "stupendous." In 1939 sportswriter Stanley Frank observed, "The Football season marks the open season on suckers—big snappy fellows always hooked by the same bait." The football cards, he said, had produced an "All-American madness" whose stacked odds provided the bettor a "one way ticket to the poorhouse." Another journalist dug deep into the burgeoning football parlay card racket and estimated that a typical runner working for a "betting commissioner" would distribute some 2,000 cards a week in his assigned territory. With the typical commissioner supervising a dozen or so runners, his weekly handle, made up largely of fifty-cent or one-dollar bets, would approach $10,000. Sports betting, now extended far beyond the racetracks, had become big business during the depression years—"a vast commercialized and heavily capitalized outlaw business," as the *Christian Century* editorialized with stern disapproval.[15]

Although established urban betting syndicates quickly climbed aboard the football betting phenomenon, the *Saturday Evening Post*'s Martin suggested that many of the individuals who had created this new phenomenon were a cut above the horse race crowd. Many had college educations and brought with them the sophistication and élan of "Wall Street types." They were, he said, "college men mostly graduated from the ivy covered halls, still interested in college football," but they were also sharp businessmen who were "adept at figuring percentages, odds, and statistical permutations." Writing from his perspective in New York City, Martin noted that many operators of the new football pools had strong ties to the stock market and had naturally gravitated toward betting on college football. "When the stock market shuddered, time hung heavy on their hands. It was an easy step from betting on a game or two every weekend to the development of football parlay cards, or pools." It was not a coincidence, he noted, that the new parlay/pool cards became commonplace in the city in 1933—the year the Great Depression reached its absolute depths. These operators easily found runners to distribute their cards, streetwise men who had experience in the numbers racket or who had worked in the lower echelons of the horse betting business. Vendors operating streetcorner newsstands were naturals to distribute the new football cards and take bets because "many of them were already running books on the ponies and also peddled baseball tickets." Consequently, the popularity of football cards "grew rapidly after 1933."[16]

One journalist in 1936 estimated that New York City gamblers alone illegally wagered $60 million a year on baseball, basketball, and football. It is important to understand, however, that the great percentage of that handle was returned to winning bettors; only about 5 percent of the money remained with the bookies as compensation or with their brokerage services. But the bookies clearly held the higher ground in their ongoing game with their clients: they enjoyed a clear statistical advantage. As a writer for the *American Mercury* explained, "Professional gamblers have reached their prominent status in and out of their trade through constant and studied devotion to the Great God Percentage, and not to any special favors bestowed by the Goddess Luck. . . . There ain't no such lady."[17]

That the percentages were skewed to benefit the bookies was testimony to the lack of mathematical skills possessed by most casual bettors. Journalist Martin's comment about the "betting commissioners" who operated the new football cards being "masters of percentages" was apt: by decreeing that all tie games were wins for the pools, the betting commissioners gave themselves a significant advantage. While they paid 50–1 for a nine-pick card, the odds should actually have been 511–1; while the minimum five pick typically paid 10–1, it should have been 31–1. With such odds, Martin noted, the pools seldom lost money, at most one or two weeks during the season. Bettors tended to gravitate toward the pools, but most bookies also accepted bets on individual games based on the traditional odds system. With a dozen or so runners in the field, in a typical autumn the small-time football commissioner, after paying off winners and remunerating his runners, would earn between $35,000 and $45,000—at a time when the average American family earned less than $2,000 per year.[18]

With such large amounts of money at stake, of course, the timeless motivation of greed sometimes got the upper hand. A bookie might merely disappear after a particularly big handle came in on Friday night, leaving his clients, being engaged in an illegal activity, with no legal recourse; but he had best never show his face in town again. Regular gamblers always knew who their bookie was, having selected him on the basis of character and trust.

During the 1943 season, one clever Harvard student, a member of the Crimson football team, put an interesting twist on the many possible angles posed by the new football betting phenomenon. Hired as a knowledgeable football expert by a Boston "commissioner" to set his weekly odds, the student, having proved his talent and gained the trust of his employer, late in the season slipped a game onto the betting sheet with the odds badly skewed. The student line maker then tipped off his Harvard friends, who made a killing on the game. At least on paper. Recognizing that he had been deceived, the commissioner simply refused to pay off on that game, and the Harvard sharpies had to eat their lost wagers.[19]

What was the attraction of betting on college football? For starters, many sports fans who attended football games or listened to radio broadcasts discovered that if they had money riding on the outcome, the experience was considerably more exciting. Others merely wanted to support their alma mater with a bet on the Big Game. In addition, thanks to radio, millions of fans developed a strong attachment to one of the three institutions that played national schedules: Notre Dame and the two military academies. Because of its success under head coach

Knute Rockne during the 1920s, Notre Dame attracted its famed and staunchly dedicated "subway alumni," devoted Fighting Irish football fans who had never attended the institution, let alone set foot on the South Bend campus. Of course, many subway alumni were Roman Catholics, but many were not, attracted by the school's winning ways, which they had learned to appreciate from listening to their games on the radio. Notre Dame's unusual policy of permitting any radio station or network to broadcast their games without charge—an altruistic gesture intended to demonstrate that the Fighting Irish teams were not to be corrupted by commercialism—led to their games being featured across the nation on hundreds of radio stations. This produced a large and loyal national following that exists to this day.[20]

Such loyal fans as these were not hesitant to put money down with their local bookies on their favorite team. To the amazement of sportswriter Stanley Frank, such fans were not even overly disappointed when their team lost. "Every football bettor firmly believes he will win, whether it is football or basketball," he observed, but a substantial number of those who tended to bet only on college football were set apart from other gamblers because of their emotional loyalty to their alma mater or favorite team: "The football bettor actually seems happy about the whole thing, even when he loses."[21]

This was never so true as with the vast amount of betting that surrounded the annual showdown between Army and Notre Dame. This particular rivalry, because it often determined the mythical national championship, became so intense that after the undefeated Cadet and Irish squads played to a 0–0 tie in their famed 1946 "game of the century" before more than 70,000 fans in Yankee Stadium, school officials mutually agreed to cancel the series despite the enormous ticket sales. The danger of having the game influenced by big-time gamblers seeking a betting edge by bribing players had become too great a possibility. In that year sports experts estimated that Americans were now betting $100 million dollars on college football, 10 percent of that amount on the Army–Notre Dame game. Even FBI Director J. Edgar Hoover was concerned, and he issued a much repeated statement: "We are unalterably opposed to any attempts by doubtful characters to move in on sports. We are opposed to any lessening of standards that apply in sports. . . . There's too much at stake."[22]

5

The Point Spread Revolution

The popularity of college football betting—whether it was betting the odds on a single game offered by a bookie or playing a parlay/pool card—quickly spread to college basketball. During the 1930s, especially in the Midwest and Northeast, interest in college basketball increased substantially. In 1939 the National Collegiate Athletic Association (NCAA) held its first national tournament (won by the University of Oregon), but the National Invitational Tournament, held at New York City's Madison Square Garden, was considered the more prestigious tournament. In 1934 a New York sportswriter by the name of Ned Irish, impressed by the standing-room-only crowds he saw squeezed into small college gymnasiums in the city, began promoting college basketball games in Madison Square Garden. He was so successful that he left journalism to promote college games full-time, eventually rising to the position of acting president of the Garden. His famed doubleheaders routinely drew sellout crowds, and by 1940 New York City had become the capital of college basketball. Promoters in other cities soon caught on, and Boston and Chicago attempted to compete with Irish. However, he had so firmly established his Madison Square Garden games in the public mind that New York reigned supreme in the rapidly growing world of college hoops.[1]

Ned Irish's success projected heretofore obscure East Coast basketball teams, especially those located in the New York City area, into national prominence. By the eve of the Second World War such teams as Long Island University, City College of New York, New York University, St. John's, Manhattan College, and Seton Hall enjoyed an enhanced status and were frequently listed in the national rankings. Strong teams from other regions vied to be invited to the Garden to play the local teams. The basketball powers of the day—Kentucky, Kansas, Notre Dame, Bowling Green, Missouri, Toledo, Stanford, Indiana, DePaul, Bradley, and a host of others—were eager to challenge one of the eastern giants and bask in the limelight of the Big Apple. Following the war, Irish put on twenty-five doubleheaders a year at the Garden and extended his promotions to civic arenas in Buffalo and Philadelphia. It was now possible for a visiting team to do a three- or four-game sweep of the East Coast under Irish's promotions and never set foot on a college campus. The commercial prospects available on the East Coast were alluring to athletic directors and coaches nationwide, and Irish became the most powerful figure in college basketball. During the war his doubleheaders remained a focal point for sports fans, and their popularity grew exponentially with the arrival of television in the years immediately following the war.

The rapid ascendancy of college basketball coincided with the emergence of the single most important development in the history of sports betting: the introduction of the point spread betting system. The origins of the point spread idea are murky, and there are several conflicting theories about when the concept was first introduced and by whom. Perhaps—as in the seventeenth century when Newton and Leibniz, each working in ignorance of the other, created the calculus at approximately the same time—so too did more than one gambling genius independently develop the point spread. The most plausible explanation is that it originated with—or at least was refined and popularized by—Charles K. McNeil, a native of Connecticut, the recipient of a bachelor's degree in history from the University of Chicago, and a man blessed with a special talent for understanding complex statistical and probability problems.[2]

McNeil originally pursued a career as a prep school teacher in Connecticut and as a college instructor in Chicago, but by the early 1930s he had taken a position as a securities analyst in Chicago. An avid baseball fan, in the evenings he devoted himself to mastering the nuances of baseball statistics and probabilities, a talent that soon led him into the company of bettors eager to take advantage of his expertise. On most summer afternoons he could be found in the gamblers' section of the bleachers at Wrigley Field or Comiskey Park, applying his keen probability skills in a practical manner. An old-time Chicago gambler recalled that "McNeil could always be found in one of three places—the Gym Club, Wrigley Field or Comiskey Park. . . . We'd sit in the bleachers where the gamblers gathered, and they not only bet on the outcome of the game but would bet McNeil on the batters reaching first or second base, or scoring, inning by inning." As Robert Boyle writes, during the 1930s sports gambling in Chicago was "widespread and wide open."[3]

The hub of Chicago's sports gambling was the famous downtown Gym Club, located on Rush Street. Here McNeil became friends with the veteran professional sports gambler Billy Hecht. At age fifty-two in 1942, the diminutive Hecht was at the top of his game. A modest and quiet bachelor who in his time had operated drug and liquor stores and managed traveling ice- and roller-skating shows, Hecht was well known as a shrewd sports handicapper who was connected with the big-time players. Before the 1940 trial of Moe Annenberg, he had been quizzed by federal investigators about his involvement with Mont Tennes and the horse race wire business, but he was not called to testify at the trial. More than once Hecht managed to avoid indictment on criminal charges for his gambling activities.

By the mid-1930s the scholarly McNeil had realized that his ability to handicap sports events enabled him to earn more from his wagering than from his day job. So he left the securities business and turned his full attention to handicapping. He was so successful that Chicago bookies put limits on his bets, which prompted him to open his own sports book in the early 1940s.[4] It was during the war years that he began to offer an intriguing new betting format to his customers, something he called the "wholesale odds system." It is likely that he obtained portions of the concept from Hecht, who in turn, some contemporaries suggest, had gotten some of his ideas from the notorious Ed Curd, a nationally known oddsmaker and gambler who lived in Lexington, Kentucky, and specialized in handicapping horses but also did considerable business in human sports. A friend and associate of the famed University of Kentucky basketball coach Adolph Rupp, Curd boldly operated out of the Mayfair Bar in downtown Lexington, booking bets and placing them himself via telephone with bookmakers elsewhere. (In the 1960s Curd was forced to flee the country to avoid prosecution on violation of interstate gambling charges and never returned from his hideaway in the Caribbean.) But while Curd and Hecht are believed to have contributed to the development of the new betting system, it was McNeil who refined it and first offered point spread betting out of his own sports book.[5]

The new system provided the ultimate answer to the perplexing problem American bookmakers had been wrestling with since the late nineteenth century: how to generate equal amounts of "action" on a contest in which one of the participants was an overwhelming favorite. Even lopsided odds could not generate equal amounts of wagers on both sides of a contest if the underdog team had no realistic chance of victory. Bookies were exposed to huge losses if too many bettors bet on a victorious underdog at steep odds and, conversely, were faced with the prospect of losing money despite low odds when an avalanche of bettors cashed in on a sure winner while the underdog attracted only limited money. To protect himself in these instances the prudent bookie would refuse to accept bets on certain lopsided games, but this often irritated his customers, who might take their business elsewhere.

The solution to this dilemma introduced by McNeil was devilishly simple: instead of offering odds on the two teams, he sought to even out the betting by requiring the favorite to win the contest by an established number of points. The underdog merely had to narrow the final margin to less than the "point spread." For example, if the University of Missouri football team was established as a 6-point favorite over archrival Kansas University, then the Tigers had to win by 7 points or more in order for bettors to collect; conversely, a bet on Kansas would pay off if the Jayhawks lost by 5 points or less. McNeil initially offered his customers a 2-point "split" line, a ploy that worked to the benefit of the bookie. If a team, say Missouri, was listed by McNeil as a 6/8 favorite over Kansas, then it meant that if you bet on Missouri, the Tigers had to win by 8 points; if you bet on the underdog Jayhawks, then you got 6 points. If the final score fell on a 7-point differential, then the bookie kept all monies bet. McNeil and other shrewd lines makers seemed to be able to set lines that hit that magic middle figure quite often. Naturally, gamblers fought to have the split line eliminated, and under the pressure of competition between bookies it disappeared by 1950.[6]

The beauty of the point spread was that even a hopelessly lopsided contest could be made attractive to bettors by giving the underdog team a substantial number of points (it is not unusual to see some college basketball games with point spreads of 20 points or more; each autumn Saturday a few mismatched college football games have spreads that reach well beyond 40 points). The point spread provided the next logical evolutionary step for bookmakers seeking ways to even out the betting handle to protect their vigorish. Admiral Henry John Rous of London had begun the process in mid-nineteenth-century England when he introduced the idea of placing additional weights on the better racehorses to make less talented horses attractive to gamblers. The idea of requiring favorite horses to carry a weight handicap—hence the origins of the term *handicapping*— did not work as well as anticipated, and so shortly before the twentieth century bookmakers introduced the concept of offering different odds on horses based upon their records and reputations; if a strong favorite won, its backers won relatively little in comparison to those who held a winning ticket on a long shot.

In their pioneering 1978 book on how to bet on football games, two respected sports betting authorities, Gerald Strine and Neil Isaacs, do not mention McNeil and state that the point spread was introduced during the 1920s. However, they provide no evidence to support their contention. One prominent sports betting figure whose career spanned the second half of the twentieth century, Mort

Olshan, has written that the spread was introduced during the late 1930s, but he too offers no supporting facts for his claim; by the time Olshan entered the handicapping profession as a young man in 1948, the system was already widespread.[7] In his novel about the 1951 college basketball gambling scandal, the sports journalist and historian Charles Rosen suggests, again without documentation, that the point spread was widely used in the New York City area during the 1930s.[8] On balance, the available evidence points to McNeil as the key person who introduced the revolutionary point spread system, although he quite likely benefited from the thinking of Billy Hecht and Ed Curd.[9]

McNeil's "wholesale odds system" was an instant hit with his customers, and it was rapidly adopted across the country. The system was even more of a hit with bookies, because if the spread was set correctly it generated approximately equal amounts of money wagered on both teams. It also enabled them to offer more wagering opportunities, because games that previously they would have been forced to "take off the board" because of an obvious mismatch could now be made attractive to bettors. The point spread thus made it theoretically possible for an astute line maker to render the most lopsided of contests dead even in the eyes of bettors, thereby stimulating considerable wagering on a team that earlier would have attracted few, if any, takers.[10] And, of course, equal monies wagered on a contest assures the businessman-bookie of earning his commission.

So although the origins of the point spread remain, to use Olshan's word, "foggy," within a few years after the Second World War the new concept had swept all before it, gaining widespread acceptance by bookies and players alike. In his authoritative book *The Scandals of '51*, journalist Rosen quotes a veteran bookie that the point spread was "the greatest discovery since the zipper."[11] Indeed, it was the equivalent of the dawning of a new age. Within a few years the point spread became the dominant wagering format for football and basketball and sparked a marked increase in the level of action on those sports. The venerable sports pool cards, which had produced high profit levels for the "commissioners" merely by requiring a bettor to pick five or more winning teams, now also incorporated the spread, making the bettors' challenge that much greater and the bookies that much more financially secure.

The widespread adoption of the point spread was helped by the support of the nation's leading sports gambling authority of the time, the consulting and publications firm operated out of Minneapolis by Leo Hirschfield. His magic numbers were disseminated nationwide via several publications that were released by the innocuously entitled company Athletic Publications, Inc., a subsidiary of Hirschfield's Gorham Press. Because a badly skewed line could prove disastrous to Hirschfield's bookie clientele, he and his associates approached their craft with utmost care. They operated, *Collier's Magazine* wrote in 1947, "one of the most intricate businesses in the world."[12]

In the 1930s Hirschfield had chosen to establish his enterprise in his home-town because of its central location in the nation's heartland, making it possible to ensure timely mail delivery for his publications. Also, long-distance telephone service was sometimes problematical at the time, and Minneapolis seemed to offer the most consistently reliable service—and Hirschfield's staff handicappers were dependent upon obtaining up-to-the-minute information from their many contacts across the nation. His company also offered what was probably the nation's first telephone non–horse racing sports information service to a select group of subscribers. From the mid-1930s until 1961, when he ceased operations in the face of new federal antigambling laws, Minneapolis was recognized as the capital of America's sports gambling. One of Hirschfield's key associates was none other than Billy Hecht, whom he had lured out of Chicago to help him put out the authoritative "Minneapolis Line." Hirschfield's company not only set the odds and point spreads for thousands of bookie clients but also published widely subscribed team scouting reports and weekly tout sheets for bettors that analyzed the upcoming contests and recommended which teams to bet on. The most prominent of these publications was the nationally circulated *Green Sheet.* Hirschfield's myriad endeavors focused on human sports, leaving the field of horse racing to Walter Annenberg's *Daily Racing Form.* Hirschfield concentrated on college football and basketball during the fall and winter and on major league baseball during the summer.[13]

Hirschfield's profitable operation rested squarely on the validity of the infor-mation he provided in the *Green Sheet* and on the accuracy of the "Minneapolis Line" he distributed to bookies. Although it was widely rumored that he had a veritable army of paid "bird dogs" scattered across the nation to provide him with the latest inside information, that was not the case. Mort Olshan, at the time a youthful handicapper, recalls that "sure, we talked to people [who] were experts with a real lowdown on the local scene. Thus is the way with handicappers now, it was the [same] way then." Hirschfield's was a small operation, usually four line makers working independently who met with the boss on Monday mornings and together hammered out the betting lines for the week. Olshan says that Hirschfield possessed "the quickest brain I ever encountered"; he never followed teams or games closely "but intuitively . . . would know if a game was out of line."[14] The accuracy of Hirschfield's service became legendary in betting circles. The *New York Times* sports columnist Arthur Daley once ruefully reflected on that reputation: "If Joe Zilch, the star at Siwash, falls down the cellar stairs in the privacy of his home and injures his little toe, the syndicate knows about it before he has picked himself up off the floor. And the odds will fluctuate accordingly. It's positively unbelievable the information that the Minneapolis group can obtain."[15]

Although all of his bookie clients operated outside the law, Hirschfield's was a legitimate business. He merely sold information and opinions to his clients and so was not actually engaged in gambling. Bookies paid him twenty-five dollars a week for a telephone service that provided them with a betting line that they hoped would attract equal action on a contest and keep them from taking a big hit. Gamblers eagerly subscribed to his newsletter, which provided articles analyzing upcoming games, offered tips on the art of handicapping and money management, and, of course, suggested teams that had the potential of beating the spread. The *Green Sheet* was an early prototype of contemporary sports tout publications. As the article in *Collier's Magazine* noted ironically, "Hirschfield's enterprise is legal, but his clients aren't."[16]

The point spread provided a boon for bookies, making their business a little less risky and, even more important, stimulating sports fans to match wits with the line makers, resulting in larger betting levels and greater profits. But it also produced a major set of problems for the sports involved. Before the point spread system was introduced, gamblers seeking to fix a game had to convince a player or players to lose a game they were expected to win. Now it was possible for would-be fixers to suggest to players that they did not have to "dump" (lose) a game but merely win the contest by fewer points than the point spread. Hence a new phrase, "shaving points," entered the lexicon of the American sports world in the years immediately following the Second World War.

Because the final score of a basketball game could be easily manipulated by one or two key players, college basketball became the sport most susceptible to a point-shaving scam. Charles Rosen's many contacts in the netherworld of New York City gambling confirmed to his satisfaction that gamblers had "fixed" many college basketball games during the 1930s, or in the curious parlance of the gambling world, had "done business." It is likely that the "business" he alludes to during the 1930s in fact involved dumping of games—that is, players taking payoffs from gamblers to lose a game so that their benefactors could clean up on favorable odds—not beating a point spread.

During the latter years of the war, a few sporadic allegations surfaced in the press about bribery of college players, but sportswriters, coaches, and administrators quickly denounced such accusations as unfounded and sensational. When solid evidence *was* presented, the example was quickly dismissed as an isolated aberration. No one, it seemed, wanted to kill the new economic dynamo that big-time college basketball had become. In 1944, before the NCAA tournament final game between Utah and Dartmouth at Madison Square Garden, a gambler had the temerity to knock on the hotel door of the Ute's head coach, Vadal Peterson, and ask how much it would take for him to let Dartmouth claim the national championship. According to witnesses, Peterson responded by uncorking a punch to the prospective fixer's jaw and unceremoniously dumping him in the hallway, although the coach later claimed he merely slammed the door in his face. (Led by All-American Arnie Ferrin, Utah eventually beat the Indians 42–40 in overtime.)[17]

Typical of the reaction of college basketball's establishment, a defiant Ned Irish proclaimed his disbelief of Peterson's story and demanded proof that a bribe had been offered. Irish did make a highly visible, although obviously contrived and artificial, move by placing a phalanx of thirty-six detectives near the players' bench and locker rooms to keep known gamblers at bay during the championship game.[18] He later had his chief of security draw up a list of gamblers who attended Garden games but claimed he himself did not know any of the persons on the list. "I heard talk about betting and I read something in the papers, but I myself had no knowledge [of gamblers and gambling]."[19] Of course, any illicit contact between players and gamblers would occur far from the public venue of courtside, but Irish apparently took satisfaction in his visible, if ineffectual, public relations ploy.

The forceful disclaimers issued by Ned Irish and college basketball's elite coaches and administrators came a cropper a season later when the New York City police arrested five Brooklyn College players for conspiring with three gamblers to dump a game. On the evening of January 29, 1945, detectives working robbery detail were on stakeout in Brooklyn when they saw five young men approach the house of a man suspected of being the fence for a gang of teenage thieves operating in the Brooklyn garment district. While the five men, who turned out to be members of the Brooklyn College basketball team, denied having anything to do with the string of robberies, they readily informed the detectives that they had accepted bribes ranging from $1,000 to $2,000 from Henry "The Mustache" Rosen and two associates to lose an upcoming game against Akron scheduled to be played in Boston Gardens. They also revealed that they were in negotiations with the trio to "control" a second game against St. Francis College scheduled for Madison Square Garden in mid-February. The resultant public outcry included calls to shut down the Madison Square Garden doubleheaders and to require college teams to play their games on campus. Ned Irish, his lucrative enterprise threatened, issued a reassuring statement that he believed the arrest of the Brooklyn Five would "discourage any future attempt by gamblers to reach the players" and again denied knowing anything about the existence of gamblers at the Garden. Irish also had "no comment" upon reports that he personally received 10 percent of all gate receipts for the games he promoted.[20]

Even after the Brooklyn College revelations, including the conviction of the three fixers and the expulsion of four of the players—one player could not be expelled because, much to the embarrassment of college officials, he had never been enrolled—the notoriously cynical New York news media adamantly refused to accept that gambling threatened college basketball. Newspapers gave the incident only cursory attention and as soon as the guilty were punished, they failed to pursue the possibility that other schools were involved. They accepted at face value the many disclaimers advanced by coaches and administrators that this was an isolated case. Like millions of other willing believers, they too had been brainwashed by the vast public relations campaign long mounted by college presidents, athletic directors, coaches, sports information officers, and boosters that college athletics produced student athletes with only the highest standards of ethical behavior. Especially outspoken in this regard was the famed coach of national powerhouse City College of New York, Nat Holman, who repeatedly emphasized that despite "having heard rumors" about fixes, he had never seen any solid evidence to that effect. "Until I have factual proof about this gambling, I am going only to look on them as just rumors. I have never had any factual proof. The boys on my team at no time have ever been approached."[21]

But college officials could not say that they hadn't been warned. Not only had the attempted bribe of the Utah coach made the news, but the veteran head coach of Kansas University, Forrest "Phog" Allen, had several months earlier bluntly told his peers and the sports world that college basketball was poised for a major embarrassment unless strong corrective measures were taken. He feared an impending "scandal that would stink to high heaven." Allen urged his fellow coaches to be on the alert and sharply criticized the NCAA, coaches, and athletic directors for "having failed utterly to protect college athletics from the stigma of professional gambling," primarily by permitting games and championship tournaments to be played in large off-campus arenas in cities where gamblers operated openly. After the Brooklyn College revelations, he told the press, "Intelligent people have known all along that big-time gamblers were getting to college basketball in the East. . . . Instead of facing the facts and acting, our national athletic bodies, to save face, have been meeting and denying that these conditions exist when every well-informed person knew better."[22]

The reaction to Allen's comments by Harold S. Olsen, head basketball coach at Ohio State and chairman of the NCAA tournament committee, was typical. He challenged the validity of Allen's comments, taking issue in particular with his recommendation that the NCAA tournament be moved away from New York City: "I heard no voice raised from Kansas [when the tournament was scheduled for New York]. As a matter of fact, Allen's team played in Madison Square Garden only a year or two ago and under the auspices of Ned Irish. . . . Just because a couple of kids are stupid enough to accept bribes doesn't mean that there's anything wrong with basketball."[23]

Even such a respected figure as Phog Allen could not shake the college basketball establishment out of its unwillingness to confront impending disaster. His impassioned speeches were dismissed as the rantings of a Midwesterner engaging in traditional anti–New York City rhetoric, and his suggestion that General Douglas MacArthur be appointed the "czar" of college basketball drew only sighs of disbelief. Nat Holman, proclaimed by the New York media as college basketball's best coach, conceded that "the playing of the games at the Garden is big time and has increased the responsibility of the coaches," but this falsely implied that there was heightened vigilance. So the basketball establishment effectively circled the wagons, and everyone seemed to be reassured. As *Newsweek* accurately observed, Phog Allen's "cries of 'Fire!' were interpreted generally as cries of 'Wolf!' "[24]

It is noteworthy to remember that the Brooklyn College episode involved the dumping of games. In 1945 New York college basketball betting was still based upon odds on winners and losers. However, the introduction of the point spread was about to greatly increase the likelihood of games being fixed. College athletics was about to be shaken to its very foundation. Phog Allen was far more prescient than he or anyone else would have liked.

6

Doing Business

The wise guys in New York City knew all about it. So too did many sportswriters and coaches—even knowledgeable fans. Yet no one stepped forward to put a stop to the craziness. What they knew but would not say was that some of the best players on the nation's best college basketball teams were routinely "doing business." That is to say, they were shaving points or dumping games in return for a payoff from gamblers. In fact, the evidence is overwhelming that college basketball players in New York City had been doing business ever since the 1930s, if not before, and that those who should have known about the practice did know, or at least had major suspicions, but did nothing about the problem. The failure of coaches, athletic directors, journalists, and players to expose the practice helped make what would have been an unfortunate but relatively minor event one of the biggest sports betting scandals of all time, equal in impact and significance to the 1919 World Series fix.

The surreal atmosphere surrounding the college basketball scandals of 1951 has been the subject of an informative and accurate account by Charles Rosen in a popular journalistic-style book, *The Scandals of '51*, published in 1978. Not content with this factual study, and in an attempt to explore the elusive factors that led players to take bribes and sportswriters and coaches to refuse to expose the scam, Rosen explored the human dimension in a novel, *Barney Polan's Game*, published in 1998. Rosen knows basketball from the inside like few other writers in America, having played four years at Hunter College (1959–62), and briefly in the semiprofessional Eastern League (1962–63). During the early 1980s he served as an assistant coach to soon-to-be Chicago Bulls coach Phil Jackson, who was then coaching the Albany Patroons of the Continental Basketball Association.

It is 1950 and Rosen's main fictional character, veteran sportswriter Barney

Polan, knows in his heart that things are out of control, but he tries to convince himself that the big games he covers at Madison Square Garden are on the up-and-up. In one critical scene in the novel, he's talking in a bar with Ray Pulaski, a top college player back in the depression years of the 1930s, who tells him that he and most of the other top players had been on the take. "I shake my head again, more energetically this time, trying to swallow some cold, heavy lump that's suddenly formed in the back of my throat. 'I don't want to hear it, Ray. I swear I don't.'" But Ray lays it out for him in agonizing detail, describing how he and his peers tanked games for a few hundred dollars forked over by small-time gamblers. "According to Ray, college basketball players 'from all over the country' have been in league with gamblers since the mid-thirties. Among dozens of others, Ray specifies Mickey Gorton, Chris Roberts, and the Foley twins—all of them currently playing in the National Basketball Association. 'If they ever gave pro players lie detector tests, then the N.B.A. would be out of business the next morning. Believe me Barney. The Celtics can still be bought for the right price and so can the Zollner Pistons.'"[1]

Ray proceeds to describe games and circumstances that overwhelm Barney's stubborn, heartfelt denial. Ray continues his assault, recalling his playing days under Coach Whitey Mack: "So Whitey said that he knew we were doing business and that despite how much he loved us, if he ever suspected anything crooked, he'd turn us right in to the D.A. . . . And you know what, Barney? We paid him no mind. We went right on shaving points as if he'd never said a word. . . . Anyway, Whitey knew we still were turning tricks, but he never said anything or did anything. That's because everybody was doing it. Wherever there was a game on the boards, there were players taking money." Barney says that the conversation puts him "in agony." He plaintively asks, "Tell me Ray. How could you ever do something like that? You must've known it was wrong." Ray's response is devastatingly simple: "We did it because we needed the money, Barney, that's the first thing. Times were bad back then. And like I said, because so many guys were doing it, Barney. So many guys in so many schools that it almost seemed okay. You know what, Barney? You were a chump if you didn't go along."[2]

This compelling dialogue aptly captures the essential truths that contributed to the greatest crisis in American college sports. A true sports fan as well as a seasoned sportswriter who's used his magic fingers at his clunky typewriter to help create many a sports hero, Barney Polan is devastated to learn that the ennobling myths upon which American sports were built turn out to be nothing more than an enormous sham. The best players, even the fabled Ray Pulaski, have sold their souls for gamblers' money. No, "everybody" was not "doing business" during those heady days following the Second World War, but the number of culprits was far greater than the few names of star players that were eventually flashed across front-page headlines. For Barney, the disillusionment is so great that shortly after the last players are sentenced in federal court for conspiring to fix games, he suffers a massive stroke and is forced to retire. From his wheelchair he ruminates on how the scandal has spread far beyond New York and how many sportswriters have sought to explain away the players' culpability. "Oh yeah. The Big Fix. Turned out the problem was not confined to New York. Exactly sixty-seven players from sixteen colleges were eventually implicated, including Ralph Beard and Alex Groza of the Indianapolis Olympians, who'd been rigging ball games as undergraduates at the University of Kentucky. The real tragedy is that mushy hearted sportswriters like Jimmy Cannon had nothing but sympathy for those double-dealing bastards. Sure. Why not feel sorry for Benedict Arnold, too?"[3]

Like Rosen's fictitious sportswriter, most American sports fans reacted with a mixture of anger and disappointment as the story unfolded in 1951. The players were viewed as traitors to their teams, their colleges, and their fans. They had openly defiled one of the enduring myths of the American Way of Life, a powerful set of values that provided sports fans with the warm and fuzzy assumption that college athletes were honorable young "student-athletes" who gave their all for the alma mater on the field of play, all the while dutifully attending classes, studying hard, and earning degrees. They were society's specially anointed princes, young men who learned from their wise and good coaches the lessons of hard work, sportsmanship, teamwork, and sacrifice in preparation for the "game of life." For a time, outraged fans and politicians eager to exploit the situation demanded major reforms in college athletics.[4] But the public had a short memory, and when President Harry Truman fired General Douglas MacArthur in April, and the messy academic cheating scandal at West Point exploded in August, public attention was effectively deflected. Basketball got out of the headlines and off the hook. The public's attention was further refocused by Senator Joe McCarthy's shrill accusations about Communist infiltration of the federal government, the dismal stalemated war in Korea, and the arrival on the political scene of a new savior in the form of war hero General Dwight D. Eisenhower.

Under this cover of distraction, the college basketball establishment blithely went about its business, suffering only minimal damage. For the nation's growing army of sports gamblers, it was also business as usual. Wiser for the experience, bookies now were alert to the possibility of the fix. Assured that players no longer were "doing business," gamblers continued to place their bets, confident that their handicapping skills would enable them to overcome the true odds and beat the spread. Almost like magic, the college game returned to normalcy.

Other than for the thirty-three implicated players, whose reputations were severely damaged and professional basketball prospects destroyed, there was relatively little collateral damage. Ned Irish, the flamboyant public relations guru, was finished as a college basketball promoter because Madison Square Garden lost its role as the capital of college basketball. But Irish moved on to other lucrative opportunities. The NCAA moved its annual national tournament finals out of Madison Square Garden and has never permitted a return to New York City. One of Irish's premier productions, the National Invitational Tournament, lost much of its luster and was never again viewed as a premier college tournament. Such perennially nationally ranked teams as City College of New York, Long Island University, New York University, and Manhattan College dropped off the game's radar screen, and only St. John's University—whose curious ability to avoid any implication in the scandals still raises eyebrows—would continue its major college basketball program. With television now making the college game more accessible to fans, and aided by brilliant public relations campaigns by the college sports establishment, the game continued to grow in popularity. Within a few years the scandals of '51 had been all but forgotten.

For a time, however, it seemed that the scandals might severely affect the future of commercialized college basketball. Within a year after the story first broke, in early 1951, thirty-three players, including several All-Americans, were exposed. *Sporting News's* Player of the Year, Sherman White, the star center for Clair Bee's top-ranked Long Island University Blackbirds, was one of those who confessed to participation in the conspiracy. A handful of players actually served short jail sentences, but most were given probation by compassionate judges. All, however, had their professional futures ruined, and most carried heavy baggage with them throughout their lives. The scandal would dominate the sports news from January 18, 1951, when the first *New York Journal American* headlines broke the news, until the following autumn, by which time judges had pronounced sentence on the last group of implicated players, and especially upon the primary fixer, one Salvatorre Tarto Sollazzo, Sicilian immigrant, convicted felon, ex-con, part-time honest jewelry dealer, sometime fence for stolen jewelry and other goods, habitual horse player, and a miserable picker of basketball winners at Madison Square Garden. Sollazzo received a stiff eight-to-sixteen-year sentence from federal judge Saul Streit and served twelve years before being paroled. Antigambling moralists took some satisfaction from learning that, despite his many fixes, Sollazzo nonetheless lost an estimated $250,000 on college basketball.[5]

Law enforcement officials eventually said that forty-nine games had been fixed by thirty-three players from seven universities. Those games were played in twenty-three cities in nineteen states. An estimated ninety games had been discussed by players and gamblers, and $72,950 had been paid in bribes. These figures, however, were only the tip of the iceberg. In March of 1953 District Attorney Frank Hogan, apparently under serious political pressure, called off his investigation and dismissed the grand jury that was looking into the scandal. Hogan claimed that although additional conspirators might be identified and prosecuted, the purpose of his investigation had been served. He told the press, "There have been hopeful signs which indicate that colleges which have commercialized their athletic programs have taken to heart some of the hard lessons learned by this investigation." As Rosen caustically commented, "The D.A. was wishfully whistling down a sewer."[6]

Beyond question, had law enforcement officials pursued the case with continued vigor, the numbers of conspirators would have been much greater. Not only did the district attorney halt his investigation when it seemed to be gaining momentum, but elected prosecutors and judges in the Midwest showed little interest in investigating local teams and their star players, whose popularity with the public remained high. It was noted that Hogan, a devout Catholic, seemed especially reluctant to follow up leads pointing to St. John's University. Rosen and others have long wondered why St. John's went unscathed despite persistent rumors about its players' deep involvement; rumors floated around the city that Hogan backed off under strong pressure from powerful leaders of the New York City Catholic diocese. Rosen quotes one "ex-dumper": "I played for St. John's around that time, and a lot of the guys on the team were involved with [gamblers]. We were no different from anybody else."[7]

The well-known coaches of involved teams also mostly escaped unscathed. Only the famed Clair Bee of Long Island University had his coaching career ruined. Within a week after four of his players were arrested, the LIU board of trustees suspended the season and slashed athletic budgets to ensure that future Blackbird teams would compete in a much less high pressured environment. Bee was soon forced to resign his well-paid position as coach and assistant to the president. Ironically, not only was Bee a highly acclaimed coach and winner of national championships, he was also the author of several authoritative coaching manuals and texts. An energetic athletic entrepreneur, he commanded large fees on the lecture circuit where he spread the gospel of the importance of sports as providing an ethical foundation for future leaders of society. He was also the author of a best-selling series of eighteen novels aimed at the teenage market. The hero of these novels was Chip Hilton, a diligent high school athlete who repeatedly overcame adversity to help his teammates win state championships in three sports while also being a top student who worked part-time in a drugstore to help his widowed mother make ends meet. After leading Valley Falls High to championship after championship, he moved on to the State U, where he continued his straight-arrow winning ways.[8]

In his own coaching career, however, Bee did little to cultivate an environment where real-life Chip Hiltons could compete for the love of good sportsmanship. Bee himself was anything but a model mentor. In reality he was a coach who recruited ruthlessly with little concern for the established rules (including holding high pressure scholarship tryouts), who manipulated players psychologically to squeeze the last ounce of production out of them, and who cared not a whit about their academic success.[9] At least he admitted—sort of—his shortcomings in a much-read article in the *Saturday Evening Post*: "Public confidence in college basketball is shattered and the fault is partially mine. I was so absorbed in the victory grail that I lost sight of the educational purpose of athletics."[10]

While Bee had to move on to other pursuits, that masterful self-promoter Nat Holman of CCNY managed to save his lucrative career even though the evidence is overwhelming that he knew that his players were shaving points. Immediately after the scandal broke, Holman launched a shrewd public relations campaign, blaming his "boys" for deceiving him. He argued in *Sport* magazine that while he had his "suspicions" about other teams, he simply could not force himself to believe that his own team could also be involved. "I couldn't be suspicious of my boys. No coach could and still do a job." Lacking hard evidence, Holman said, he could not take action. A leading professional player with the New York "Original" Celtics during the 1920s, and then a successful college coach, Holman had long promoted himself as the greatest basketball mind in the world. He encouraged sycophantic sportswriters to refer to him as "Mr. Basketball." Even a casual observer of the scandals, however, had to inquire how such an experienced coach of such superior ability was unable to recognize the blatant tactics of outstanding players in tanking games while less knowledgeable fans filled the air at the Garden with angry cries of "Fix!" But Holman adamantly contended that he had been fooled by devious players, and his many friends in the sports media quickly adopted his self-serving rationale as gospel.[11]

Confronting skeptics on the Board of Education, which oversaw City College, Holman forced those audacious enough to question his integrity and judgment to accept his contention that he could be found culpable only if he had known explicitly of wrongdoing and had failed to take appropriate action. That he was at least guilty of not acting in the face of enormous evidence to the contrary greatly irritated some board members, but his strategy, bolstered by his media supporters, carried the day. Unable to find a reason to fire Holman, the board cut the basketball budget and forced the Beavers to play at a less competitive level. No longer able to compete for national honors, "Mr. Basketball" eventually retired on his own terms from CCNY in 1960. He was inducted into the Basketball Hall of Fame in 1964 and continued to be in demand as a speaker, even serving as a consultant to the State Department, heading up its program using basketball to spread goodwill abroad.[12]

While Bee was forced out of college coaching and Holman was subjected to serious questioning, other coaches of teams swept up in District Attorney Hogan's net endured little criticism. One, the imperious "Baron" Adolph Rupp, head coach at the University of Kentucky, did suffer the embarrassment of having his 1952–53 season canceled by the university for the unstated (but fully understood) reason of having failed to protect the school's good name from gamblers. When the scandals first broke, Rupp arrogantly told the press that fixers "couldn't reach my players with a ten-foot pole." They could, of course, and the culprits included three of the most talented players ever to wear the school's famous blue-and-white uniforms: Alex Groza, Dale Barnstable, and Ralph Beard, real-life heroes who had led the 1948 Olympic team to a smashing victory and had gone on to star in the NBA with the Indianapolis Olympians. Another Wildcat player, the seven-foot All-American center Bill Spivey, was implicated by circumstantial evidence but never formally charged.[13]

After a year in exile, a revenge-minded Baron Rupp ran up the score on hapless opponents to emphasize that no points were being shaved anymore and went on to win the NCAA tournament. Demonstrating the essential coaching truth that winning solves most problems, Rupp remained as popular as ever in the basketball-crazed Bluegrass State. Closely connected to the state's political and economic elite, Rupp not only survived but thrived. Today the Wildcats play their games in the posh 23,000-seat Rupp Arena in downtown Lexington. Only a few naysayers point out that at the time of the scandals, one of Rupp's best friends and associates was Lexington resident Ed Curd, the nationally recognized big-time gambler, handicapper, oddsmaker, and horse wire entrepreneur whose career ended with a year in federal prison for income tax evasion.[14]

Coaches at the two other implicated midwestern schools also were beneficiaries of a forgiving public and understanding administrations. Forddy Anderson continued to win games at Bradley University before going on to Michigan State, while Gerry Bush of Toledo, widely recognized within the coaching profession as a renegade recruiter, continued his winning ways when the locally elected prosecuting attorney declined to investigate his program, refusing even to bring charges against the Rocket basketball players whose names popped up prominently in Frank Hogan's investigations.[15]

⚑

Ned Irish's statements in 1945 that the Brooklyn College revelations would discourage future attempts by gamblers to suborn players were obviously misguided and self-serving. On the contrary, the popularity of the new concept of the point spread virtually invited corruption of a game that lacked adequate institutional and NCAA oversight. The point spread made it possible for players to rationalize making a few miscues to lower their team's victory margin because they were not actually "dumping" a game, merely making the game's final score a little closer than the line set by bookmakers. The rewards were attractive to many poor college athletes. They could pick up several hundred, even a couple of thousand dollars, for merely missing a few shots or making a bad pass here and there. And the victims—those who had made illegal bets with bookies on the favored team—had no legal recourse. If the shaving was done with finesse, only the perpetrators would know. It can be argued that only the best players could have pulled off point shaving; it took real skill to miss shots, to get beat while playing defense, to throw an errant pass, or foul an opponent to send him to the free throw line at a crucial juncture—and make such deceptions look like legitimate efforts. And if Nat Holman can be believed, to fool some of the nation's best basketball coaches in the process.

The roots of college basketball's gambling problems can be traced to the 1930s, when several major resorts in the Catskill Mountains, located just a few hours' drive north of New York City, offered basketball games as part of their summer entertainment package. These outdoor games featured many of the nation's top collegiate players. The rivalry between the resorts evolved into an informal summer league with high-caliber play. The "Borscht Belt League" proved enormously popular with guests. The players were ostensibly hired by the hotels as waiters and bellhops, but in reality their jobs were to entertain the customers by playing basketball. Not only were they well paid, but many of the fans were eager to give them gratuities for their efforts on the courts. In this relaxed summer resort environment, gambling flourished among the clientele. For some reason, much of the betting revolved around picking the total number of points scored by both teams. It was common for the players to accept substantial payoffs from grateful bettors if they could manipulate the final minutes of a game so that the final score landed on a certain number. Thus they learned the subtle art of shaving points and fixing games.[16]

This was summer, after all, and the games were relatively low-key and unofficial. No harm, no foul—just good old fun and games. Many of the best college players were veterans of the recently ended war. Anything but innocent eighteen year olds, they readily accepted the largesse showered upon them by the vacationers. These players brought a healthy cynicism to their college basketball experience; they noted in amazement the large incomes their big-name coaches were pulling down while they themselves were struggling to get by on scholarships and modest stipends. The summer games in the Catskills became so popular that New York City sportswriters covered them. Not so innocent as the fictitious Barney Polan, these streetwise reporters recognized the familiar faces of Broadway gamblers seated at courtside—the same faces they knew as regular attendees of Ned Irish's doubleheaders during the winter months. The friendly interaction between known gamblers and players was so open that, as one sportswriter bluntly commented in the *New York Post*, "any sportswriter worth his salt had to know what was going on."[17] The *Saturday Evening Post* agreed, acidly commenting in 1951, "And the sportswriters who might have been expected to evaluate this phenomenon critically, were so intoxicated by their new sense of importance—so vitiated by their allegiance to [Ned] Irish—that, far from questioning, they joined enthusiastically in the general hoorah."[18]

Not surprisingly, the connections made in the Catskills carried over to the games played during the collegiate basketball season. The wise guys—astute gamblers who worked diligently at handicapping—recognized the telltale signs that too many players were doing business and refused to bet on games at the Garden. The famed Milwaukee gambler Sidney "Shoebox" Brodson had shied away from these games for years, and Leo Hirschfield, accurately perceiving what was transpiring from his distant perch in Minneapolis, refused to set a line on many New York City games for fear of a fix.[19] Nonetheless, the audacity of gamblers anxious to score a big payday became ever more palpable, and the rumors continued to grow with each passing season. Powerful, nationally ranked teams would win several games convincingly and then barely defeat an outclassed opponent. Star players missed easy layups or tossed wild passes into the seats. Actually, the shaving of points was not an easy thing for many players to do because they were so conditioned to react instinctively to game situations. Sherman White told the *New York Times* in 1998 that the most successful point shavers did their real work while playing on defense, where their efforts could not be easily spotted. By not blocking out an opponent on rebounds, by being a half step slow in making a defensive transition, by failing to fight through a screen, it was possible to permit outclassed opponents easy opportunities to score.[20]

Sometimes, however, efforts to keep a game close were so blatant and contrived that even casual fans smelled a rat. Many a game at the Garden was accompanied by cries from irritated fans of "Fix!" and "What are they paying you?" In one memorable episode, an angry bettor who had made the mistake of backing Holman's CCNY team when the fix was in, angrily approached the CCNY bench shouting, "You guys are dumping!" before being hustled away by Garden security. Sometimes the effort to shave points became almost comedic when players on both teams were simultaneously attempting to shave points for different gamblers! "It could get messy out there when the other team was shaving too," one player recalled. "We knew when we purposely threw away a pass, and we'd get it right back."[21]

Coaches and Madison Square Garden officials repeatedly issued statements of complete denial. By 1949, however, the rumors had grown to the point where one of the nation's leading weekly magazines, the *Saturday Evening Post*, published an article by the highly respected sportswriter Stanley Frank openly raising the question of scandal, noting with concern that Leo Hirschfield's *Green Sheet* frequently refused to set lines on major games being played in New York City.[22] As we note in chapter 7, bookies need to rely on an honest game if their carefully constructed point spread line is to hold up.

As Murray Sperber comments in his penetrating study of the structure of big-time intercollegiate athletics, many persons in basketball's inner circle had to know what was going on.[23] So it is significant that it was an individual who had little interest in, or knowledge of, college basketball who pricked the festering boil. Max Kase was the sports editor of the *New York Journal American*, but his interests lay elsewhere—with the horses and baseball. His curiosity aroused by suggestive comments picked up from his reporters covering the college basketball beat, Kase became even more suspicious after conversations with his many acquaintances in the gambling community. He also understood that his sportswriters were not only friendly with players and coaches but also heavily dependent on them for leads and information. So he wisely turned the story over to the newspaper's crime reporters.

Kase's suspicions were confirmed when Manhattan College center Junius Kellogg agreed to cooperate with police to arrest two former Manhattan College players for offering him a $1,000 bribe to shave points. Buttressed with this strong evidence, Kase called on New York District Attorney Frank Hogan and gave him a few days to take action before he published his findings. Hogan moved quickly and on January 18 made his first arrests, bringing into custody three CCNY players, Ed Warner, Al Roth, and Eddie Roman. New York detectives arrested them at Pennsylvania Station at 2:30 A.M. when the team returned from

Philadelphia after trouncing Temple University by twenty-five points. At the time of the arrests Hogan had only circumstantial evidence, but in this pre-Miranda era when law enforcement officials enjoyed much greater freedom in questioning suspects without defense attorneys in attendance, the detectives told each player that their teammates being questioned in adjacent rooms had already confessed; within hours all had started to talk. Hogan had his hard evidence and quickly arrested Tarto Sollazzo and his go-between, former Long Island University star player Eddie Gard.[24]

For a time it was like a row of dominos falling. Within a few days after the first headlines broke, players at LIU, Manhattan, and NYU were arrested. Although Sollazzo was the primary fixer of games involving LIU and CCNY, using Gard as his contact man with players, other gamblers operating independently of Sollazzo were implicated in fixing other games. There was apparently no coordination of the efforts and, it is noteworthy, no involvement by New York's famed crime families. All of the fixers were petty gamblers and hangers-on who had discovered they were dealing with poor and, in some cases, naive college students eager to pick up a few bucks. Bradley star Gene Melchiorre later said, "None of us had any money. We justified our decisions to go along . . . by saying that the colleges were making plenty out of us. We agreed to go along with them again. We argued to ourselves that what we were doing was wrong, but not too wrong."[25]

Just as the players rationalized their actions, so too did the coaches, who had failed to take preventive action despite persistent rumors, and even some specific charges, about fixes. Nat Holman's masterful defense was based upon his shock that his "boys" had deceived him. Clair Bee followed the same line of defense, with much less success, and laid the blame on his players, saying plaintively, "A coach has to believe in his players or he might as well quit." Toledo University's Gerry Bush fended off criticism by citing the premier names of Holman and Bee: "There never was a question in my mind that my boys were absolutely clean. If great coaches like Clair Bee and Nat Holman could be fooled by their players, then so could I."[26]

Many midwesterners offered up the standard image of New York as a place of crime and evil, suggesting that the culture of the city had somehow tricked their gullible star players into making an innocent mistake. Fans suggested that the actions were not really *that* bad: "Who cares how many points they win by, as long as they win?" one fan wrote to the *Toledo Blade*, while others suggested, "Heck, let's forget the whole thing," and "They didn't throw any games, did they?" A columnist in the *Toledo Times* editorialized, "I want to emphasize that the ballplayers did not actually throw any games, and that the university was not hurt one iota in the won and loss column. . . . If the fixer is hurting anyone, it must be a fellow who is doing something he shouldn't be doing—betting on the outcome of a game." Kentucky's Adolph Rupp engaged in some interesting spinning of the facts and the massaging of moral principles when he rushed to the defense of Alex Groza and Ralph Beard: "The Chicago Black Sox threw ball games, but these kids only shaved points. My boys were the inexperienced victims of an unscrupulous syndicate."[27]

Although such prominent star players as Ed Warner of CCNY and Sherman White ended up serving jail sentences, the great majority of the players received probation or suspended sentences. Sollazzo's point man, former LIU backcourt star Ed Gard, received a three-year sentence, and several others had their jail time dropped if they joined the military. The gamblers were all sentenced to jail for one to three years, with the exception of Sollazzo, who ended up spending the next twelve years doing hard time at Sing Sing. Presiding over most of the trials was New York federal district judge Saul Streit. After handing down his final sentences, Streit stunned the college athletic establishment with a scorching condemnation that included everyone *but* the gamblers. He called for a far-reaching reform of "this evil system of commercialism and overemphasis" on intercollegiate athletics that was leading to the "moral debasement" of universities, their coaches and players.[28] For a time, at least, the NCAA and its member institutions were on the defensive. And grown men—much like the fictional Barney Polan—had their trust in intercollegiate sports shaken to the foundation.

7

Senator Kefauver Slays His Dragons

Judge Saul Streit's acidic commentary on the state of intercollegiate athletics reflected a widespread perception in American society that sports gambling was growing too rapidly and posed a serious threat to the public weal. This apprehension was exacerbated by the fear that the spread of gambling was the sinister work of organized crime. The reasons for the growing concern about gambling were complex, but essentially it resulted from inaccurate, self-serving comments by politicians and law enforcement officials that were amplified by uncritical journalists. Just as Senator Joe McCarthy found a large audience of believers for his charges of communist infiltration of the national government, so too did several political figures find their names in headlines when they trumpeted accusations that American cities were being taken over by powerful crime organizations. Throughout the twentieth century the American public was buffeted by news reports of notorious crime bosses. Sensational stories of highly lucrative criminal enterprises backed up by murder and beatings became a staple of news and entertainment media. However, it was not until after the Second World War that local crime organizations were identified as being part of a larger, and therefore more frightening, conspiracy. Americans discovered the Mafia about the same time they learned about the allegations of traitorous activities by such notorious figures as Alger Hiss and Julius and Ethel Rosenberg.[1]

The Prohibition era of the 1920s produced an avalanche of news reports about the doings of bootleggers. Bloody shootouts between rival gangs became the stuff of radio programs and motion pictures. The gruesome St. Valentine's Day massacre in Chicago was etched upon the minds of the entire nation, and in many circles Al Capone became a quirky type of folk hero. Following repeal of the Eighteenth Amendment, media reports often detailed real and fantasized stories about the "Mob." After the war the stories became even more sinister with reports about a secret society dominated by a few "dons" from powerful "crime families" that wielded enormous power through a highly secret national crime syndicate known as the Mafia.

Americans were fascinated by revelations of how a Sicilian secret society had become a powerful force in the American underworld. Americans love conspiracies, the bigger and more sinister the better. It did not take long for information and speculation about this heretofore unknown organization to spread across America like a prairie wildfire. Within a few years most Americans had become convinced that the Mafia had its tentacles deeply embedded in the nation's economic and political infrastructures, that its origins lay in Sicily, that it had been brought to America by criminal immigrants, and that it posed a dire threat to society. The molders of popular culture—journalists, novelists, filmmakers, radio networks—reported and exploited the legends that had developed around the family-based secret societies of Sicily. A secret organization that uses violence, wields power, and penetrates government and business naturally creates fantasies and encourages exaggeration. By 1960 the American people had accepted as gospel sensational reports about the Mafia, the Black Hand, the Cosa Nostra—new and ominous names for what had previously been known merely as The Mob, The Outfit, The Gang, or The Syndicate.[2]

Few observers noticed that such terms were not used by top officials in the Department of Justice. When hard-pressed, these officials would readily agree that local criminal organizations did exist, often enjoying strong influence in the political and economic structure of large cities. But they were curiously silent when it came to corroborating the existence of a powerful, secret, national organization operated by a few dozen "crime families " of Sicilian descent that raked in millions and millions of untaxed dollars from such enterprises as prostitution, narcotics, hijacking, labor racketeering, loan sharking, the numbers racket, extortion, and gambling. It is not without significance that FBI Director J. Edgar Hoover—the nation's most famous crime fighter with an unquestioned ability to exploit a public relations opportunity—was conspicuously absent from the ranks of those proclaiming the existence of any national crime organization.[3]

Hoover's boss also had major doubts. In 1950 Attorney General J. Howard McGrath testified before a Senate subcommittee looking into organized crime that he had no documentation on the existence of a national crime organization. When queried by the committee chair, Arizona Democrat Ernest McFarland, about the influence of a "national crime syndicate," McGrath simply stated that he was not prepared to say that such an organization existed. Pressed by the startled senator, McGrath unequivocally said on the public record: "We do not have evidence that there is any such thing. . . . I could not, with any degree of fairness, or honesty, say that we know, in the Department of Justice, that there is any great national syndicate presided over by any great czar." The attorney general went on to affirm that the Justice Department was naturally well aware of many criminal organizations in major cities whose operations included "gambling and horse racing," but from all appearances they seemed to be acting independently of each other.[4]

McGrath was noticeably reluctant to use the term *Mafia*. But since his understated comments did not mesh with public perceptions or with the ambitions of politicians, they were ignored by those eager to believe that a vast criminal conspiracy threatened the American Way of Life. Public opinion, fed by politicians, thus came to accept not only that the Mafia existed but also that it derived its primary source of income from gambling profits generated in illegal horse parlors and through a clandestine national system to "lay off" big bets. Although most of the activities attributed to the Mafia fell within the domain of state and local law enforcement, national leaders thirsting for publicity grabbed onto the fact that the interstate network of "horse wires" provided (legally) by AT&T and Western Union supplied Mafia outposts across the nation with the information essential to operate their outrageously profitable gambling operations.[5] One of the prized powers of Congress is to pass laws regulating interstate commerce. The best example of organized crime operating across state lines was the horse wires. So into an environment of overheated public opinion charged a band of intrepid politicians eagerly in search of headlines, focusing on the horse wires and uncritically accepting ever more outlandish estimates of gambling monies being sucked into Mafia coffers.

Taking advantage of this opportunity was an extraordinarily ambitious career politician from Tennessee. Estes Kefauver had no background in the area of organized crime, but he knew a hot-button issue when he saw one. Motivated by a desire to become the first southerner to run for the presidency since fellow Tennessean Andrew Johnson, Kefauver responded to the urging of Philip Graham, publisher of the *Washington Post*, to undertake an investigation of organized crime.[6] Only one of several would-be senatorial crime busters, Kefauver succeeded in winning a bitter intra-Senate struggle for the opportunity to chair a special investigative committee created by Congress in May of 1950 only after Vice President Alben Barkley broke a 35–35 tie in the Senate.[7]

The Special Committee to Investigate Organized Crime in Interstate Commerce lasted for two years and demonstrated the power to influence public opinion inherent in the new communications medium of television.[8] The committee was the product of intense partisan in-fighting fueled by growing public concern over organized crime. Bare-knuckle politics lay behind the struggle over the role and composition of the committee. For years Republican leaders had wanted a committee to investigate the relationship between Democratic city political machines and local criminal activities. This interest had naturally intensified when Harry Truman, himself an alumnus of the infamous Pendergast organization of Kansas City, assumed the presidency in 1945. In early 1950 a gangland-style killing of two Democratic leaders in Kansas City provided additional incentive for a committee that would prove embarrassing to Truman, even if chaired by a Democrat.[9]

A native of the small eastern Tennessee town of Madisonville, the lanky, bespectacled Kefauver had been a star lineman on the University of Tennessee football team in the 1920s and had gone on to Yale Law School and the practice of law in Chattanooga before being elected to the House of Representatives in 1938. Ten years later he triumphed in a hotly contested primary election over the candidate supported by the notorious Memphis machine led by boss E. H. Crump to win a seat in the Senate. Clearly harboring dreams of higher office, and despite having demonstrated no previous interest or expertise in the subject of organized crime, Kefauver won a tough battle with Senator McFarland to chair the committee. He also had to fight off a determined effort by Nevada senator Patrick McCarran to scuttle any committee that might endanger his state's primary industry. The other members of the special committee were Republicans Alexander Wiley of Wisconsin and Charles Tobey of New Hampshire, and Democrats Lester Hunt of Wyoming and Herbert O'Conor of Maryland. The cherubic seventy-year-old Tobey provided much of the color as he delivered himself of many an outraged outburst of indignation and mortification as police officers and state attorneys general related tales of criminal activities within their jurisdictions.[10]

The subsequent two-year investigation provided a case study of a congressional committee seeking evidence to support its a priori conclusions. From the beginning the committee focused on the unchallenged, but wrong, perception that gambling provided the primary source of revenue for "organized crime." In particular, the committee accepted as gospel that the key to shutting down organized crime was to find a way to halt illegal interstate betting on the horses. In effect, the committee was operating on a premise that perhaps had some validity a quarter of a century earlier, but in an age of reliable long-distance telephone service, television, and a threefold increase in the number of legal horse tracks around the country, the horse wire services were already declining rapidly in importance, soon to be rendered as obsolete as buggy whips.[11]

There were, then, two misperceptions undergirding the committee's operation: (1) that there was a unified national organized crime syndicate, and (2) that it derived its primary source of revenue from the transmission of data regarding horse races and from its handling of "lay off" bets, a system whereby bookmakers sought to balance their books to avoid overexposure on a particular horse by placing bets with other bookmakers. Attempting to prove what its members believed at the onset of the hearings, the Kefauver committee played a major role in misleading public opinion about the nature and structure of sports gambling in America.[12]

Kefauver took his show on the road to sixteen cities, interviewing mostly police officers, prosecuting attorneys, and city and state officials—true believers who had good reasons to support the idea of organized crime. Criminal justice experts have long appreciated that it takes a healthy crime wave to generate higher budget appropriations for law enforcement organizations. Committee members essentially elicited the information that supported their presuppositions, and when testimony to the contrary was given, as by Milwaukee sports gambler Sidney Brodson, it was simply ignored.[13] The committee did, however, make for great television. The daytime viewing audience was enormous: when local gangster Frank Costello was hauled before the committee—where he repeatedly invoked the Fifth Amendment and refused to permit his face to be shown on television—New York City's electric utility faced brownouts due to the drain on the electricity supply. Unfortunately for Kefauver's political ambitions, the connections the committee uncovered showed no evidence of a national criminal conspiracy, only the cozy relationships that existed between local crime organizations and local branches of the Democratic Party.[14]

Such relationships were there for all to see during testimony in such Democratic strongholds as Kansas City, St. Louis, Chicago, Miami, and New York City. Powerful Democrats, beginning with Truman himself, were not amused. Nor were they pleased that Kefauver was getting large television audiences while exposing their party's embarrassing association. It was no surprise that the party's power structure gave Kefauver a chilly reception when he ran for the presidential nomination in 1952.[15]

Ultimately the committee, like so many other congressional investigations, ran its course, reveled in the headlines generated, and then disbanded without producing an iota of legislation. All nineteen of the committee's legislative proposals failed to become law. But the publicity surrounding the committee's activities did intensify what the political scientist William H. Moore calls the "postwar crime scare."[16] The Mafia, lack of concrete evidence of its existence notwithstanding, was here to stay. The committee's final report not only reaffirmed its belief in the Mafia but perpetuated the unfortunate ethnic stereotype that organized crime in America was almost the exclusive bailiwick of Italian immigrants and their descendants. As noted in chapter 2, the so-called American Mafia or underworld contained many prominent members of Eastern European Jewish descent; clearly a "pure" Mafia would not have accepted anyone other than Sicilians. Although it had gathered no substantive evidence to support its conclusion, the Kefauver committee nonetheless stated: "There is a sinister criminal organization known as the Mafia operating throughout the country with ties in other nations. . . . The Mafia is the direct descendant of a criminal organization of the same name originating in the island of Sicily. . . . The Mafia is a loose-knit organization, . . . the binder which ties together the two major criminal syndicates as well as numerous other criminal groups throughout the country."[17]

The committee also included in its final report the false assertion that "gambling profits are the principal support of big-time racketeering and gangsterism. These profits provide the financial resources whereby ordinary criminals are converted into big-time racketeers, political bosses, pseudo businessmen, and alleged philanthropists." These conclusions were based upon inflated estimates and erroneous assumptions about the volume of business being done by mob-connected bookies. Stating that organized crime in 1950 took in between $15 and $30 billion annually from its gambling activities, the committee fell into the trap of accepting as fact wild assumptions and pie-in-the-sky estimates. In 1950 the Gross National Product was $286 billion; thus the committee was asserting that illegal gambling alone accounted for about 10 percent of the GNP, a "dizzying concept" according to Richard Sasuly, an astute student of American horse racing. As he notes, "Illegality invites wild estimates. The estimator feels no fear of correction, and his guess is based upon the policy he promotes."[18]

Because its mandate was interstate commerce, the Kefauver committee concentrated its attention on the horse wire network, already an out-of-date system rapidly moving toward obsolescence. William Moore provides ample evidence that the committee's obsession with the horse wire meant not only that it focused on irrelevant data but that it severely misled the press and the public. "While Kefauver and his staff pored over seemingly endless testimony and records on the underworld structure as reflected in the racing-news wire services, the Committee neither inquired into the social and economic causes of crime nor considered the advisability of legalizing gambling." Several scholarly studies of the Kefauver committee's work and legacy all lead to the same conclusion: it was grounded upon erroneous assumptions, it was extraordinarily selective in its examination of evidence, it produced no new information not already in the possession of law enforcement agencies, it perpetuated and expanded the grossly misleading ethnic stereotyping of American citizens of Italian descent, and it did nothing to curb the operations of local crime organizations. In short, it was nothing less than politics as usual.[19]

The assumptions underpinning the committee's investigations were holdovers from the 1920s and 1930s. Senator Kefauver and his colleagues, none of whom had any expertise in gambling, were oblivious to the dramatic changes occurring in the world of sports gambling. They never stopped to consider the obvious: that all but the most compulsive gamblers will eventually, if they continue to lose, look elsewhere for action. As *Newsweek* columnist John Lardner sardonically put it in a humorous evisceration of the Kefauver assault on gambling: "A great many horse players do not die broke." If the profits earned by bookmakers were so huge, he wrote, then most bettors would have forsaken the horses for other venues. Lardner also reminded his readers that the 15 to 20 percent taken by the tax man from each and every pari-mutuel race was a major factor in the failure of horse bettors to fare better.[20]

The Kefauver committee failed to appreciate that, the tax man's grab notwithstanding, a healthy portion of any race betting handle is returned to winning bettors. They also did not take into consideration that the number of legal racetracks had grown from a relatively small number during the 1920s to thirty major tracks in 1950, and that state agencies, in search of additional revenues, had routinely liberalized the number and length of racing meets held each year. Since the 1920s there had been a threefold increase in the number of races run each year. This meant that more horse players had more legal venues at which to put their money in play; conversely, the money that was bet with illegal books was much less.

The expanding size of legal horse racing had come in the wake of two slowly evolving trends: a growing tolerance of gambling as a legitimate recreational outlet, and a healthy appreciation among legislators of the revenues that can be generated from a tax on each and every race run on the pari-mutuel system. Attendance at the tracks naturally increased as a majority of states offered some form of legalized racing. Almost anyone who wanted to bet on the horses now had an opportunity to do so at a betting window sanctioned by a state government. The increased pari-mutuel handle added increased revenues to state budgets from Florida to California, and it cut deeply into the profits of the illegal horse rooms allegedly operated by the "Syndicate."

The Kefauver committee also failed to consider the enormous, if undocumented, growth in wagering on human sports. Contrary to the long-standing truism among bettors "Never bet on anything that talks," bettors were finding increased satisfaction from their wagers on football, baseball, and basketball. The structure of the systems governing those games gave gamblers a better opportunity to win money. For starters, the bettor had to select a winner from a field of two, not eight or more. Instead of the 15 percent to 20 percent that went into state treasuries from each pari-mutuel race, sports bettors had to contend with the much more favorable 9 percent vigorish charged against winning bets (based upon the bet $11 to win $10 concept). Savvy bettors also appreciated that once they got their money down on a game, the odds or point spread could change, but not for *their* wager. The conditions of their bets were set in concrete; not so on a pari-mutuel bet. At the track, the final odds would not be known until post time, so those betting on a horse might see the value of their investment decline (or improve) depending upon monies subsequently bet on the race.[21]

The fact that none of the committee members or staff were knowledgeable about gambling, and sports gambling in particular, became evident as the hearings ran their course. The allure of the point spread, which turned every football and basketball game into an intellectual challenge with innumerable variables to consider, was something the Kefauver committee never understood. Nor should it be underestimated that this intriguing new way of betting was introduced at the same time that the American people welcomed television sets into their living rooms and taverns. Had committee members taken into account the emerging changes in the patterns of American life created by television, they would have recognized just how outdated was their obsession with horse wires and illegal offtrack horse rooms. By 1952 nearly every bar and one-third of American homes were equipped with a black-and-white television set. More than 75 percent of private residences would have a set by 1960.[22] Kefauver's political fortunes were greatly accelerated by the vast coverage his crime hearings received and the huge audiences they generated. That he and his associates failed to recognize that television was rendering the horse wire services and the world they had created obsolete is ironic indeed.

8

The Brave New World of
the Modern Bookie

The star witness appearing before the Kefauver committee hearings in the late winter of 1951 seemed to come straight out of central casting—handsome, dark-haired, nattily dressed, self-assured, articulate almost to the point of glibness. Sidney Brodson proved to be a most improbable witness before the high-profile committee, unlike the many unwilling and uncomfortable leaders of organized crime syndicates whose highly publicized appearances before the committee attracted such enormous television audiences and press coverage.

The hearings had exposed in dramatic fashion the nasty face of organized crime to Main Street America. As an engrossed American public followed the deliberations, the Kefauver hearings proved to be one of the first great demonstrations of the power of the new medium of television, what David Halberstam has called "innately explosive drama." Most Americans had never before confronted the term *Mafia*, which was now being thrown about by committee members and the media. Although Americans had long been aware that local crime organizations were active in many cities, deriving enormous income from many unsavory and illegal activities, the grim realities of a supposed tightly knit national crime syndicate were now being described in vivid detail to a stunned citizenry sitting securely in their living rooms. *Life* magazine vividly captured the significance of the event: "The U.S. and the world had never experienced anything like it. . . . For days on end and into the nights they watched with complete absorption. . . . Never before had the attention of the nation been so completely riveted on a single matter."[1]

The timing of Brodson's appearance before the committee could not have been better. Just a few weeks before he appeared, the American people had been shocked by the arrests of CCNY and LIU basketball players for accepting bribes from gamblers to throw games. By the time Brodson testified, it was evident that before the district attorney completed his investigation, the scandal was going to spread far beyond the confines of New York City. The members of the Kefauver committee apparently assumed that Brodson would describe the connection between sports betting and organized crime, highlighting the negative impact of sports betting on society. In particular, they hoped that he would shed light on the interstate nature of gambling, exposing a sordid and corrupt system funneling millions of dollars each week into the hands of the Mafia. Not so, as it turned out. Although the forty-five-year-old Brodson impressed those in the Senate hearing chamber and the millions watching on national television with his extensive knowledge and dapper appearance, his answers were not what the committee had expected or desired.

Impressively buttressing his comments with facts and figures, Brodson painted a picture of sports gambling that differed sharply from popular stereotypes. He portrayed sports betting, as he and other professionals practiced it, as a highly sophisticated enterprise that was based on hard work, information gathering, statistical analysis of data, and creative insight. As far as a national crime syndicate skimming off enormous profits was concerned, Brodson professed no awareness of such activity. By the time he was finished, the standard image of sports gambling as a shady and damaging enterprise had become much more complex—colored in many hues of gray rather than black and white—and the perceived role of organized crime within the sports betting world had been diminished.

There was, according to Brodson, no connection between organized crime and the basketball scandal. He decried the recent college basketball "fixes" that had made headlines across the country, not because star athletes had sold out to gamblers, but because the image of his profession had been damaged. Ironically, he noted, illegal sports betting could prosper only if the wagering public had faith in the integrity of the system. The perception that college basketball games were fixed would drive away gamblers, especially the serious ones who played with large amounts of cash. The key to success for a bookie, Brodson told the committee, was maintaining an impeccably honest operation at all times. Even if a bookie had ties to organized crime, the first order of business was to assure the betting public that the games were on the up-and-up. Unless gamblers were convinced of that essential fact, they would simply walk away, greatly reducing the bookmaker's potential profit.[2]

The primary attraction of betting on sporting events, Brodson emphasized, was that it provided an opportunity for an individual gambler to match wits with other savvy bettors. Careful betting was an intellectual enterprise in which research, unemotional analysis of data, and a disciplined approach to money management were crucial to success. The overwhelming percentage of sports bettors, including himself, viewed it as a cerebral challenge in which the bettor used information gleaned from many sources and then made a calculated decision. Taking note of the recent arrests of star college players, Brodson stated that he had personally avoided wagering on basketball games played in the New York City area for several years, especially the high-profile games promoted by Ned Irish in Madison Square Garden. He said that he, like other "serious bettors[,] realized something was wrong with a lot of Garden games when suddenly the games started going contrary to form."

What had happened in the scandals, Sidney Brodson insisted, was a distinct aberration within the world of sports betting. As a rule, he said, over the past two decades he had found the bookies around the country to be reliable, honest businessmen. "It is my opinion than 100 professional gamblers would constitute a better credit risk than 100 businessmen," he told the committee. "The gambler has no stock in trade except his reputation and once that is gone he is bankrupt."

Brodson's confident, polished presentation reflected an extensive education that included an undergraduate degree from the University of Illinois and a law degree from the University of Wisconsin. He lived in an upscale Milwaukee suburb with his wife and three children. Brodson was gently prodded by New Hampshire Republican Charles W. Tobey to explain why he had abandoned the practice of law to take up a new career, one Brodson identified as "businessman bettor." Brodson responded that when he opened his law practice during the early years of the Great Depression, he found business to be slow. Out of boredom, he began to handicap sports events and place bets with a local bookie. He found that he was very good at picking winners. As he routinely beat the odds he came to realize that his time could more profitably be spent handicapping games than practicing law.[3]

Brodson explained to the committee how he made his betting decisions. He always thoroughly researched each wager he made and dispassionately analyzed the data to determine those games where the odds or point spread gave him a decided advantage. Unlike the "sucker bettors," whom he dismissed with derision, Brodson did not simply put his money on his favorite team or his alma mater; rather, his bets were well-researched, calculated "investments." Within the gambling fraternity, he had acquired the nickname "Shoebox" because he would often appear at a betting emporium carrying his carefully guarded research notes in a cardboard shoe box. By 1940 "Shoebox" Brodson had become so proficient at beating the odds that he abandoned his law practice to devote himself full-time to his new enterprise. Although he had to place his bets with illegal bookies, he had found a way to provide his wife and three children with a comfortable living, better than he could by practicing law. Cavalierly dismissing the moral and legal issues surrounding his profession, Brodson averred that he was at worst engaging in a victimless crime. To his thinking, that some of his bookies might be connected to urban crime syndicates was incidental, as long as they paid off when he won—which apparently was more often than not.[4]

After the Second World War Brodson opened an office devoted strictly to his new vocation. He hired a full-time assistant and, during college football and basketball seasons, put on several part-timers as well. Their primary task was to assemble as much information as possible from a wide range of sources about upcoming games. In a typical week Brodson's assistants plowed through upward of a hundred daily newspaper sports pages in search of bits of information that could provide a betting edge—injuries, team morale, weather, special rivalries, officiating, coaching subtleties, idiosyncratic home field advantages, and a multitude of other nuances and special circumstances that might affect the outcome of a game. Like his research assistants, Brodson also spent hours each day on the telephone, culling information from a national network of informants he had developed over the years who provided him with useful local information that would not make the national news services. He had learned that unpredictable and unquantifiable psychological factors could very well affect the outcome of a game (a star quarterback who had had a death in his family, a stellar lineman who had just been suspended for breaking training rules, an All-American running back whose girlfriend had dumped him just before the big game).

If properly armed with this array of statistical and subjective data, evaluated in an orderly, objective fashion, Brodson discovered that he had a big edge over recreational gamblers and bookies alike. It was not so much gambling as taking calculated risks like any prudent investor buying stocks. As his profits grew, Brodson confessed that he was forced to develop contacts with a large number of bookmakers across the nation, since some had grown wary of his skills in picking winners. "My telephone bill last year was $15,000," he said.

Of course, Brodson was dealing with illegal bookmakers, and he acknowledged that his bets were illegal under state and federal law. Nonetheless he argued that his adopted profession was widely misunderstood. In fact, his career fit well within the American work ethic. He emphasized to the Senate committee that he viewed his wagering as an occupation, one that required him to invest heavily, in both time and money, in obtaining accurate and useful information. Like the vaunted heroes of American capitalism, he had to take risks with his pool of investment capital, and he always faced the possibility of sustaining serious losses. He also pointed out that like any successful entrepreneur, he had to establish a prudent system of money management and a long-range investment strategy. He seldom bet on more than five games on any business day. After becoming convinced of the integrity and soundness of a particular situation, he would bet between $500 and $2,000 on a game; the greater the advantage his research indicated, the larger the bet. Brodson told his transfixed audience that by the late 1940s his capital had increased to the point where he was betting nearly $1 million a year, making an annual profit of about $200,000.

Brodson's testimony challenged many of the long accepted stereotypes of sports betting. He himself was anything but a slovenly dressed, cigar-smoking, beer-swilling, shifty-eyed gambler who hung out in sleazy pool halls. Instead, he cut a natty figure, "dressed in a dark gray suit, white shirt and a black tie," the *New York Times* reported, and "was a composed, communicative witness," parrying with the committee and its counsel "as one lawyer to another."

Pressed by Senator Alexander Wiley of his home state of Wisconsin about the desirability of eradicating sports betting, Brodson responded with a strong rebuttal, presenting arguments on behalf of gambling that had never before reached the general public. There were, he said, definite social benefits to be derived from gambling on sporting events. It should not be outlawed, he said, but rather legalized, regulated, and taxed like other businesses. He argued that it was a legitimate enterprise that embodied the essential values of the American free enterprise system, rewarding hard work, intelligence, research, and judgment.

Sports gambling also provided, he suggested, millions of Americans a genuine and rewarding leisure avocation. Beyond the intellectual challenge of beating the odds, he said that he and millions of Americans simply enjoyed the excitement of placing a bet on a sporting event. Certainly, he noted, many states recognized as much by legalizing and heavily taxing horse racing; if gambling were prohibited, attendance at races would be minuscule at best. By having a bet riding on the outcome, the individual's involvement in a game naturally became more meaningful and intense. In short, to millions of Americans, placing a bet on a football game was not morally wrong. It was fun.

Any effort to eliminate sports gambling from American life, Brodson warned, would be doomed to suffer the same ignominious fate as the Eighteenth Amendment. "It's like prohibition taught us. You can't make people believe that a popular idea is wrong merely by legislating against it. Where there are evils or graft connected with that idea, you can and should control and regulate it to remove the evils, but you can't kill the idea itself if the people want it."

Brodson was a prototype of an individual who would become much more prominent in the postwar era: a well-educated professional urban male who found in sports gambling a pleasurable and potentially profitable leisure activity that provided intriguing intellectual challenges. Sports gambling in postwar America would continue to attract the preponderance of its adherents from the ranks of non–college educated, working-class males, but the new handicapping challenges presented by the concept of the point spread, coupled with the G.I. Bill–generated increase in the number of college students, resulted in more male college graduates placing wagers on college football and basketball games, a practice that many had begun during their undergraduate days.

The changing demographics of sports gambling, as reflected in the compelling testimony of Sidney Brodson, can be traced to many such factors, but beyond question a driving force in this process was commercial television. The impact of this new entertainment medium on many aspects of American society has been described and interpreted by a small army of scholars, social commentators, and journalists. Its effect on the structure of American sports was no less revolutionary. By the middle of the 1950s it had already demonstrated its power to control both professional and amateur sports. Network executives now changed the time and location of events to attract larger viewing audiences, often to the inconvenience of the stadium audience. Professional leagues and college athletic directors scheduled more games to attract higher broadcast fees, and rules were changed to make contests more appealing to the television audience. New professional leagues were founded based on the potential of attracting television revenues. The number of college football bowl games began to proliferate, ultimately reaching twenty-five postseason contests. The regular college football season was extended from nine to ten and then to eleven games, and the number of games basketball teams played increased by 25 percent between 1960 and 2000. The number of teams invited to the NCAA postseason tournament was expanded from sixteen in 1960 to sixty-five today. Professional baseball, football, and basketball also substantially increased the number of their franchises, thereby increasing the number of regular season games and the length of their postseason play.

Each autumn weekend college football games filled the airwaves, and by the end of the 1950s professional football had come of age as a result of its popular appeal to television audiences. College and professional basketball also became a regular feature during the winter months. The televised broadcasts of major league baseball games in the 1950s produced a disastrous decline in the minor leagues from sixty leagues to twenty by 1970, and in the process destroyed the long tradition of "town ball" played by semiprofessionals and amateurs across the country. The major league games also suffered through the 1950s with slumping attendance that was attributed to fans staying home to watch games on the tube. Boxing became a high-profile sport for a few years during the '50s, but the greed and stupidity of promoters and television executives in oversaturating the market had virtually ruined the sport by the early 1960s. And so-called junk sports like roller derby and wrestling filled many an hour on local broadcasts.[5]

Viewers loved televised games. The contests were free, the view was better than from a stadium seat, and the dialogue provided by announcers and "color commentators" was sometimes entertaining. And the beer in the refrigerator was colder and a lot cheaper than at the ballpark. Not only did the American people watch televised games, but they increasingly bet on them. The relationship between the advent of televised sports and the increase in sports wagering is unquestioned. Millions of casual fans who had heretofore exhibited only passing interest in sports became hooked. As they watched games on the tube they formed opinions about the teams. Substantial numbers of the new fan base also liked to support their opinions about an upcoming game with hard cash. Not only did they consider themselves capable of handicapping a game, but they also discovered that they derived more enjoyment out of a televised game if they had some money riding on its outcome. What Senator Kefauver and his crime-fighting colleagues failed to perceive was that television was rapidly putting the old horse wires into moth balls. Wherever there was a television set, there was a new type of sports wire service. By 1960 Western Union had shut down its horse telegraph operations. The popularity of horse racing in the United States, in fact, had peaked and entered a period of slow but steady decline.[6]

Television dramatically changed the world of sports betting by democratizing the process and opening up sports for all to see. It gave everyone a chance to scout teams and to ponder future wagers. Coupled with the steady expansion of sports reporting in daily newspapers, television provided the information that gave a new generation of gamblers confidence — sometimes false — in their own abilities as handicappers. The fundamental laws of economics soon took over: as the supply of gamblers increased, so too did the number of businessmen willing to respond to their demands. The traditional bookie operating out of a horse wire room as part of a local gambling organization was replaced by a new breed of bookie who largely ignored the ponies and concentrated on the team sports regularly shown on television — baseball, football, and basketball. This new breed of bookie often operated as an independent agent, or sometimes in partnership with a limited number of associates. Whether old style or new, bookies were not difficult to find, even if one were a visitor to a strange city. As the political scientist Oswald Jacoby wrote in 1950, "In a strange town one would ask the hotel bellboy or elevator man. The news dealer would probably know. . . . So might the policeman on the beat, although this procedure is not recommended. If the bettor finds a bar or cigar store in which a radio is

tuned at track time to racing results, he should have no trouble in establishing contact."[7]

The new dynamics of sports betting were thus largely the product of the
postwar innovations of television and the point spread. Contrary to the out-
moded views of the Kefauver committee, sports gambling in the United States
was moving away from large organizations and into a new era where small
entrepreneurially inclined bookies operated lucrative businesses, in most cases
free from the control of local crime organizations. Although traditional historical
documentary sources about the average American bookie are thin—the typical
bookie does not routinely deposit his papers and account records with the local
historical society upon retirement—it is nonetheless possible to patch together
from published sources and interviews a reasonable composite profile of the
modern bookie.

As the interests of bettors moved away from horse racing and toward team
sports, the role of the bookie underwent a profound transformation. Operating
independently and often thinly capitalized, the new bookie would begin to
service a small group of clients, many of them acquaintances, in his urban
neighborhood. Often only in their twenties, these businessmen-bookies ran their
operations out of their homes and apartments, from behind counters of candy
stores and newsstands, in the back of the corner pool hall, at the bar in the
neighborhood tavern, out of a college fraternity house. They had few overhead
costs and paid no taxes on their operation. They began on a small scale, booking
bets with low limits with friends and acquaintances, slowly expanding their list
of clients through referrals. A lone operator might typically build up a list of
twenty to fifty regulars.[8]

If he is properly motivated and well disciplined, it is not too difficult for a
bookie to build a client base sufficient to earn himself a comfortable middle-
class income. Capital seldom proves to be a problem, and many bookies report
having started out with only a few thousand dollars in the bank. Some of the
more intrepid actually begin booking bets without a bankroll, counting on the
inability of bettors to beat the odds or point spread. In reality this is not so daring
as it might seem. Experience has taught bookies the essential article of faith that
you can count upon the average sports bettor to lose money over a reasonable
period of time, certainly over the length of a football season. The major threat
to a bookie is a customer who goes on a hot streak. As one bookie notes, "The
easiest way for a bookie to go broke is for a big-money client to get hot. Those
things happen, you know. Just let one or two of my big bettors go on a winning
streak and you won't see me smiling and spending the way I do."[9] But while
there are many tales told of big winners, the number of bettors who can win

consistently is small indeed. One of those men, the legendary Lem Banker, now in his seventies, reports that he has always operated on a thin margin of wins over losses. He says that in his lifetime of betting he has known very few bettors who can pick 60 percent winners over a season. And with the bet $11 to win $10 system, a winning bettor has to pick 52.38 percent winners simply to break even.[10] Thus the bookie, well schooled in the laws of averages and probabilities, confident in the line that he puts on the board, and armed with the knowledge that most bettors operate on emotions and not hardheaded analysis of the facts at hand, knows that he is going to make good money each and every season.

If a bookie's business grows into a several-person operation, overhead costs increase with the renting of a small office with several telephone lines.[11] Although many bookies make their rounds to see customers face-to-face, most do business over the telephone. A single operator in New York City in the late 1940s, for example, booked about $500 a day during baseball season from a clientele of "ordinary" young men who worked as clerks, salesmen, truck drivers, bookkeepers, and waiters. In the 1990s on a football weekend an established bookie operating independently may easily have between $10,000 and $50,000 in play on individual game bets limited to $2,000.[12]

These new-style bookies build their businesses on the basis of time-honored business ethics applicable to any legitimate enterprise. In a very real sense, they embody the spirit of the capitalist ethic. They provide a service that is in demand in the free marketplace; they must keep good records to prevent disputes with customers; they have to pay off all winners regularly (usually done on a weekly basis on Monday or Tuesday), at which time they also collect on losing bets. Depending on circumstances, they might extend credit to customers considered reliable, although it is understood that one of the costs of doing business is that they sometimes have to write off bad debts. The successful bookies work long hours, often seven days a week. There is always some "action" to be booked, even on Christmas Day. This is why some bookies only do one or two sports. Many prefer football because it attracts the greatest bettor interest. Also, most games are played on Saturdays and Sundays (although since its inception in 1970 Monday Night Football has become a major betting attraction); this gives them a few days midweek when they can turn off the telephone or accept bets only during specified times.

Although they operate outside the law, bookies don't view themselves as criminals. They uniformly say that they provide a service that is much in demand. They know their clients and have a good relationship with them, not unlike a doctor-patient relationship. Many compare themselves to stockbrokers. Yet the bookie lives in a world where the values of law and ethics are blurred, where they are both admired and reviled. Although they treat their clients with respect and cultivate a positive and friendly relationship, the nature of the business is adversarial. Experienced bookies confess that they often privately view each client as a sucker to be taken, or as one bookie stated, "the boob out there who exists only to be fleeced."[13] The bookie recognizes that each bet booked means either profit or loss. When forced to confront the ethics of their profession, most fall back on the rationale that they do not force anyone to place bets, and that if they were not in the business, someone else would be. As one New York City bookie told a reporter: "Guys will always bet, so why shouldn't there be people like me to book for them? Betting is one of the reasons this town is the kind of place it is." A San Francisco bookie summed it up simply, "After all, it's a service business."[14]

If the bookie is successful, he might be invited to join ranks with other bookies. Or he might simply expand his own business, using a form of franchising not unlike that which swept through America's mainstream economy after the war. A friend or customer who is deemed trustworthy might be enlisted to help out part-time as business grows, especially on those days, such as football weekends, when the telephone rings off the hook. This assistant, usually called a runner—like the old-style runners employed by the old gambling bosses—is also used to hit the streets to make a weekly visit to clients to settle up accounts. The runner is encouraged to build his own list of clients, and as his productivity increases, so does his cut of the profits. Over several years a bookie who exhibits good skills in dealing with people, in managing capital, and in keeping records might build an organization of several associates, who in turn might then develop their own subordinates.[15] Thus the system follows the lines of such successful "direct option" or "multilevel marketing" giants as Mary Kay Cosmetics, World Book, Tupperware, and Amway. As the marketing expert Richard Bartlett noted in a 1994 book on the subject, "You want to find a product line [or service] to sell that you believe in. . . . The rest is up to you—your enthusiasm, your determination, your hard work, and your integrity."[16] Bartlett identifies the modern-day bookie's perfect prescription for success.

The analogy between the direct-sales business and the successful bookie who takes on associates is instructive, and it is true as well that many in the direct-sales business do not become wealthy; many eager young salespersons soon retire from the field, and the turnover of bookies is also large. The pressure and hard work demanded of bookies mean that many go broke for a variety of reasons, such as lack of discipline, inattention to detail, poor record keeping, or simple bad luck. Despite the money to be made thanks to the statistical advantage of the

11/10 rule, it is also true that the bookie operates on a thin margin of profitability. Miscalculations on just one big game can create an overnight disaster.

Given the lack of hard data and the differing conditions in various cities, it is impossible to generalize with complete confidence about the personalities of bookies and the nature of their operations. But although each one is unique, as a group they share several defining characteristics. They tend to be gregarious, deeply interested in sports, and have been (and sometimes still are) bettors themselves. Although bookies come from every ethnic and racial group, the preponderance are Caucasian and male. In a society ever more committed to gender equity, it remains true that the field is heavily male dominated. The number of women bookies has remained infinitesimally small; the few women active in the field have largely worked in clerical and communications roles — accepting and logging bets placed by telephone by established clients.

Like the Avon saleswomen, bookies begin their careers at the bottom level. As in an earlier era, many learn their craft hanging out in pool halls or at newsstands where sports gambling is a routine part of daily life. One of the most famous of twentieth-century sports gambling figures, Jimmy "the Greek" Snyder, served a lengthy apprenticeship as a teenage runner for a Steubenville, Ohio, bookie, often handling bets on high school football games.[17] Lem Banker of Las Vegas learned the ins and outs of gambling very early in Union City, New Jersey, where his father booked bets out of his candy store.[18] Scotty Schettler, the innovative operator of the Stardust Casino sports book in the 1980s, was drawn into the sports betting world as a teenager in suburban Pittsburgh, and one current-day gambling entrepreneur operating a large Internet gambling information and tout service started out working for his uncle, who booked "about $40,000 a week during football season" in New Haven, Connecticut, during the 1980s.[19]

While once it would have been accurate to say that most bookies had limited formal educations — many not even graduating from high school — within the past few decades college graduates have entered the field. They got their start on college campuses, booking bets for fraternity brothers or dormitory pals, doing business in the snack bar of the student union or in a campus beer-and-pizza joint. In addition to the traditional lure of adding excitement to the outcome of sports contests, college bookies know that the possibility of arrest is low, of conviction even lower. They also know that their profits fall below the radar screen of state and federal tax officials, and whatever profit they take goes directly into their pocket free from the IRS. In recent years the growth of sports gambling on college campuses has attracted attention, leading NCAA officials and university administrators to view it with apprehension. The entry of college graduates into the field is a reflection of the large profits to be realized with relatively little risk of losing money or being arrested. Such bettors are often subscribers to expensive tout and informational services, read several sports pages each week, log on to one of many sports betting Internet services, and love to talk sports with other men at watering holes and workout clubs.

The major difficulties in a bookie's life stem from the possibility of arrest and the awareness that bettors can go on inexplicable winning streaks. However, the bookmaker can normally approach his business with the reassurances provided by history: Few bookies are arrested, and if they are, the justice system is usually lenient. More important, over a season, the great majority of bettors lose. The cautious and well-organized bookie prudently sets limits on the bets he takes—the limit being driven by the size of his own operation—and he is quick to make adjustments in his line when a savvy "wise guy" client goes against the conventional wisdom on a game. A limit is also intended to keep the player active. "Bobby," a college-educated bookie in New York, told an interviewer, "We have a five-thousand dollar limit on any one bet. We don't want our customers going broke. We need to do a volume business."[20] A typical small-time bookie in the 1990s usually will take no bet over $2,000 per game, many less, whereas larger operations, such as "Bobby's," often have limits that are higher. On special occasions, a bookie will be faced with the dilemma of having a prime client who wants to take a plunge on a particular game. Then he either has to take a calculated risk of accepting the bet or run the other risk of driving his client into the arms of a competitor. The option he might take, however, is to book the bet and then "lay off" the money with another bookie. Although much has been made of the lay-off business by political investigations into organized crime, many bookies tend to take the risk of accepting the bet themselves, based on their experience that the customer is often on the wrong side of the game.[21]

Although the ideal situation for the bookie is for his books to be balanced at game time, that is seldom the case. In most instances at kickoff or tipoff time the bookmaker has some of his own money in play on every game; he is in effect betting against his customers. But the power of the vig, the bet $11 to win $10 system, provides him a significant overall edge, as does the tendency of all but the professional "wise guys" to bet their emotions or simply to encounter a run of bad luck. Thus "Bobby" seldom worries about balancing his books and prefers to consider himself not a broker working for commission but as an active player who has a piece of the action. He is willing to take a position on a game, using the 11/10 vig as his hedge. "Bobby" says that "our feeling is, in the long run, the vig will take care of us." As "Smiley Joe," a small-time operator in New York, told a reporter in 1947, "Just let a guy keep betting me steady and I'll break him."[22]

But the new brand of bookie who considers himself a combination of Jimmy the Greek and Michael Milken knows that all sports gamblers do not lose. Lem Banker has made a comfortable six-figure income betting legally in Las Vegas for more than three decades, and so have many other crafty gamblers, like "Clyde," who have discreetly stayed out of the limelight. Casino insiders readily acknowledge that the only game in a modern Nevada gambling palace in which the house faces the real possibility of losing money over the long haul is in the sports book. But shrewd bookies like "Bobby" know who the talented gamblers are, and when one of these gamblers comes in heavy on a game, they spring into action, since the word will soon get out about, for example, "Clyde's" informed bet. Knowing that they will be deluged with bets on one side, bookies quickly adjust the line on the game away from "Clyde's" position to keep their own books balanced. "Bobby" often immediately gets on the telephone to place substantial bets himself with other bookies on "Clyde's" pick. This sophisticated form of the old "lay off," referred to as "scalping," protects Bobby's position by giving him the chance to win big on his own bets, thanks to "Clyde's" reputation for picking winners. "Buy cheap, sell expensive" is the way "Bobby" describes his formula for success.[23]

Thus in the half century following the introduction of the point spread, it has been possible for a reasonably skilled bookie to make a comfortable living from his bookmaking if he provides year-round service. Generally accepted estimates made by federal officials in the late 1990s placed the number of professional bookies at 250,000. Many contemporary bookies tend to specialize in only one or two sports. Some will open up shop when the NFL preseason games are played and close down operations after the Super Bowl in January. Others will do multiple sports, but the biggest variable is horses. Some provide horse betting as a courtesy to their best clients, but as more and more racing venues have opened with increasingly longer seasons, and with offtrack betting legalized in many states since the state of New York first permitted offtrack betting in 1964, betting on horse racing has steadily declined for street bookmakers.

As we have seen, the stereotypical Hollywood version of the bookie as a hardened criminal, part of a vast criminal organization, is not supported by the available evidence. The local criminal organization—if there is one—has usually not been an active participant in sports betting since the demise of the horse wire rooms a half century ago, for the simple reason that the business does not offer the high rate of return of other enterprises. For a long time the numbers racket was much more lucrative than sports betting, but between 1960 and 1987 thirty- seven states drove the numbers racket from the streets by going into competition with the mob by establishing state lotteries. These government-operated games are nothing more than a much better organized, highly computerized, legal variant of the old numbers scam operated by urban crime organizations. The numbers racket operated on the principle of the economies of scale by converting small amounts of money pried from very large numbers of poor city dwellers into very large profit margins, and state governments operate state-run lotteries on the same principle. Significantly, less than 50 percent of all dollars bet on state lotteries are returned to the participating public; about 95 percent of the dollars bet on team sports contests are returned to winners.

Consequently, urban criminal organizations in recent decades have looked elsewhere for their income, focusing their operations on such time-tested and lucrative venues as prostitution, loan-sharking, drug peddling, extortion, hijacking, and old-fashioned burglary.[24] In some instances, especially during the immediate postwar years in the larger cities, the local gang might have leaned upon bookies for a percentage of their take—"Smiley Joe" paid the "syndicate" of New York City $175 a week to permit him to operate safely—but the organizations seldom ran sports books as an important part of their portfolios. In fact, if bookies had to pay protection money to operate—what they called "rent"—it was more likely to be forked over to local law enforcement personnel than to the mob.[25]

Violence makes only a rare appearance on the sports gambling scene. The standard Hollywood version of the bookie sending out a 250-pound gorilla to work over a player whose account is in arrears is uncommon. Physical violence might frighten off other customers, for one thing, but it simply is not the way bookies operate. Very few kneecaps have been broken or even noses bloodied if a bettor skipped out on paying his bookie after a losing streak. Undoubtedly a stiffed bookie can become one angry individual, but unlike the appliance or automobile dealer, he does not have the option of the services of a collection agency, repossession, or legal action in small claims court. He might try to pressure the gambler-in-arrears with the threat of notifying his wife, friends, or boss. Social pressure can work sometimes, other times not. But most bookies simply write off the loss and put out the word that the client is not good for his losses.[26]

Just as the structure of sports betting has evolved since the Second World War, so too has its relationship with local law enforcement. The record is incomplete, of course, but it is clear that some members of the local constabulary, including patrol officers and their supervisors, regularly received payment from bookies. In return, they permitted the bookie to go about his daily routine. The amount of payment was based on the size of the bookie's operations. For example, "Smiley Joe" reported in 1947 that he routinely paid the several policemen who patrolled his neighborhood ten to twenty dollars a week to look the other way; another cop placed a verbal "bet" with him each week and collected if he won, but Smiley Joe wryly noted that he "wouldn't dream of asking him for the money if [he] lost the bet." Other big-city sources indicate that large bookie operations at that time paid up to $1,000 or more per week in "rent" to local authorities.[27]

As the second half of the century unfolded, however, this casual system of small-time bribes has apparently declined, although it has definitely not disappeared. This decline occurred for several reasons, the primary one being that as public salaries became more respectable, the unwritten expectations that policemen would supplement their incomes via petty graft has tended to disappear. Law enforcement has also undergone major reforms that have produced a much higher quality officer, better educated, better trained, possessed of higher ethical standards. Law enforcement has become much more professional, and consequently the so-called rotten apples have tended to disappear as higher standards were set for recruits and as extensive training programs and rigorous performance evaluations were implemented. Law enforcement has also been subjected to a heightened external evaluation process, from elected officials wary of being tainted with corruption, from spokespersons for neighborhood and ethnic groups, and from an aggressive post-Watergate media that is ever on the alert for any form of public corruption.

There is no question that the police know the names of bookies working on their beat.[28] But with the growing acceptance of gambling of all types, law enforcement has tended to wink at bookies, occasionally harassing them but not engaging in a concerted effort to run them off the streets. They recognize that the bookie is an integral part of neighborhood life, and many citizens would be upset if their gaming provider were put out of business. Occasionally a crackdown is ordered, designed to mollify a moralistic politician or to respond to a series of investigative articles in the local newspaper. Even then the booked bookie usually gets off with probation, or perhaps a fine of a few hundred dollars, and is almost never sentenced to jail time. Those few bookies who do end up in court invariably receive misdemeanor sentences, not felonies. Mention of the Internal Revenue Service creates a much more nervous response from a bookie than the mention of the local district attorney or vice squad.[29]

Although profits are to be made, the life of a bookie is often very stressful. Peter Alson's 1996 novel, *Confessions of an Ivy League Bookie*, describes the intense pressure in a large boiler room operation in New York City, where those in charge place one subordinate into competition with another, where the pressure to recruit ever more customers is intense, and where the fear of making a bookkeeping error produces many an anxiety attack. Fear of being set up for arrests by rivals—as eventually occurs in the novel—adds another level of intimidation and pressure. Operating outside the law and having to conceal one's means of livelihood from family and loved ones takes its toll. In Alson's novel, apparently based on personal experience, a fledgling novelist is brought into a boiler room operation where the cigarette smoke is thick, the language crude, and the pressure palpable when several telephones are ringing just before kickoff time. Real-life bookies, unlike the romanticized and sanitized version in Damon Runyon's short stories, do not lead a carefree life. They know they are operating on the margins of social acceptance and beyond the limits of the law.[30]

Thus the role of the street bookie has changed with the times. Changes in public sentiment have led to the rapid decline of horse racing as a major part of a bookie's operation, while the popularity of football and basketball has become ever more prominent. Technology has also changed the nature of the business, and bookies are forced to deal with clients who have access to (sometimes) informative tout sheets that provide detailed betting advice. Technological advances have led many a bookie to incorporate computers into their operation, and by the 1990s they were doing increasing amounts of business on cellular telephones or by FAX machines. As offshore sports books opened up in large numbers during the mid- to late 1990s, bookies faced a new and formidable competitor who accepted credit cards, offered toll-free telephone service, and accepted bets via the Internet. Like other traditional American businesses in the new era of the Internet, the traditional bookie now has to deal with the fact that his local operation is subject to worldwide "dot.com" competition.

9

The Lengthening Shadow of Scandal

Authorities on professional football tend to agree that the dramatic overtime 1958 NFL championship struggle between the Baltimore Colts and the New York Giants was one of the greatest professional football games ever played. Whether it was the "game of the century" is open to serious and continuing arguments at many a sports bar. About one point, however, there can be no doubt: this game clearly established the enormous power of television as a sports communications medium. Not only did it help propel football past baseball as the nation's most popular spectator sport, but it greatly stimulated interest in betting on professional football, luring millions of new gamblers whose only contact with the game would be as a member of the television audience.[1]

Played on the Sunday afternoon that fell between Christmas and New Year's Day, the game attracted an overflow crowd of 60,000 to Yankee Stadium, and a nationwide audience estimated at 40 million. In the waning moments of the game, Baltimore Colts quarterback Johnny Unitas coolly led his team on a late fourth quarter drive that began at the Colt fourteen-yard line and culminated in a field goal by place kicker Steve Myhra with only seven seconds left to play. His twenty-yard kick through the uprights (the goal posts were then placed on the goal line and not on the end line) forced a sudden-death overtime. In the overtime period, after the Giants were forced to punt, the stoop-shouldered Unitas once again led his team down the field, deftly connecting on passes to receivers Jim Mutscheller and Raymond Berry, and handing off the ball to running back Alan Ameche, who chewed up substantial yardage on draw and trap plays. The overtime drive began at the Colts' twenty-yard line, with the Colts eventually making a first down inside the Giants' eight-yard line. Then for three consecutive plays head coach Weeb Ewbank confounded football experts by not opting to kick a near-certain field goal to win the championship. Ewbank's judgment was rewarded, however, when on third down Ameche crashed off tackle for a one-yard touchdown run, giving the Colts the NFL crown by a 23–17 score.[2]

Before the game, as one writer observed, the Baltimore Colts players were "working men, tradesmen, glamorous only when compared with miners and factory workers," but afterward they were "legends, genuine folk heroes." The game was, NFL commissioner Bert Bell said, "the greatest game I've ever seen," and the veteran New York Times sports columnist Arthur Daley termed it an "utterly mad affair" that demonstrated "how completely pro football has arrived." It was great made-for-television high drama. Sports television had come of age.[3]

This exciting overtime game is widely considered the pivotal event that began the rapid transition of professional football into the nation's most successful, lucrative, and popular spectator sport. In the wake of this game, professional football, which had operated for three decades on the fringes of sports respectability, became a hot item. After undergoing a period of franchise instability—there were more than fifty major changes in franchise ownership or team location between 1945 and 1960—the NFL entered a time of continuous expansion (from eight teams in 1946 to thirty-two in 2000) with the value of each franchise increasing from about $500,000 in 1955 to $300–$800 million in the first year of the new millennium. Emulation is one of the most precious forms of approval. Just two years after the dramatic Colts victory, the newly formed American Football League fielded a rival eight-team operation based largely on the premise that it could succeed even if it was not popular at the box office—the crucial factor was securing a lucrative television contract. This assumption proved to be right on target, and upstart network ABC was more than happy to take a flyer on the new league.[4]

The pivotal New York–Baltimore game is also significant as a milestone in the evolution of sports gambling. More than forty years later, this famous game has never quite shaken serious, if unproven, allegations regarding the influence of gambling on the outcome. The unanswered question regarding the game is this: if Ameche had not scored on third down, would the Colts have gone for the sure win with an easy field goal attempt or would they have attempted to score a touchdown?[5]

Colts owner Carroll Rosenbloom was well known as a gambler, given to making large wagers. It was widely reported that he and a friend together placed several bets, totaling an estimated $1 million, on the slightly favored Colts in the championship game. The early line opened at 3½ and went up in some quarters to 4 and even 5 points. Many observers wondered why the Colts, once they were in easy field goal range during the overtime period, did not immediately kick a field goal rather than risk a fumble or pass interception. The decision to go for the six-point touchdown, especially after making a first down inside the Giants' ten-yard line, seemed especially puzzling. After the game, however, when word leaked out about Rosenbloom's enormous bet, many cynics suggested that he ordered Coach Ewbank to go for the touchdown because a three-point field goal would have left him the proud owner of the league championship trophy but $1 million poorer. Everyone connected with the Colts' play calling in that game, including Unitas and Ewbank, denied that Rosenbloom had interfered with their decision making. They noted that Myhra had missed a field goal earlier and that he was not the most reliable of place kickers, while Ameche was known as a sturdy running back who rarely fumbled. On the other hand, there is solid evidence, according to investigative reporter Dan Moldea, that Rosenbloom had not only made a large bet on the Colts but had given more than 3 points. Moldea admits that there is no clear evidence that Rosenbloom influenced the decision not to kick a field goal, but he implies that such might be the case.[6]

No matter. The essential fact is that many people believed that gambling had helped determine the outcome of the most famous professional game in history. At the heart of these speculations stood the new system of the point spread and how it created new expectations and pressures upon coaches and players. Now fans were concerned about not only whether their favorite team won a game but also whether they beat the spread in the process. The cold reality, NFL executives now understood as never before, was that professional football and gambling were, like siamese twins, inextricably connected.

Speculation about this one high-profile game must be placed within a larger context, however. Throughout its early history, professional football, like professional baseball, was often subject to rumors and accusations that its games were decided not on the field but by gamblers operating behind the scenes. The first established instance of a fixed football game was between the Canton (Ohio) Bulldogs and the Massillon Tigers in 1906; the Canton coach and a key Massillon player apparently worked out an agreement whereby Canton would win the first game and Massillon the second in a best-out-of-three championship series so as to produce a large number of ticket sales for the final game.[7]

When the National Football League was established in 1922, by changing the name of the two-year-old American Professional Football Association, its leadership was indeed dominated by well-known gamblers. Tim Mara, a New York City trackside bookmaker, purchased the New York Giants in 1925 for $500 even though he had never seen a football game in his life. Charles Bidwell, whose close association with the Al Capone gang in Chicago was well established and who was reputed to be an active gambler as well as a racetrack owner, purchased the Chicago Cardinals franchise in 1932 for $2,000. Art Rooney of Pittsburgh operated a tavern that was a popular watering hole for gamblers and bookmakers in the Steel City; Rooney himself once boasted that he had won $256,000 in two exquisite days of picking winners at the Empire City and Saratoga tracks in New York. And so it went throughout the infant NFL. Team owner and later commissioner Bert Bell was known for his gambling interests, as was Detroit Lions owner George Richards. But as Rooney once told a journalist, "Bookmakers in those days were such a different brand of people from what they are today. They were great people. They had class."[8]

As Dan Moldea makes clear, the early history of the NFL was closely linked to gamblers and gambling. This was not all that unusual, given that the same was true of the early ownership of Major League Baseball franchises. The attraction of "sportsmen" to the prospect of owning professional teams was natural. One authority noted, "The promoters of the NFL knew that bookmakers were a type extremely susceptible to new forms of investment" related to professional sports. When the rival All-American Football League was established in 1946, the preeminent franchise was purchased and operated for eight years by the well-connected Cleveland native, taxicab operator, gambler, and horse wire entrepreneur Mickey McBride. The Cleveland Browns, coached by one of football's most innovative and successful coaches, Paul Brown, dominated the new league, and when the Browns joined the NFL in 1950 they promptly confounded football experts by winning the conference championship behind the inspired play of quarterback Otto Graham, fullback Marion Motley, and a host of talented teammates.[9]

Browns owner McBride had assembled his original cache of capital as a hard-nosed circulation manager for William Randolph Hearst's *Cleveland News*. On more than one occasion McBride employed the services of mobster Moe Dalitz and his Mayfield Road gang when force was deemed necessary in the *News'* circulation wars with the established *Cleveland Plain-Dealer*. Just two months after Moe Annenberg shut down his Nationwide horse wire service in 1939 in preparation for his trial on income tax evasion, McBride opened up its replacement in the form of the Continental Racing Wire, which he unloaded several years later to concentrate on his primary investment, operating a taxicab business that enjoyed a monopoly throughout the Cleveland metropolitan area.[10]

During these formative years of professional football, it was not unusual for the NFL to be afflicted with rumors of bribed players and fixed games. One major instance occurred in 1943 when two reporters for the *Washington Times-Herald* published rumors that were making the rounds in the nation's capital that star Washington Redskins quarterback Sammy Baugh was associating with known gamblers. This association, reported the *Times-Herald*, perhaps explained why the Redskins had been upset by the heavily underdog Pennsylvania "Steagles" (during the war the Philadelphia Eagles and the Pittsburgh Steelers fielded a joint team). Redskins owner Preston Marshall angrily offered $5,000 to anyone (including *Times-Herald* reporters) who could present hard evidence that any member of his team either gambled on football or was associated with known gamblers. The *Times-Herald* could not produce such evidence and hurriedly backed off the story. But the possibility that such a star player might have been on the take received extensive play across the country. For his part, "Slinging" Sammy Baugh, now ensconced in the Football Hall of Fame, later admitted that he had known gamblers but stated to an interviewer, "I never made one damn bet in my life on a football game. I made one bet in my life on a horse race. It lost, and I [decided] that I was never going to bet again."[11]

In 1946 the NFL was rocked by confirmation of reports that four gamblers, apparently led by Alvin Paris, a gambler from Elizabeth, New Jersey, had attempted to bribe two key members of the New York Giants before that year's conference championship game. One of Paris's accomplices, interestingly enough, was Harvey Stemmer, who had been convicted the previous year for attempting to fix Brooklyn College basketball games. Just hours before the kickoff, District Attorney Frank Hogan announced that quarterback Frank Filchock and running back Merle Hapes had been offered $2,500 each to lose the game and had also had $2,000 bets placed on the game on their behalf. Hogan had uncovered the bribe offer via a wiretap he had on Paris's telephone. Hapes, whose name was mentioned on the wiretap tape, was suspended by Commissioner Bell, but quarterback Filchock was permitted to play because he denied receiving any bribe offer. Filchock later recanted and admitted receiving the offer but said he did not report it because he had rejected it out of hand.[12]

Filchock, obviously shaken by the hurried investigation that occurred just hours before kickoff, threw six interceptions along with two touchdown passes as the Giants lost 24–14. Following the conviction of the four gamblers, Bell suspended both Filchock and Hapes indefinitely, and they soon signed to play in the Canadian Football League. Filchock later joined the Baltimore Colts in the new All-American Football League and in 1963 was named head coach of the Denver Broncos of the American Football League, where he lasted two years before being fired after a 3–11 season.[13]

The attempt to fix the championship game, coming as it did on the heels of the unsubstantiated but widely publicized speculation about Sammy Baugh, threatened the future of professional football. Consequently, the league owners charged Commissioner Bell with rigidly enforcing a new set of policies that prescribed a lifetime banishment from the league for anyone associated with a team if he bet on any professional football game or failed to report any bribe offer, even if it was merely "by insinuation or by implication" and not an outright offer.[14]

Bell took his charge seriously and immediately hired a covey of undercover agents to monitor off-the-field relationships of players and to monitor the betting lines that were increasingly coming out of Las Vegas. He also quietly opened up communications with established gamblers and bookmakers, in particular the key oddsmakers in Leo Hirschfield's Minnesota offices. Of major interest were unusual moves of the betting line—a major indicator that a fix had been made. Bell's son later told Dan Moldea that his father had a special telephone line by which well-placed gamblers and handicappers could call him to report such line movements. Bell kept the names of his contacts to himself, or as his son said, "He took to the grave with him the names of his contacts in the underworld." Bell knew, of course, that established professional gamblers abhorred a fix and the possibility that some fixer would interfere with their ability to handicap the outcome of a game. The NFL would continue to use such contacts among handicappers and bookmakers as a way of being alerted to a fix. Later, the NCAA would also avail itself of the information on the flow of monies bet on games in Las Vegas's biggest sports books.[15]

It was within this larger context that Commissioner Bert Bell looked on from his private box as the Colts beat the Giants in the overtime championship game. He would die a year later, but he had put in place strong policies and procedures to protect the rapidly maturing NFL from the scourge of gamblers eager to arrange a sure thing.

⚑

Meanwhile baseball was in the doldrums. Attendance was down all across the major leagues, and the number of minor league teams was shrinking at an alarming rate. The attraction of horse racing had peaked and begun a slow but inexorable slide in popularity that continues to this day. Although boxing enjoyed a brief but spectacular run thanks to high television ratings in the mid-1950s, by the end of the decade its popularity as a television spectacle had waned substantially, and the sport was relegated to the margins of the legitimate sports world. Only the spectacular and controversial career of the charismatic Muhammad Ali would postpone its decline. Boxing had long been popular in New York City, largely because of its appeal to gamblers, but continuing rumors about fighters taking a dive at the behest of gamblers (who might also be their owner/managers) had soured many professional gamblers on the sport as a betting medium. Because of the constant rumors and allegations regarding fixed fights, many gamblers looked elsewhere for their action; more important, many bookies, weary of having their oddsmaking undercut by a fix, simply refused to book boxing.[16]

On the plus side, however, college basketball had recovered from the scandals that had rocked it to its foundations in 1951. Professional basketball, long a minor factor on the American sports scene, now featured such dynamic star attractions as Wilt Chamberlain, Bill Russell, and Bob Cousy, plus a host of other talented players. The professional game was catching on, the beneficiary of the powerful eye of the television camera. Bookies now found themselves doing more and more on college and professional basketball and football than on the horses or baseball, a sport that did not lend itself to the point spread.[17]

College basketball remained a major focus for wintertime gambling, and memories of 1951 were largely forgotten. But shortly after his release from prison for his central role as Salvatore Sollazzo's contact man during the scandals of '51, former Long Island University basketball star Eddie Gard told a journalist, "I don't ever want to hear about basketball again, but mark my words, all the rest of you will be hearing plenty about it. I've got to wonder if anybody ever stopped doing business. So it's only a matter of time. It'll all come out again someday and some other poor bums will do time in the can."[18]

The words of this ex-fixer were prophetic indeed. It took only ten years for an even larger event to shatter the complacency that had settled over the NCAA after the fixes had disappeared from the front pages in mid-1952. Once again it was New York District Attorney Frank Hogan who revealed the scandal when he announced on March 17, 1961, that he had arrested two small-time gamblers, Joseph Hacken and Aaron Wagman, and charged them with attempting to fix games with players at Seton Hall and the University of Connecticut. Soon Hogan had hard evidence about point shaving at four other New York City colleges: Brooklyn College, NYU, Columbia, and St. John's University.[19]

By the time his second investigation into college basketball had run its course, Hogan had fingered forty-nine players associated with twenty-seven universities in eighteen states, although, again, knowledgeable insiders felt he had only scratched the surface of this festering sore. This time the conspiracy ran deep into the heart of Dixie, and such major institutions as Tennessee, South Carolina, Alabama, North Carolina, Mississippi State, and North Carolina State were embarrassed by the actions of a handful of their players. It was truly a coast-to-coast scandal; the University of the Pacific in Stockton, California, was also implicated. At least sixty-seven games had been affected between December of 1957 and March of 1961, when Hogan broke the story. On the surface the story was not much different than in 1951, but this time the fixers were more sophisticated in their work. They established a relationship with a player and then waited until he signaled them when a fix would occur. In an interesting twist, the fixers sometimes worked with players on losing teams; then the complicit players would make certain that their team lost by more points than the spread. In the earlier scandal, it was invariably the favorite team that failed to cover the spread.

Players professed that they did not think they were doing anything really wrong. NYU guard Ray Paprocky told the press that, in addition to time-consuming basketball, he was married and an expectant father who had been enrolled for sixteen credits while working an eight-hour shift in a cannery to make ends meet: "I was aware that what I did was wrong, but if I were in the same circumstances, I'd do it again. Not because I'd want to, but because I'd be forced to. It was better than robbing a bank." A Columbia player, Fred Portnoy, sounded a similar theme: "I knew it was morally wrong, but I just didn't think of it as criminally wrong. I know I never would have done it if there had been a real threat of jail. But I didn't have too much loyalty to Columbia. I knew we didn't have a good team, so what difference did it make if we lost by ten points instead of five?"[20] Inflation apparently had not yet affected the shaving business; the typical payoff remained about $1,500 per player per game.[21]

At the center of the mess was former Columbia University All-American and (for a very brief time) NBA star player 6'6" forward Jack Molinas. Molinas had had a long involvement with illegal gambling and fixed basketball games. Having grown up on the streets of New York, he joined the Ft. Wayne (now Detroit) Pistons in 1953 and was so impressive in the first few months of his rookie season that he was named to the league's All-Star team. But he never played in the All-Star game because he was found to have been placing bets via telephone with a New York City bookie on professional basketball games, including Pistons games. He told the press, "I always bet on us to win. I have never done anything dishonest in my life." But he was in clear violation of league policy prohibiting betting on any game by a player or league official, and he was banned from the NBA for life by President Maurice Podoloff, who was shaken by the first gambling scandal to hit the league.[22] An apparently contrite twenty-one-year-old Molinas, who had won about $400 on an estimated six different bets, told the press, "I was silly. I'll never bet again." But he lied. He was in fact a compulsive gambler. He escaped criminal prosecution when league detectives could not convince a grand jury that he had actually placed bets against his own team and was conspiring to shave points.[23]

In 1961, now twenty-eight and the possessor of a law degree and a member of the New York State Bar,[24] Molinas sued the NBA for $3 million in damages, alleging that he had been damaged under federal antitrust laws and arguing that the league had conspired to deny him his livelihood by leveling excessive punishment for what he termed "minor transgressions." Ironically, his suit apparently stemmed from his inability to control his gambling: he needed the money to cover his gambling debts. He had also become deeply involved in fixing college games. His fixes did not always pan out; in one notable instance he reportedly lost $80,000 on a game he thought he had bought. Molinas had apparently committed himself to a long career as a fixer. He worked hard at establishing relationships with some of New York City's top high school players with the clear intent of exploiting these young men in future fixes, including the naive and innocent New York City high school superstar Connie Hawkins, whose college career was ruined and professional career severely jeopardized simply because he had been befriended by Molinas. Hawkins never was offered or took a bribe, but it was clear that Molinas was laying the groundwork to later approach Hawkins when he reached the college varsity level at the University of Iowa.[25]

At the antitrust trial in early January of 1961 brash young attorney Jack Molinas told federal judge Irving Kaufman that his suspension from the NBA was unjustified: "The punishment given me is more than commensurate for the acts performed." The highly respected jurist denied the claim, finding that no antitrust laws had been violated. Kaufman went on to assert that every professional league required strong antigambling policies, adding that the NBA policy was "about as reasonable a rule as could be imagined" and that "it was absolutely necessary for the sport to exhume gambling from its midst for all times in order to survive." In his concluding remarks, Judge Kaufman said, "One can certainly understand the reluctance to permit an admitted gambler to return to the league and again participate in championship games, especially in light of the aura and stigma of gambling which has clouded the sports world in the past few years."[26] His final words should have resonated across the American sports world: "Viewed in this context it can be seen that the league was justified in determining that it was absolutely necessary to avoid even the slightest connection with gambling, gamblers, and those who had done business with gamblers, in the future."[27]

It took some time following Hogan's first indictments in March 1961 to nail the primary conspirator, but by the following year Hogan had assembled incontrovertible evidence that the "master fixer" of this epidemic of scandals was former basketball star turned attorney Jack Molinas. For months Hogan had followed up his leads, using hidden cameras, wiretaps, and extensive detective legwork to put together the pieces. Aaron Wagman, a longtime associate of Molinas's, confessed, as did several implicated players. But Molinas knew his law: he could not be convicted on the testimony of co-conspirators, and Wagman and the players were co-conspirators. However, Molinas himself had offered a bribe to Bowling Green University player Billy Reed, and to protect himself he decided to serve as Reed's lawyer. In the secure confines of his office, the arrogant Molinas carefully instructed Reed how to lie to the grand jury about his role in fixing games. But Reed had already cut his own deal with Hogan and was wearing a wire that captured every incriminating word. Consequently, in February of 1963 Molinas was convicted of conspiracy, bribery, and subornation of perjury and given a ten to fifteen year sentence. Judge Joseph Sarafite told Molinas at the time of his sentencing, "In my opinion you are a completely immoral person. . . . You callously used your prestige as a former all-American basketball player to corrupt college basketball players and defraud the public."[28]

His legal career over and any dreams he had of returning to the NBA gone, Molinas served four years of his sentence before being paroled in 1968. He later resurfaced in California, reportedly engaged in producing pornographic films. He was killed in what the press called a "gangland" shooting in 1975 when he was shot in the neck by a sniper while standing in his Los Angeles backyard at 2 A.M. Police theorized that the shooting was related to the beating death of his partner in a fur-importing business the year before which netted Molinas a $500,000 life insurance payment. His federal trial for shipping pornographic materials across state lines was scheduled to begin just a few weeks after his murder at the age of forty-three.[29]

The fixing uncovered by the scandal of '61 was much bigger and more sophisticated in scope and design than the amateur conspiracies of 1951, but the reaction of the media and the public was strangely muted. Charles Rosen attributes the indifferent response to a public "weary of corruption." Perhaps. Once again the coaching establishment professed its ignorance of the fixes, and the NCAA, according to *Sports Illustrated*, seemed to be reverting to its traditional response by "display[ing] more eagerness to bury scandals than to expose them." Despite the lessons of 1951, the NCAA had not responded, the magazine editorialized. "College athletics demand close supervision. The NCAA, like supervisory bodies in various pro sports, should have a security arm whose members are perpetually on the lookout for possible trouble."[30] A few months after Molinas entered prison, the story had disappeared from public view, soon to be buried in the history books.

🐾

If 1963 was not a good year for college basketball, it was no better for football; both the professional and collegiate games were hit with serious allegations regarding gambling. In March of that year the *Saturday Evening Post* dropped a bombshell when it reported the bizarre story of an Atlanta businessman who claimed that while making a local call his line was mistakenly connected to a long-distance conversation between University of Alabama head coach Paul "Bear" Bryant and the athletic director and recently deposed head coach of the University of Georgia, "Weeping Wally" Butts.

According to George Burnett, a forty-year-old Atlanta insurance salesman, while making a local business call on September 13, 1962, he heard some strange sounds on the line and then was mysteriously tapped into a conversation between Butts in Athens, Georgia, and Bryant in his office in Tuscaloosa, Alabama. For about fifteen minutes he listened to the two men discuss football. According to Burnett, the conversation began with Bryant asking authoritatively, "What have you got for me?" Almost immediately, Burnett perceived that Butts was revealing to Bryant inside information about Georgia's game plan for the opening game eight days hence. As he listened, Burnett furiously took notes. Those notes remained in a bureau drawer until the following January, when Burnett shared them with a friend who then informed the second-year Georgia head coach, Johnny Griffith.

Fully aware that Butts was less than enthusiastic in his support of him, and convinced that he had betrayed him by revealing game plans, Griffith immediately went to senior university officials and demanded that his boss be fired. Two years earlier, in the wake of a series of losing seasons compounded by damaging revelations about his personal life (public marital infidelity, excessive drinking, frequent sightings at sleazy Atlanta night spots, a misguided political endorsement in the 1960 gubernatorial race of a blatant segregationist, and a well-known friendship with a big-time Chicago gambler), Butts had been forced out after twenty-two years as head coach. Butts had also speculated disastrously, losing large sums of money on a Florida land development deal. Surprised and upset that his former assistant coach had excluded him from all phases of the team's activities, Butts was apparently torn between his devotion to the school and his animosity toward Griffith, who was attempting to create a better public image for the Bulldogs football program by distancing himself and his team from

Butts, who was slated to retire officially on June 30, 1963. Thus, by the time of the most important telephone call of his life, according to James Kirby, "Butts was on a collision course with disaster. Personally, professionally, and financially his life was a shambles. He was reckless and vulnerable."[31]

The university undertook a thorough and secret investigation of the allegations, but it produced nothing conclusive, although it did find that on the afternoon in question there had indeed been a long-distance telephone call between Butts's office and Bryant's that lasted sixty-seven minutes. When Burnett took and passed a lie detector test, and Butts angrily refused to submit to a similar test, university officials were understandably concerned. Later, however, Bryant easily passed a similar test. (Polygraph tests in 1963 were believed to have about 80 percent accuracy.) As to the lengthy telephone conversation, coaches around the country rallied to their colleagues' defense, noting that coaches are notorious conversationalists during the season: "If I'm in trouble about something the week of a game," Arkansas head coach Frank Broyles said, "I'm liable to call every coach in the country and talk all day, just to put my mind at ease."[32]

Butts angrily resigned as athletic director, saying, "They asked me to take a lie test and I didn't think that was right. I figured I'd just resign now instead of June." At this juncture, convinced that Georgia officials were not going to take decisive action against Butts, Burnett's attorney contacted the *Saturday Evening Post*, which agreed to pay the salesman $6,000 for his story and his fourteen pages of handwritten notes. Perhaps not coincidentally, the *Post* was currently bracing itself for a $500,000 libel suit from Bryant regarding an exposé it had published accusing him of using brutal coaching techniques.[33]

The lengthy article appeared on March 23, 1963, and was written by senior writer Frank Graham Jr., although it was later revealed that several of the more inflammatory words had been inserted later by editors. The main thrust of the article was that Butts had provided Bryant with inside information in order to benefit by betting on the Crimson Tide beating the point spread; the magical figure had fluctuated the week of the game between 14 and 17 points. The Tide rolled to victory by a lopsided 35–0 score, outplaying the Bulldogs in all phases of the game. Graham emphasized that Butts had recently taken a $70,000 loss on a land investment deal in Florida, and that his animosity toward the university and Griffith was intense. Revenge was also a motivating factor, Graham alleged. He acknowledged that a sophomore-dominated Georgia team was hopelessly outmanned by Alabama's powerful team (Alabama would go 10–1, losing only to Georgia Tech 7–6 when its attempt at a two-point conversion failed). But Graham provided no evidence that Butts or his gambling friend, John Scoby of Chicago, had placed any bets on the Tide to beat the spread.[34]

Butts and Bryant immediately sued. Butts's libel case went to trial in August, after a federal judge in Atlanta insisted it be tried before the football season began. According to attorney James Kirby, whose 1986 book examines the case in detail, the Curtis Publishing Company's defense was poorly presented, while Butt's attorney effectively elicited testimony that the *Saturday Evening Post* had been suffering from declining subscription rates, advertising revenues, and profit margins. Dramatically quoting from the article, attorney William Schroeder (himself a former Notre Dame football player and onetime freshman coach at Georgia) emphasized key words that had appeared in the article: "fixer," "fix," "corrupt," and "sell-out." He forced the publisher of the *Post* to admit that he had established a new policy to publish "sophisticated muckraking" articles in order to improve circulation. The purpose was "to provoke people, to make them mad," editor Clay Blair admitted under Schroeder's aggressive cross-examination.[35]

Although the five-day trial produced conflicting testimony, and although both sides suffered setbacks from the evidence presented, the atmosphere in the courtroom was unmistakably hostile to the publisher for engaging in muckraking journalism. The big winner was Bear Bryant, who gave impressive football jargon–laden testimony, emphatically denying any wrongdoing. The defense did not provide any tangible evidence that the notes Burnett had taken of the conversation contained any information useful to Bryant, it produced no evidence to support the contention that Butts had sought to manipulate the point spread, and it presented no evidence that either Butts or Bryant had bet on the game themselves or had used third parties to place bets for them.

Observing the trial for the Southeastern Conference, Kirby watched, listened, and reread trial transcripts. By the trial's end, he concludes, "The case against the *Post* for its shoddy, reckless journalism was overwhelming. The callous indifference that the magazine had shown for the consequences of its rush to publish a scoop cried out for a remedy." That remedy was shocking— a $3 million punitive damage award to Butts, plus $60,000 in compensatory damages. This was later reduced upon appeal to $400,000.[36]

College football had been stained but not seriously damaged by this strange case. The media tended to treat it cautiously but with marked skepticism about the allegations. Coach Bryant emerged an even more popular coach and public figure in Alabama, even though he quietly settled his own suits with the *Post*. In his detailed study of the case, Kirby decides that the truth will probably never be known. He points out that the *Post* and its attorney were in possession of unused information that should have enabled them to mount a much better defense. He suggests that had its lawyers properly argued the case, the *Post* could have obtained a dismissal of Butts's suit on technical grounds. Nor does he completely close the door on the possibility that Butts had shared useful information with Bryant. Kirby's fascinating book poses a series of questions about this case but provides no definitive answers.[37]

Although the legal battle in Atlanta revolved around gambling, that central issue was often lost in the legal maneuverings of a libel suit. The role of gambling was much clearer in the case of the National Football League, an extremely image-conscious organization that had entered into a period of rapid growth. For years the NFL had mounted a strong antigambling campaign. Like organized baseball, the NFL had in place a clear policy that anyone connected with a team—players, coaches, administrators—were subject to severe penalties if they gambled on any NFL game. In early 1960 the club owners had made the improbable selection of thirty-three-year-old Los Angeles Rams general manager Pete Rozelle as their commissioner to replace Bert Bell. Rozelle's appointment was greeted with considerable skepticism because he lacked experience and because his expertise lay not in management and finance but in public relations.[38]

On April 17, 1963, Rozelle dramatically resolved any concerns that he lacked the backbone to direct the league when he shocked the sports world by suspending two of the NFL's best players, Paul Hornung and Alex Karras, for a minimum of one year. Both players had violated the league's policy against gambling. Green Bay Packers popular halfback Hornung was arguably the best player in the league, a former Heisman Trophy winner at Notre Dame and, with a salary of $30,000 and endorsement and speaking income of another $20,000, one of professional football's highest paid stars. Karras, a former All-American from the University of Iowa, had become a perennial all-league defensive tackle with the Detroit Lions.[39]

Their gambling, in and of itself, was small-time stuff. Hornung had been betting since 1959, placing relatively small bets of $100 to $500 on college and professional games. The star running back had long been associated with gambling in his hometown of Louisville and was often seen at Churchill Downs betting on horse races—permissible under NFL guidelines. He told the press that he probably "broke even" on his football bets. Hornung placed his bets by telephone with a friend, a man named "Barney" Shapiro, he had met in San Francisco but who had relocated to Las Vegas to operate a pinball and coin machine company. For several years he and Hornung would talk by telephone during the season; Shapiro might ask, "How do you think the Packers will do this week?" and Hornung would tell him to bet on the Packers, laying the points against the spread. This was, technically, inside information, but Hornung later told an interviewer that he was merely showing faith in his team. Hornung had Shapiro place his bets for him in Las Vegas books, frequently betting on the

Packers to beat the spread. "Not once did I ever bet against us. But if I chose not to place a bet on us one week, there was a reason why. Just too tough a game or something."[40] No one ever asked Shapiro if in those instances he took Hornung's deferral as a signal to bet against the Packers.

According to NFL investigators, Karras had bet much less than Hornung— $50 bets on six games. It was his widely known associations with prominent Detroit gamblers that probably led Rozelle to deal so harshly with him. In announcing the suspensions, Rozelle emphasized that the real danger lay in the fact that the two men were talking to gamblers and exposing themselves and the league to suspicions of foul play. Additionally, Rozelle levied fines of $2,000 each on five members of the Detroit Lions who had each placed one $50 bet on games that did not involve the Lions.[41]

Rozelle emphasized that neither player had bet against their own teams or in any way attempted to shave points or fix games for gamblers. "There is absolutely no evidence of any criminality. No bribes, no game-fixing or point shaving." He went on to say, "There is no evidence that any NFL player has given less than his best in playing any game. There is no evidence that any player has ever bet against his own team. There is no evidence that any NFL player has sold information to gamblers. There is clear evidence that some NFL players knowingly carried on undesirable associations which in some instances led to their betting on their own team to win and/or other National Football League games."[42]

Hornung was contrite and teary-eyed when he told the press that he had "made a terrible mistake." Karras, however, was angrily unrepentant: "I haven't done anything that I am ashamed of and I am not guilty of anything." He had been given, he complained, "a life sentence for running a red light." Rozelle emphasized that Karras's "pattern of betting and off-field associations constitute serious breaches of his player contract and of the constitution and by-laws of the league."[43] He was particularly concerned about Karras's continuing association with known Detroit organized crime and gambling figures, including his ownership of a bar these individuals frequented.

While some fans reacted negatively to Rozelle's decisive handling of the case, most sports commentators approved of his strong leadership. The journalist Tim Cohane, writing for *Look* magazine, praised Rozelle for taking a stand against gambling by courageously suspending two of the league's best players, and for dealing directly with "the gambling angle continually tormenting football with suspicion and rumor." Although Cohane noted that most of these rumors— including the one regarding the overtime strategy used by Carroll Rosenbloom's Baltimore Colts in the 1958 championship game—were "unfounded and often crackpot," they nonetheless presented Rozelle and his league with a problem that had to be confronted.[44]

What did not make the news, however, was a hostile exchange between Hornung and Rozelle when the commissioner first confronted the star halfback with the evidence his investigators had uncovered. Hornung angrily refused to take a lie detector test, telling Rozelle that if he were forced to do so he would volunteer to appear before the ongoing Senate investigations on organized crime being conducted by Senator John McClellan and state on the record the names of the many NFL players he personally knew were also gambling on league games. He later said that in early 1963 he told Rozelle, "If we go down to Washington your ass is in trouble if I talk about how many guys I know who are betting. Don't have me go to Washington and raise my right hand."[45] Rozelle assured him that he did not want that to happen, and the lie detector test was canceled. The ever-smooth public relations man turned commissioner did not want a scandal of major proportions to smear the league's image; rather he hoped that making an example of Hornung and Karras would bring an end to violation of the league's antigambling policy.

Rumors regarding gambling and fixed games continued to plague Rozelle. They surfaced repeatedly between 1966 and 1970 and invariably focused on the Kansas City Chiefs and its all-star quarterback, Len Dawson. Las Vegas books frequently took Chiefs games off the board when "unusual" or "unnatural" money came in on particular games. Behind the scenes the Department of Justice, the Internal Revenue Service, and the NFL conducted ongoing and extensive investigations. The irony of the allegations was that during this period the Chiefs had a strong team and enjoyed winning seasons. Not incidentally, they also often beat the spread.

Out in Las Vegas, like all bookmakers, Jimmy "the Greek" Snyder was closely monitoring the situation. Like others, he heard the rumors that Dawson was receiving telephone calls from a Detroit underworld figure and well-known sports gambler, Donald "Dicey" Dawson (no relation). Len Dawson became a marked man, but the level of his play belied any point shaving. Time and again he denied any gambling connection when interrogated by NFL officials, although he readily admitted that he had met the Detroit gambler through his friendship with Detroit Lions quarterback Bobby Layne. In 1968 Len Dawson agreed to Rozelle's suggestion that he voluntarily take a polygraph test regarding Dicey Dawson and gambling, a test he passed without any problems. Meanwhile in Detroit, Don Dawson was alleged to have made several casual statements about his close relationship with the Chief's quarterback, invariably on the eve of a big game.[46]

This long-simmering episode came to a boil in January of 1970 when the Len Dawson–led Chiefs prepared to play the Minnesota Vikings in Super Bowl IV. The betting line, which seldom moves more than 2 points after it is posted, fluctuated wildly. It opened with the Vikings a 3-point favorite, but quickly soared to 9. Obviously, something was amiss. A few days before the game, NBC-TV reported that a Detroit federal grand jury was about to subpoena NFL figures regarding point-shaving allegations and specifically mentioned that one of those persons was Len Dawson. Even the nation's number one football fan, President Richard Nixon, got involved, calling the Chiefs' head coach Hank Stram to tell him, "I know there is nothing to the rumors about Dawson. He shouldn't be upset about them. Would you tell him that for me?"[47] Rozelle hurriedly released a statement affirming his confidence in the integrity of the Chiefs, and for the first time publicly mentioned the polygraph test that Dawson had passed in 1968.

Len Dawson was apparently able to put the allegations out of his mind as he prepared for the game, in which he led the Chiefs to a 23–7 upset victory over the heavily favored Vikings. He completed twelve of seventeen passes, one for a touchdown, suffered only one interception, and was named most valuable player of the game. The investigation thereupon collapsed. Some observers believe that NBC's breaking of the news had soured the investigation.[48] But out in Las Vegas, Jimmy the Greek had taken his own reading of the curious event.

Like other oddsmakers, Snyder had over the years noticed "unnaturally big money" coming in on Kansas City games, money that had made its way to Las Vegas via circuitous routes. His sources traced those monies back to Detroit and to friends of Dicey Dawson. What Snyder detected was an elaborate conspiracy designed to manipulate the point spread so that Don Dawson and his associates could "middle" a game and make a killing without taking a risk. Supposedly he did this by manipulating public opinion with his carefully orchestrated comments about his alleged—and apparently fictitious—telephone conversations with Len Dawson. As Snyder's biographer explains the scam:

Jimmy knew what was happening to the line. Say that the Chiefs were favored by seventeen over Denver, and Dicey Dawson took the points. His friends, the people around him, would say, "Dicey talks to the quarterback. He knows something. . . ." The line would drop to sixteen and their friends would start betting, and soon it goes to thirteen. The suckers would come in and the line would fall to eleven. The fellow in Detroit [Dawson and associates] would bet that—take Kansas City and lay the points—and now he had the game middled. He was on both sides with maybe a six-point spread. That was beautiful—for him.[49]

In this scenario, Don Dawson and his associates very likely would have ended up with equal amounts of money bet on both teams. If the difference in the final score ended up between 11 and 17—in the middle—they would win on both bets; if not they collected on one of the bets and broke even. Getting a middle is every professional gambler's dream, but few have been as creative as the boys from Detroit seem to have been in making it happen.[50]

Snyder and other Las Vegas bookmakers had originally made Minnesota a 3-point favorite, but when the allegations surfaced, he estimated that gamblers would calculate that the distractions would hurt the Chiefs and so would bet the Vikings. He and his peers moved the spread upward; finally it leveled off at 9, and the subsequent flow of monies balanced out. After the game was over—as after the previous year's Super Bowl, when he had made the Baltimore Colts an overwhelming 16-point favorite over the underdog New York Jets—he and other bookmakers were criticized for "missing" the final point differential so badly. In both instances, when the underdogs won handily, Snyder was made the butt of jokes about how far off he was. Like all competent oddsmakers, however, in setting his line he was taking into consideration how the public would react. He was not in the business of picking winners. He was seeking what is called in the business a "splitter" number, a line that would generate equal monies on both sides.[51]

As a result of increased interest in betting on televised sports, daily newspapers began to print the point spreads, often under the title "Las Vegas Line." Public attitudes toward gambling were changing: states started to run lotteries, and increasing numbers of state political leaders began to look toward casino gambling as a way to alleviate pressures upon state budgets. All of these factors turned national attention to the desert state of Nevada, where gambling, including sports wagering, was legal.

10

Bugsy, Lefty, and the Boys
in the Nevada Desert

The popularity of betting on sports teams coincided with the rise of legalized gambling in Nevada. This development was a momentous event in a large western state with a small population. It had enormous impact on the future of gambling in the United States. The legalization of gambling in the Silver State was unplanned and proved to be more of an afterthought than anything else.

In part, it was a desperate attempt to stimulate a severely depressed economy in a state that had historically lacked a stable economic base. Riding a spectacular boom in silver and gold mining, Nevada was prematurely admitted to the Union three days before the presidential election of 1864; President Abraham Lincoln wanted a little electoral insurance from the potential 40,000 staunch antislavery voters clustered along the Comstock Lode in northwestern Nevada. By 1880 the mining bonanza had run its course, and the bulk of the wealth had been siphoned off to San Francisco by several major bankers, investors, and mine operators. Despite several subsequent mining booms, Nevada's population in 1900 had dipped to just 42,000, and its critics in Congress—disturbed by the state's heavy congressional clout resulting from having two senators and one congressman representing so few citizens—were in full cry. They denounced Nevada as a "rotten borough," and state leaders had to fend off the ignominious possibility of having its statehood revoked. More than one powerful congressional leader would have liked nothing more than to return Nevada to territorial status, or perhaps to merge it with Utah or California.[1]

Things did not improve much for Nevada during the first three decades of the twentieth century. Its economy proved insufficient to support stable growth, and so in the depression year of 1931, Nevada's cautious and conservative politicians took a chance on gambling. No one at the time envisioned the luxurious hotel casinos that would soon be rising out of the sagebrush, nor did they anticipate the economic bonanza that gambling would produce. No one in their wildest dreams conceived of the development of Glitter Gulch in downtown Las Vegas or the world-famous Strip springing up along the two-lane highway leading south of town toward Los Angeles. Nevada's provincial, rural-dominated legislature was merely looking for a new source of tax revenue and for a modest boost in tourism. In 1931 Reno, located just a few miles from the California line in the northwestern part of the state, was the state's largest city with about 16,000 residents. Las Vegas, 450 miles to the southeast in the southern tip of the sprawling state, was a mere blip on the map with slightly more than 5,000 residents; its economic activity revolved around its primary roles as a railroad water stop and county seat. Nevada also boasted the nation's smallest capital, Carson City, which had a population of just 5,000. The entire state's population hovered at just 96,000, and the future looked anything but bright.[2]

Over the previous fifty years state leaders had tried many approaches to get a firm economic base established. Various mining booms in Goldfield, Tonopah, McGill, Beatty, and Rhyolite set off spurts of economic expansion, but these bonanzas did not provide long-term stability. Gold and silver reserves were exploited, and then gave way to copper mining. Several boomtowns sprang up overnight, with populations of several thousands, only to see all of the residents depart with the exhaustion of the ore deposits or a decline in commodity prices. In 1907 Goldfield reached an estimated 18,000 residents, but by 1930 its population had fallen to less than 300. Nevada's arid climate and broad expanses of alkali soil precluded serious farming, and the vast stretches of sagebrush offered precious little natural feed upon which to launch a major ranching economy. Even the much heralded Newlands irrigation project, built early in the twentieth century in northwestern Nevada with federal funding, failed to approach the promises and predictions of boosters that it would "make the desert bloom."[3]

When conservative Republican governor George Balzar signed the gambling bill into law he did so over sharp but futile opposition from religious and women's groups. This historic event, however, merely capped more than sixty years of legal flirtation with gambling. Many rationalized legalization by noting that it merely made legal a form of popular entertainment that Nevadans had always practiced, no matter the current wording of the law. Gambling was an integral part of the state's life—a legacy of the mining frontier, where it had become firmly integrated into the state's social fabric. Gambling was originally legalized in 1869, when the legislature overrode Governor H. G. Blasdel's veto. But in 1910, under intense pressure from moralistic progressive reformers, the legislature declared most forms of gambling illegal, and it made all gambling illegal in 1913. Two years later, however, under heavy lobbying from saloon and gambling interests, the legislature changed course slightly by making some card games legal. In the next fifteen years, determined gambling and business interests attempted every biennial legislative session to obtain passage of a "wide-open" gambling law, but without success.[4]

By 1931 gambling in Nevada essentially meant poker and blackjack, craps, roulette, and an occasional tug at a "one-armed bandit"—the mechanical slot machines that had made their appearance about 1900. Nevadans seldom bet on sports, the two exceptions being the brief horse racing season held each September at the Reno fairgrounds and sporadic high-profile prizefights.

The primary impetus for an open gambling law came from Reno and Las Vegas businessmen who operated legal card shops and from hotel and restaurant owners who hoped for an increase in tourism. A second group supporting the legislation included the town and county officials who needed a new source of tax revenue. In a time before widespread use of political polls it is impossible to determine public sentiment, but it is clear that strong opposition existed, led in Reno by the editorial pages of the *Evening Gazette* and the *Nevada State Journal*. Many church leaders were hostile, as were reform-minded women's groups. Many Nevadans feared (correctly) that passage of legislation would produce national condemnation of the state, and they warned of a rise in crime and social problems. A few prescient critics even predicted an influx of big-time gangsters from eastern cities. More pragmatic citizens, however, rationalized that legalization of gambling would merely give legal sanction to the widespread gambling that routinely occurred in the back rooms of taverns and restaurants across the state, especially in Reno and Las Vegas.[5]

Because of the strong opposition, it is not surprising that no member of the legislature wanted to be identified as the leader of the legalization movement; even after passage, no prominent political figure stepped forward to take credit. The decisive influence of politically connected businessmen such as Reno banker and hotel owner George Wingfield was unquestioned. This former saloon owner and dedicated gambler had built the foundation for his wealth in the rambunctious mining town of Goldfield early in the century. Now operating the Nevada National Bank out of his office on Virginia Street, he had become a powerful and sometimes ruthless man and was the unquestioned political boss of the state. Wingfield's leadership proved instrumental in lining up legislators in the months before the convening of the session.[6]

Opponents of legalized gambling might well have been in the majority, but they lacked the insider political clout of its proponents. Significantly, no concerted opposition came from the business community. One of the few advocates who had the courage to step forward was Las Vegas real estate developer

Thomas Carroll, who took out an advertisement in newspapers across the state presenting what he called a "New Idea" to make Nevada "The Playground of the United States." Carroll clearly perceived the future: "We can make wide-open gambling the biggest industry in the state, so that it with horse racing and tourist traffic, will bring more millions of dollars into Nevada than . . . any other industry we now have."[7]

Early in the legislative session several copies of a bill floated around the state capital for weeks before freshman legislator Phil Tobin, a rancher from Humboldt County, finally introduced the bill. The *Reno Evening Gazette* glumly took note of the legislative groundswell of support for legalization on January 24, but grumbled that "no one will admit having been approached to offer such a bill." The *Gazette* observed that despite the lack of sponsors for a legalization bill, "all legislators profess a lively interest in one." Although eager to satisfy the demands of important business interests and campaign contributors, most legislators were also deeply concerned about voter retaliation in the next election.[8]

A quarter of a century later, basking in the glow of the economic boom that his bill produced, Tobin claimed that he and he alone had come up with gambling as a means of generating new tax revenue and, as he curiously said, of preventing illegal gambling money from leaving the state.[9] The actual vote on Assemblyman Tobin's bill revealed a healthy 2–1 majority in both legislative chambers. The secret support within the legislature and the quick signing of the bill by Governor Balzar on March 19, protests of angry Mormons and Methodists notwithstanding, indicate that, far from public view, the legislative wheels had been carefully greased.

Not coincidentally, Governor Balzar also signed into law that same March day a bill reducing the waiting period for obtaining a divorce to just six weeks. Throughout much of its history Nevada had imposed a modest six months' residency requirement to be eligible for a divorce. It was reduced to three months in 1927 after the neighboring state of Idaho, having taken notice of Nevada's divorce-driven economic boomlet, had passed a three months' residency law of its own. In signing both bills, Balzar revealed how desperate Nevada had become to find solutions to its severe economic plight. As predicted by its critics, Nevada's unconventional anti-depression measures immediately produced moral denunciations from across the nation.[10]

Governor Balzar and the legislature might have been acting in the best economic interests of their state, but their actions also reinforced a negative image that Nevada had gained during the heyday of the Victorian era. The legislature had never bothered to make prostitution illegal since it became an important part of the social life of Virginia City during the Comstock days;

by custom, the matter of prostitution was left to the county commissions to decide as a "local option." Nevada's liberal approach to divorce had produced a minor economic boom for Reno lawyers and guest ranch operators.[11] Nevada's toleration of boxing—the blood sport was outlawed nearly everywhere else in the country—added to its outlaw image. Nevada had provided one of the few safe locations for the holding of championship bouts until about 1920 when boxing was legalized in New York. Nevadans had eagerly accepted the money paid out by high-roller fight fans who came to the state to witness, and bet on, a major bout.[12]

Thus well before 1931 and the legalization of casino-style gambling, prize-fights, prostitution, and easy divorce had already set Nevada apart from the other forty-seven states. The addition of legal gambling sealed its fate as the "sin state," an image it would not completely shake by the end of the twentieth century. Interestingly, in 1931 Governor Balzar had distributed to every daily newspaper in the United States a pamphlet proclaiming the virtues of Nevada's lifestyle under the intriguing title of *Nevada Liberalism*.[13] Nevada thus embarked on a curious political trail, commingling an intense economic and political conservatism with an extraordinary streak of permissive social liberalism. By 2000 the rest of the nation had largely caught up in the matters of divorce and gambling, but Nevada still held its dubious monopoly as the only state to permit the operation of legal brothels.

If there was ever a case that proved the rule of unintended consequences, it was Nevada's decision to legalize gambling. Three-quarters of a century later, the state's population had increased twentyfold, propelled almost completely by the tourist-driven casino business. Las Vegas became not only one of the nation's most rapidly growing cities, but also one of the most famous in the world, recognized for its unique entertainment, its wide-open twenty-four-hour gambling, its luxurious hotels, its towering electric signs, and its easy-come, easy-go atmosphere. Between 1931 and 2000, the population of Clark County grew from 5,000 to 1.5 million. The gambling mecca that emerged in the desert of southern Nevada is one of the great economic success stories of modern American urban history.

Las Vegas's explosive growth and its image as one of the world's most popular tourist destinations have overshadowed the miracle that gambling also brought to Reno. This once-dominant Nevada city, with 18,000 residents in 1931, also grew rapidly thanks to the establishment of such famous gambling landmarks as Harolds Club and Harrah's. In 2000 Reno and its immediate environs contained 250,000 residents.[14] Reno lost out to Las Vegas in the competition for the gambling tourist dollar for several unavoidable reasons, including the lack of an abundant supply of water and the proximity of Las Vegas to Los Angeles. However, Reno lost out primarily because its more cautious residents never embraced gambling with the gusto of the people of Las Vegas. Whereas Renoites placed large stumbling blocks in front of those who sought to establish major casinos along the Truckee River and historic Virginia Street, Las Vegas openly courted those who wished to take advantage of legalized gambling and went to great lengths to encourage gambling as the primary purpose of the community.

The first decade of legalized gambling in Nevada saw little change. The slot machines and green-felt tables were moved out of the back rooms and onto the main floor of small venues in downtown Reno, Las Vegas, and the few small towns scattered across the state. Although about fifty new gambling halls opened, the largest could accommodate only a few hundred patrons. With a few notable exceptions, such as Reno's prominent Bank Club, this was low-stakes gambling. Few casino operators advertised in newspapers and journals outside Nevada. Only after Raymond "Pappy" Smith launched his famous nationwide "Harolds Club or Bust!" roadside sign campaign in 1940 did casino operators begin to exploit the potential inherent in their legal gambling monopoly.[15]

The Second World War provided the catalyst for such exploitation. By 1942 Nevada had become the location for several large Army Air Corps training fields. The military loved Nevada's mostly sunny climate and the enormous expanse of open spaces uncluttered by towns or even farms and ranches. The opening in 1941 of the enormous, hastily constructed $140 million Basic Magnesium plant in Henderson brought thousands of workers to southern Nevada, and they and bored military personnel flocked to casinos in their off-hours. The small mining and ranching towns of Elko and Ely, located in the eastern part of the state, were overwhelmed by soldiers on furlough from Wendover air base on the Utah border. The attractions were their red light districts, small gambling venues, and twenty-four-hour liquor sales. Reno, and especially Las Vegas, not only attracted servicemen from the several new air bases throughout the state but also drew thousands of military personnel stationed at many locations in California.[16]

It was during this period of rapid war-related economic growth that New York gangster Benjamin "Bugsy" Siegel first visited Las Vegas. Dispatched westward in 1937 by New York crime boss Charles "Lucky" Luciano to run offshore gambling cruises out of Los Angeles, he visited Las Vegas in 1942 with the intention of establishing a small horse racing wire service. He observed that the once somnolent dusty desert town was alive with men spending money with abandon at small casinos in downtown Las Vegas such as the Golden Nugget, the El Cortez, and the Pioneer. Siegel especially took note of the popularity of a new motel, the El Rancho, built south of town on Highway 95 leading toward Los Angeles.[17]

The sociopathic Siegel—his nickname "Bugsy" apparently came from his erratic behavior—recognized that in this isolated little community he could not only realize his dreams of becoming a major player in the world of gambling but also do so legitimately. In this windswept desert town gambling *was* legal. It was to this former New York thug a special place where he could operate openly and without fear: "No FBI man can ever as much as lay a finger on my shoulder," he exulted.[18]

After being rebuffed in his attempts to purchase several existing Las Vegas casinos, Siegel turned visionary entrepreneur, thus helping to set in motion the transformation of Las Vegas. Obtaining investments and loans estimated at $3.9 million from Chicago and New York mobsters, Siegel built the precedent-setting Flamingo Hotel-Casino on the highway just south of Las Vegas. This vaguely Mediterranean-themed resort featured a large swimming pool, opulent rooms located in two-story buildings that were spread across manicured lawns and surrounded by palm trees and extensive landscaping, luxurious restaurants, and a show room where famous Hollywood and Broadway stars performed nightly. At the core of this new complex, of course, was a large, sparkling casino.[19]

Siegel's vision of the future was extremely perceptive, but he proved to be an inept businessman. Enormous overruns, costly architectural planning errors, and Siegel's insistence on making costly upgrades during construction pushed the price to almost double the original estimate. In a rush to open the day after Christmas in 1946, Siegel overlooked too many important details. The casino did not immediately attract the level of action anticipated, and Siegel was unable to stem a huge tide of employee theft from the gaming tables. The casino dropped $100,000 during its first two weeks of operation—Siegel had erred by opening the casino before the hotel was completed—and he endured the embarrassment of having to close for two months. By mid-March of 1947, however, he had reopened, and by May the casino receipts had moved the casino into the black. But by this time he owed various mobsters more than $4 million, and his outrageous behavior and arrogance, coupled with the sense among the mobsters who had put up the money that he could not manage this large and complicated enterprise, apparently sealed his fate. Bugsy Siegel was ambushed gangland style in his girlfriend's Beverly Hills home on June 20, 1947, his body riddled with nine bullets fired from a .30 caliber army carbine at close range through a picture window. The slugs shattered his face; one eye was found fifteen feet from his body. Only thirty minutes after Siegel was cut down, several representatives of New York and Chicago crime organizations walked onto the Flamingo casino floor and assumed control. Las Vegas had come of age.[20]

Following Siegel's abrupt exit, a seemingly endless construction boom transformed this desert railroad stop. In rapid succession, one opulent hotel-casino after another popped up along the Strip like so many mushrooms in the springtime. In 1948 the Thunderbird opened, and then onetime Cleveland mobster Moe Dalitz's classy Desert Inn (1950). The Sands and the Sahara opened in 1952, and in 1955 there appeared the New Frontier, Dunes, and Riviera. The Stardust, destined to become a pioneer in establishing the standard for casino-based sports books in the late 1970s, opened for business in 1958. These glitzy casinos had nothing in common with the western or cowboy theme that had dominated the first generation of small locally owned casinos. The new venues featured luxurious accommodations, food service ranging from inexpensive buffets to luxurious gourmet restaurants, extravagant entertainment, garish electric signs, and architecture styles designed to provide an image of affluence.

A large and continuing infusion of capital from mob-related enterprises in New York, Chicago, Kansas City, Milwaukee, Cleveland, Detroit, and Miami provided the funds for the construction of these gambling palaces. Because until 1969 Nevada law prohibited corporate ownership of casinos, these were privately owned operations. And given the complex levels of ownership created by mob lawyers, no one, not even Nevada's political leaders and gaming regulators, seemed to know who really owned them. But with a euphoric wave of prosperity sweeping across the state, no one really cared. Not only did mob-related sources provide the funds to build the casinos, they also provided the managerial expertise to make them function efficiently. The first wave of professional gambling operatives to arrive in America's new gambling mecca had learned their trade in the Midwest and East in illegal gambling emporiums—experts at running fast-paced poker and blackjack games, at keeping the dice moving at the craps tables and the chips coming at the roulette wheel. They were much in demand because Nevada lacked an adequate supply of dealers and middle managers for the rapidly increasing number of casinos.

At first there was not much to attract professional sports bettors to Nevada, because a 1951 law passed by Congress in the wake of the basketball scandals made the operation of legal sports books virtually impossible. Congress imposed a 10 percent tax on all sports bets and required all bookmakers to purchase a fifty-dollar license (an absurd provision of the law if ever there was one). For a time federal agencies used the law to shut down local gambling operations, a crusade that briefly drove illegal bookies into hiding for fear of being nailed by the IRS. However, bookies soon recognized that there was little to fear from the new tax law and went back to (illegal) business as usual, discovering that television had produced a social environment conducive to increased levels of action. The gambling expert John Scarne observed that by 1954 "the pendulum began swinging back. . . . Millions of horse players needed someone to book their action, and a younger, hungrier generation of new bookies replaced the old timers who were in jail or out of business." By 1956, he reported, "there were more bookies at work than ever before," a number he placed at 300,000 by 1960.[21] These intrepid souls laughed at the gambling license requirement and concluded that the threat of prosecution was too small to prevent them from pursuing their craft.

In Las Vegas and Reno, however, casino owners compared the 10 percent federal sports betting tax and the 4.4 percent profit that the 11/10 system normally generated and decided to look elsewhere for ways to separate tourists from their money. Several modest-sized horse rooms had operated in Las Vegas casinos during the war years, but the first publicized casino-based sports book was placed in the Flamingo by that longtime horse wire entrepreneur Bugsy Siegel. It was only a small operation, though, tucked away in a corner of the casino floor, providing a nostalgic tie to the prewar horse wire rooms that had once dominated American sports betting. By the early 1950s it was gone, a victim of the 10 percent federal tax bite.[22]

After that, the only major sports action in Nevada was provided by a handful of grimy little "turf clubs." Often poorly capitalized, they opened and closed with regularity. With names like the Vegas Race and Turf Club, Hollywood Sports Service, Del Mar, Churchill Downs, Reno Turf Club, and the Rose Bowl, these small establishments offered an ambience reminiscent of prewar horse wire rooms—with peanut shells and discarded betting sheets littering the floor, and the pungent aroma of stale beer and cigar smoke contributing to the atmosphere. These clubs were often called "sawdust rooms" because workers would toss sawdust on the floor to absorb the spilled beer and dampen the odors. In these small clubs the odds were posted by hand on the chalkboard, and the owners ground out a small profit. Operators got by by manipulating the pari-mutuel take of 18 percent and illegally booking team sports bets "off book." According to former employees, these "turf" or "race and sports" clubs survived by assiduously avoiding the federal tax. A $500 bet taken from a regular customer would be printed as $5 with a telltale sign written on the ticket to denote that it was actually a $500 bet. Or a bet would be taken "off book," meaning that no formal record of it was kept on the regular books that were made available to tax auditors and state regulators. Unknown customers, who might be federal agents operating a sting, were given accurately written tickets.[23]

Jimmy Vacaro, who has long been involved with the sports betting scene in Las Vegas and during the early 1990s was director of the sports book at Steve Wynn's Mirage Hotel-Casino, explains it this way: During the 1950s and 1960s the hotels and the operators of the turf clubs held fast to a gentleman's agreement; the hotels would stay out of sports betting if the turf clubs did not attempt to introduce other forms of gambling, especially slot machines. Everyone knew, Vacaro recalls, that the turf clubs were playing fast and loose with the federal tax monies they were supposed to report. "With that 10 percent excise tax there was no way the hotels could make a profit. The little guys [in the turf clubs], on the other hand, were cutting some corners to beat the tax." He told a writer, "As a kid I'd sit around the Churchill Downs book with some of the old timers and see things happen that would never happen now in one of our operations. For example, if you were a regular customer and went to the window to bet $1,100 to win $1,000 on a football game, the guy might write the ticket for $11 to win $10. It was between you and him, you see, and that way the tax was on only $11, not $1,100. The eleven bucks is all that went though the machine."[24]

The turf clubs also knew when the feds were around town, and from 1951 until the tax was lowered in 1974 no major scandal ever took place. Nevada Gaming Control Board commissioner Phil Hannifin understood what was going on. "Back then you couldn't run a race and sports book in a casino. They were . . . on the outside and they had lots of problems. There was past-posting, and the state never got a full count. There were two and three sets of books. You'd have a guy with a chalkboard, a phone line, and a lease, and at the first sign of trouble he was gone."[25] As prominent Las Vegas handicapper Arne Lang puts it, "It's worth noting that sophisticated, high stakes bettors in Nevada, like bettors elsewhere, never paid the tax anyway."[26] In other words, they bet through illegal bookies, often working in the shadows of the turf and sports books, or they bet with the clubs with ticket writers who manipulated the system to foil the feds.

The race and turf clubs were transitional institutions in Nevada sports betting, providing the tie from the former illegal horse wire rooms to the future luxurious casino sports books. In Reno, the action was at the Reno Turf Club, located along the railroad tracks, just around the corner from Virginia Street and the world-famous Harolds Club. This operation—which in 2000 was the only one of the breed still in operation as a race and sports book—derived much of its business from out of state by soliciting telephone and mail business in men's magazines, a practice that came to a halt in 1961 when Congress made interstate betting illegal, including the transmission of sports betting information across state lines.

The race and turf clubs did make book on team sports, primarily football, but also some basketball and baseball. However, in order to make a profit and pay the 10 percent federal tax, they had to book team sports bets at the outlandish rate of 12 to 10 on a straight wager, rather than 11 to 10. This meant that the bettor had to win an incredibly high 54.54 percent of his sports bets merely to break even.[27] While wildly optimistic gamblers placed bets at these odds, the knowledgeable sports bettor recognized that the 12 to 10 virtually assured that they would emerge from a season an overall loser and so they took their business elsewhere. With the advent of network television and, especially, the major advances in the art of televising sports introduced in the early 1960s by Roone Arledge of ABC-TV— color, sideline shots, instant replay—the turf club operators recognized a rapid increase in the amount of customer interest in team sports, despite the onerous tax. This was especially true with the advent of the Super Bowl in 1967 and Monday Night Football in 1970.[28]

Eventually the overall gambling friendly environment that Las Vegas offered proved attractive to professional sports bettors. One of the first to arrive was Lester "Lem" Banker, who had grown up watching his father openly making book in his Union City, N.J., candy store and knew that a portion of his winnings went to the Union City police to permit him to operate. Banker attended the University of Miami on a basketball scholarship but never played; instead he ended up spending much of his time betting at South Florida horse and dog tracks. He soon learned that he could make more money using his handicapping skills on college football and basketball, taking advantage of less knowledgeable college students. In 1951 Banker relocated to New York City, where he moved into the mainstream of the flourishing sports betting environment. Soon he was hanging out with the big boys, including helping to "move some money" for major gambling interests, but as he puts it, "I wasn't part of 'organized crime,'" in New York. "Disorganized crime, maybe, but never the organized kind."[29]

In 1957 Banker accepted an offer from a New York gambling associate to move to Las Vegas to operate a new turf club he was opening. The Saratoga Club was located on First Street in downtown Las Vegas, but like all such clubs it operated on a razor-thin profit margin. Within months of his arrival, Banker's friend bailed out, and his successor likewise lacked sufficient capital to run the operation. After helping to close down the club, Banker moved on to perfect his handicapping skills and become one of Las Vegas's most famous residents. The Saratoga would subsequently reopen, several times, under "new management."[30]

Just as Banker found the atmosphere in Las Vegas a pleasant respite from New York, where gamblers had to operate outside the law, so too did another young gambler who had already developed a reputation for his handicapping skills in the East. Demetrious Synodinos was born to Greek immigrant parents in the hardscrabble town of Steubenville, Ohio, in 1918. This tough river town of 40,000 was wide open. When he entered high school at age fourteen Steubenville gamblers were keeping ten bookies busy, several of whom provided him employment as a runner and a card and craps dealer. "You had to bet to survive," he later joked. "I was 25 before I found out gambling was illegal." Either by luck or by instinct, as a teenager he became locally renowned for his ability to pick winning horses at tracks he had never seen. At age sixteen, with $500 in his pocket and a new "Americanized" name, Jimmy Snyder dropped out of school and headed for Florida to play the horses; within a few years he had built his bankroll to several thousand dollars.[31]

By the time he was in his early twenties, Snyder had learned a great deal about the world of gambling. He understood that casino games gave the house a statistical advantage that could not be beaten in the long run by even the most skilled of players, and he had also come to recognize that despite his demonstrated ability at picking horses, the large pari-mutuel take and the many variables that enter into a horse race ultimately made for an unattractive betting proposition. Football and basketball, on the other hand, could provide a skillful handicapper with opportunities for success. In this venue, skill, intelligence, instinct, and experience did count. In 1939 Snyder returned to Steubenville and began to develop a reputation as an uncanny sports handicapper, becoming the stuff of legend by placing bets with Chicago and New York bookies of over $100,000 on a single game—if he felt he had a decisive edge.

By the onset of the Second World War, Snyder had moved his operation to New York City, and he suffered the notoriety of being identified as one of the nation's more sophisticated sports handicappers before the Kefauver committee by witness Sidney Brodson, a person he had only met once in passing. Snyder built a wide network of friends and associates in the gambling arena and naturally began to visit Las Vegas, where, like Lem Banker, he relocated in 1957. Later he told an interviewer that, having noted that the Kefauver hearings had created a hostile environment for gamblers everywhere "except the one place where it was legal, the state of Nevada, I would take my assets and go there."[32]

"I decided," Snyder later recalled, "that the only real bankable commodity I had was my lifelong knowledge of sports and the manipulation of odds and point spreads."[33] He was soon recognized as a major player in Las Vegas, not only betting his own bankroll but also advising others. He hooked up with the Vegas Turf and Sports Club, setting betting lines. *Sports Illustrated* made him a popular public figure when it introduced him to the nation in 1961 as "The Greek Who Makes the Odds." Snyder was always ready to defend the ethics of his chosen profession. He loved to tell anyone within range that "there are more bank presidents in jail than bookmakers," and "I'm not a crook. I'm not a thief. I'm a gambler, and a damn good one." He found in sports betting a continuing intellectual challenge: "You're always matching your wits against someone else's in the sports world. Every game is a challenge, and if you win, it gives you some sort of satisfaction."[34]

On October 15, 1974, the lure of Las Vegas for sports bettors was magnified manyfold when Senator Howard Cannon, himself a resident of Las Vegas, succeeded in getting legislation through Congress reducing the 10 percent federal tax on sports bets to just 2 percent. Overnight the sports gambling scene changed dramatically. The turf clubs were now able to make a profit on sports events *and* pay the federal tax. Action at their counters immediately picked up. Understanding that the great majority of sports bettors will lose in the long run, the clubs now tended to go legit, electing to absorb the lower tax. This led to the obvious business decision by casinos to open their own sports books to compete with the turf clubs; enabling legislation was passed by the 1975 state legislature and in August of that year the Union Plaza Hotel and Casino in downtown Las Vegas opened the first casino-based sports book since the pioneering days of Bugsy Siegel's Flamingo.

A major figure in the passage of this legislation was Frank "Lefty" Rosenthal. By the mid-1970s this powerful figure had risen to a position of absolute control over the Stardust Hotel-Casino located in the heart of the Las Vegas Strip, although he never was licensed by the Nevada Gaming Control Board. Born in Chicago in 1929, Rosenthal had "been dodging trouble most of his life," according to the journalist Nicholas Pileggi. He went to work for Chicago mobsters and gamblers as a teenager and became known during the 1950s and 1960s as a major horse and sports gambler. In 1961 he was called before the McClellan Senate committee investigating organized crime and took the Fifth Amendment thirty-seven times. In 1968 he was dispatched to Las Vegas to look after the financial interests of Chicago mobsters who effectively controlled the Stardust Hotel-Casino, where they had installed a massive skimming operation that Rosenthal was instructed to supervise and protect.[35]

In 1975 Gaming Control Board commissioner Phil Hannifin convinced Rosenthal to testify before committees of the Nevada state legislature on behalf of legislation that would permit sports books to be located within casinos. Hannifin recognized the potential for additional state revenues, and Rosenthal, an accomplished sports handicapper, was more than willing to oblige. With legislative and Gaming Control Board approval, Rosenthal devoted himself to developing a new form of sports book that contrasted vividly with the sawdust clubs. When the Stardust Race and Sports Book opened in 1976 it marked him in Las Vegas as a man of extraordinary vision. Rosenthal recalls, "I knew exactly what to do. I had spent my life in [casinos] and knew what they needed. I can't tell you the hours I spent going over the design, just the hours to going over the right kind of seat to buy, the space, height, the boards, the TV screens. I wanted them to be like theaters."[36]

Instead of the seamy cramped space filled with the smells of old beer, cigarette smoke, and greasy food that had typified the turf clubs, Rosenthal created a lush environment of 9,000 square feet to accommodate 600 gamblers. He had 250 individual desks with comfortable chairs installed, and placed a bank of large television screens high on the wall to show several horse races and games simultaneously. He replaced the old chalkboards with electronic sign boards so that changes in odds or point spreads could be posted instantly. "We put in a bar measuring nearly a quarter mile of inlaid wood and mirror and the largest projection-lighted board system in the world. We had a forty-eight square foot color television screen, and since horseplayers were still our biggest bettors, we had entry boards for five separate racetracks covering a hundred and forty square feet. It was the largest and most expensive system of is kind anywhere, and we had it all. Quinielas, exactas, futures, daily doubles, and parlay betting, along with the regular win-place-show bets."[37]

Rosenthal was recognized as "the man who brought sports betting to Vegas — an achievement that made him a true visionary in the annals of local history."[38] His revolutionary Stardust Race and Sports Book set the standard for Las Vegas, and it gave his casino a major lead in catering to the needs of sports gamblers. "I was in a great position," he later recalled. "The sports books began making money for the casinos and, therefore, for the state. In some circles, I was golden."[39]

Over the next few years several other casinos followed suit, especially after a gaming-friendly Congress responded to the blandishments (and campaign contributions) of casino lobbyists by reducing the 2 percent federal tax on sports gambling even further in 1983, to just .025 percent. Even then some casino managers were hesitant to get into the sports book business because they recognized that the long-term return would be, at best, between 3 percent and 5 percent. Heavy overhead expenses and the possibility of sustaining losses on big games or fights gave them additional pause. Casino operators also recognized that sports books take up large amounts of valuable space that could be utilized much more profitably by filling it with slot machines or blackjack tables, activities where incontrovertible percentages give the house a built-in profit margin. Nonetheless, managers of major casinos also understood that they had to offer a full complement of "gaming services," and that included a lavish sports book.

They also appreciated that if their sports books enticed sports-minded gamblers into their casinos, while there they might also visit the green-felt tables or take a few tugs at a slot machine. By the late 1980s every major casino in Las Vegas, South Lake Tahoe, and Reno offered a sports book to its customers, as did many midsized casinos. By 1985 all of the small turf clubs in Las Vegas had closed, and a new era of casino sports betting was at hand. Even smaller operations in towns like Ely, Winnemucca, and Carson City saw the merit of providing sports wagering to lure customers to their tables and found a convenient way to do so by leasing space to Leroy's Sports Book of Las Vegas, which used modern computerized communications to operate more than two dozen satellite books across the state.

The importance of a sports book to a casino's bottom line was made clear by the example of the enormous 2,800-room Hilton Hotel and Casino in Las Vegas. It did not open its race and sports book until December of 1986, but when management decided to take the plunge they did so with Las Vegas–style gusto. It was the first true "super book," an enormous place, richly appointed, with several large television screens linked to satellites to bring in sporting events from around the world. Large electronic boards flashed the odds and point spreads, and 200 small workstations were provided for serious horse players who often spent the entire day handicapping horse races and placing wagers. Cocktail waitresses offered free drinks to players, and the atmosphere during major game days was electrifying as the gamblers cheered or jeered each play according to their wagers. Although Hilton's race and sports book manager Art Manteris concedes that the Hilton "SuperBook" has not generated income levels equal to other gaming venues in the casino, he argues that it has demonstrated its ability to lure additional customers to the casino. He notes with satisfaction that in 1987, the first full year of operation of the SuperBook, "there was substantial increase in hotel occupancy, slot handle, casino handle, food and beverage revenue." The casino, he concludes, "benefitted in all areas after the opening of the sports book."[40]

By 1995 there were 80 individual sports books operating in the state, the great percentage in Las Vegas and Reno but some also in such smaller communities as Elko, Fallon, and Carson City. In 2000 the number had increased to about 100 books, which took in $3 billion in bets that generated about $100 million dollars in profits. Although the books still were not viewed as major profit centers by casino executives, they had proved Rosenthal's view that they would bring into the casinos a large stream of customers, many of whom would also take a fling at other, more profitable gaming venues. Thus the plush sports books became merely one aspect of the overall service that a major casino offers its clientele.

But there is a major difference: unlike the other games where the casino has a built-in statistical advantage ranging from approximately 2 percent on blackjack to more than 10 percent on keno, it is altogether possible for the sports book to lose money. And on certain big games, such as the famous Dallas-Pittsburgh 1978 Super Bowl, when astute gamblers were able to "middle" the books as the odds changed, they have lost—big time. However, over the long run the casinos' built-in 11/10 advantage gives them a margin of safety in regular sports betting, and they routinely take advantage of naive bettors with parlay cards that carry odds and probabilities heavily skewed in the casino's favor. Further, by locking into the pari-mutuel odds established at the distant horse tracks that appear on their television screens 365 days a year, the books have an automatic take of approximately 15 percent without risk on each and every dollar bet at their counters.[41]

Thus in the 1980s did Las Vegas assume control of America's sports betting. In a city where gambling was viewed as a normal human activity, sports gamblers found a natural environment in which to pursue their craft. When Congress reduced the tax on all sports bets, the enterprise took off like a rocket. By the mid-1980s sports authorities had come to recognize that a new era had arrived. Las Vegas's major casinos became the nerve center for an exponentially expanding sports wagering bonanza, providing bookies everywhere with a reliable betting line. The nation's authoritative sports magazine, *Sports Illustrated*, which two decades earlier had presented Jimmy the Greek to the nation in a laudatory article, took an intensive second look at this phenomenon and came away deeply concerned. "Betting on football, basketball and baseball has become a huge nationwide business. Massive television exposure and the look-the-other-way attitude of league and club executives have helped propagate sports gambling's vast popularity." The enormous popularity, the magazine editorialized, was replete with potential dangers. "Nothing has done more to despoil the games Americans play and watch than widespread gambling."[42] The irony was that— as we shall see in chapter 12—while state lotteries and regular casino gambling were sweeping the nation, battle lines over the role of sports wagering were once more being drawn.

11

Setting the Vegas Line: Jimmy the Greek and Roxy Roxborough

When Leo Hirschfield shut down his Minneapolis offices in 1961 and went into retirement, the nerve center of American sports gambling was already shifting to Las Vegas. Hirschfield had filled a vital need for America's bookmakers for nearly a quarter of a century—setting odds and providing reliable information on teams—but new federal legislation prohibiting the transmittal of betting information across state lines by telephone convinced him to fold his tent and head into retirement. Hirschfield had launched his business during the late 1930s in response to the changing American gambling culture. Gamblers now were less interested in the horses; many wanted to bet on baseball, and after the end of the Second World War they were increasingly drawn by the point spread challenges offered by football and basketball. Recognizing that knowledgeable gamblers could do major damage when a bad number was put up on the board, bookmakers had eagerly signed up for Hirschfield's weekly service. His Monday morning releases, sent by telephone or telegraph to his subscribers, provided a reliable national line for nearly a quarter century. With the assistance of able associates, such as veteran handicapper Joe Katzman and the eager youngster Mort Olshan, Hirschfield was able to make the transition from the money line system (odds on winners) to the point spread without missing a beat.

Every Monday morning during football and basketball seasons, Hirschfield would quietly listen while his four lieutenants—Katzman, Carl Ersine, Jimmy Harris, and Olshan—presented their independent assessments of each game. He seldom intervened, but he wanted to know in detail how the line was being formulated. "Early Monday," Olshan recalls, "the four of us would enter the boss's office armed with portfolios containing facts and figures on the up-coming games. We would discuss one game at a time, each offering his opinion of what the odds on each game should be. . . . As might be expected with everyone extremely well informed and having access to the same data, there were seldom major differences. When there were, a lively debate would ensue, with Joe [Katzman] left to render the decision on what number would be sent out." Hirschfield apparently had full confidence in his associates and only rarely intervened once the group had reached a consensus. "The whole idea [of the process] was to come up with a line that our subscribers could use and profit by," Olshan later recalled.[1]

After Hirschfield retired, the national line soon radiated out across the land from the Las Vegas race and sports books. Although several different betting lines were reported out of southern Nevada during the 1960s—each small club set its own line—a consensus on each game quickly coalesced as the sports book managers compared their handiwork with competitors down the street; more important, they reacted to the early betting patterns of experienced gamblers whose skills they knew and appreciated (and often feared). Of course, anyone willing to book a bet can set a line. As longtime handicapper and sports book manager Bob Martin once commented, "A line originates wherever someone is capable enough and confident enough to put up some numbers."[2] Such self-appointed line makers, however, ran a large risk. When the so-called wise guys detected a weakness in a new line, they immediately pounced to take advantage of a perceived golden money-making opportunity.

The void left when Hirschfield abandoned the field was initially filled by recent Las Vegas arrival Jimmy Snyder, who for a time put up his own numbers as manager of the Saratoga Club located in "Glitter Gulch" in downtown Las Vegas. With only a handful of clubs in town, Snyder was operating within a small tight-knit community. Like all bookmakers, he kept close tabs on what his competitors were doing, and if initial lines differed substantially, the flow of gamblers' monies quickly produced a convergence. If different numbers did appear, within hours they had moved to within a half point or so of each other. When Snyder began writing his syndicated newspaper gambling column his national prestige began to grow. His line more or less became the Las Vegas standard for a few years, but his increasingly erratic line making led to his fall from grace on the streets of Las Vegas among turf club operators.

In 1961 a *Sports Illustrated* article had identified Snyder as the nation's leading handicapper.[3] Unfortunately for him, the laudatory article came to the attention of Attorney General Robert F. Kennedy, who was in the process of launching a major offensive against organized crime. Assuming that such a well-known gambler had to be tied to the Mafia, Kennedy authorized a telephone tap that ensnared Snyder discussing, of all things, the odds on an inconsequential 1962 Utah–Utah State football game with an acquaintance in Salt Lake City.[4]

Kennedy had pushed Congress to pass a law in 1961 making it a federal crime to send gambling information across state lines. Nailed by the wiretap, Snyder eventually pleaded nolo contendere and paid a $10,000 fine. He was convinced, however, that the aggressive attorney general had come after him because of a comment about the Kennedy administration Snyder had made that was picked up by the press in the wake of passage of the 1961 legislation: "They lost in Laos, they lost in Cuba, they lost in East Berlin, but they sure are giving the gamblers a beating."[5]

Knowledgeable Las Vegas insiders who witnessed Snyder's handicapping skills up close during this period all have the same opinion: he was average at best, probably mediocre when compared with many lesser known wise guys who ground out a living betting on sports.[6] However, these same insiders admit that Snyder was in a class by himself as a self-promoter. Hilton sports book manager Art Manteris wrote in 1991 that "Jimmy the Greek had more impact upon the sports gaming industry in Las Vegas than people with small jealousies are willing to admit. . . . But long before casinos got into the legal bookmaking industry—almost twenty years before, in fact—The Greek was running one of the few sports books in Las Vegas and paying thousands of dollars in taxes every month to the U.S. government."[7]

It was this special talent for public relations that Snyder exploited in a major way. From 1961 he devoted the bulk of his time and energy to promoting himself as the unchallenged guru of handicapping. In 1963 he began writing a column on sports betting for the *Las Vegas Sun* in which he "released" his favorite plays for the week. The column was soon syndicated nationally, and in 1965 he established his own public relations firm, Sports Unlimited. This new business enabled him to set lines on sports, and even on political elections, and offer betting advice. He later became the public relations director for Caesar's Palace, and thereafter engaged in a nonstop public relations campaign to establish himself in the public mind as a new type of gambling expert. In contrast, the true Las Vegas wise guys shunned the limelight and operated in obscurity, in part out of habit developed in eastern cities where gambling was illegal, but also because they profited the most when they could spot a weakness in the line and take advantage of it before others made the same discovery. Glitzy Las Vegas, where skilled gamblers were revered instead of reviled, offered Jimmy the Greek the perfect venue to establish himself as the "Wizard of Odds."[8]

By the late 1960s, however, new faces where taking control of the daily lines making, and Snyder's local reputation began to fade. This bothered The Greek not one bit, because he was already pursuing several new lucrative opportunities, which probably explains some of his erratic lines. Snyder increasingly concentrated his efforts on becoming the unofficial publicity spinmaster for the handicapping and gambling fraternity. He was irritated by the low level of respect accorded his profession by the American public, and so he frequently laced his newspaper columns with positive images of the professional gambler. He especially liked to make comparisons with the business community, commenting that there were far more stockbrokers and bankers in prison than bookies. At one point, for example, he wrote that life insurance companies are the nation's biggest gamblers, taking bets on when people will die. "Insurance companies employ highly trained mathematicians, known as actuaries, to compute the percentages in any situation. With precise formulas, they arrive at rates based on age, job, and health." Setting a sports betting line, he wrote, "isn't quite so scientific, but it works. At least for me it does." His formula was quite simple: "Knowledge $\times$ Energy $\times$ Intuition = the Odds."[9]

Setting betting lines, Snyder readily confessed, was an imperfect science. But success in the craft required a great deal of study and work, luck being the result of concerted effort. He believed that successful line setting/handicapping depended upon obtaining the relevant information and using that information correctly. However, intuition, he said, was "the most important factor of all." It "means how I react to the intangibles, what kind of gut feeling I have when I look at the whole. . . . A computer can absorb the raw material, perform the tasks of knowledge and energy, and set out a price. But it won't have the full picture, because computers can't handle the intangibles—a team's mental attitude or a politician's charisma [until 1985 sports books in Nevada could book bets on elections and other nonsporting events[10]]. It starts there, with that visceral feeling, the one you get when you look at a game and you think, 'The line ought to be six. Now why do I feel that way?'" So it all boiled down to careful analysis of the data, coupled with a dose of old-fashioned intuition. Eschewing the quantitative methods of some of his successors, Snyder once remarked, "I haven't found a computer yet that ever had a gut reaction."[11] Like most gamblers of his era, Snyder liked to talk about "feel." As he liked to say, "The three things I always had a feeling for was Bob Feller, Joe Louis, and F.D.R. I bet them whenever I could and made a fortune."[12]

By 1970 Snyder had moved beyond lines making to more attractive professional opportunities, working through his new Sports Unlimited company. He increasingly focused his energies on public relations and special events promotion. Nevertheless, he continued to set his own private line on major sports events, with the assistance of a staff that eventually grew to about twenty persons. He distributed his lines as a courtesy to friends ("to keep his name out there") well into the 1980s. Distribution of his syndicated sports column climbed by 1970 to 300 newspapers, and he also sent his line to "an unlisted number of private subscribers."[13] In distributing his "News from Nevada," he relied on the same ploy as the old horse wire operators: he was merely providing news, not inside gambling information, and therefore was not in violation of the 1961 federal legislation prohibiting gambling-related transactions across state boundaries.

For a time he served as a publicity consultant for Las Vegas's mysterious and reclusive first citizen, the increasingly eccentric if not psychotic Howard Hughes. But first and foremost, Snyder worked at popularizing and glamorizing himself as the nation's premier expert on gambling. His success in that endeavor was revealed when a nationally distributed cartoon by Jim Berry in late 1971 showed a worried President Richard Nixon commenting to an aide about his upcoming campaign for reelection: "Frankly, John, I don't care about the Gallup Poll or the Harris Poll — What does Jimmy the Greek say?"[14]

The public's awareness of Snyder and sports gambling increased substantially in the autumn of 1976 when CBS-TV signed him to an initial three-year contract to become a regular on the Sunday show preceding the network's professional football programming. His primary role was to predict winners, especially upsets, although he was prohibited by network attorneys from commenting directly on point spreads. He seized on this opportunity to become a national spokesman — albeit indirectly — for the legitimacy of sports gambling and to enhance his public image as a sophisticated handicapper and generally enlightened sports prophet. By this time he had received a presidential pardon from Gerald Ford for his 1962 felony conviction, apparently arranged by Nevada's recently elected Republican senator and former governor Paul Laxalt. Snyder obviously saw his CBS gig as an opportunity to burnish his growing reputation.[15]

Joining Brent Musburger, Phyllis George, and Irv Cross as the program's regulars, Snyder commented on sports news in general and then, in a special segment entitled "The Greek's Board," predicted the day's winners, with special emphasis on potential upsets. If he predicted an upset, that was a signal for gamblers to jump on that game by "taking the points." Millions of viewers were enthralled by the chance to see a famous professional gambler analyze games; ratings for *NFL Today* jumped when he joined the show. Snyder's run on CBS was long and successful. His prominent position as a television expert clearly elevated the status of sports betting by emphasizing the intellectual process involved for serious practitioners of the craft: extensive research, critical analysis of a mass of data, intuitive judgment, prudent money management, and ultimately taking a risk. Behind the scenes, though, Snyder was conducting a running feud with several producers and directors as well as with Musburger, with whom he reportedly engaged in two separate episodes of fisticuffs.[16]

Snyder's stature as a glamorous national television personage ended sadly and abruptly. In January of 1988, while waiting for a table at a Washington, D.C., restaurant, he made an off-the-cuff response to a question from a newspaper reporter about the physical capabilities of black athletes. When these comments—viewed by many as both racist and ignorant—were published they created a national scandal that led to his termination the following day by CBS. While many applauded his firing, millions of his fans were outraged. For a time his firing was the subject of front-page headlines and lively commentaries on the editorial page. He would later claim he was the victim of a "network conspiracy." That this sensational issue revolved around a pardoned felon whose profession was handicapping said much about the enhanced stature of sports gambling in American society.[17]

After the CBS debacle, Snyder entered a period of rapid decline. A lengthy bout of depression was accentuated by other health problems—diabetes, high blood pressure, a broken hip, and finally in 1995 a major stroke. America's most famous sports handicapper and gambler died on April 21, 1996, in the city he loved, Las Vegas, Nevada. Hundreds of the famous and near-famous attended the funeral services for the "Wizard of Odds," and he was laid to rest in Steubenville. As the eulogies poured in, there was little doubt that he had helped to elevate gambling's stature. Few could argue with one obituary: "His gift for gab was responsible for making sports betting one of the most popular forms of mainstream entertainment."[18]

Ironically, though, as his national reputation had grown, his stature among the professionals in Las Vegas had continued to decline. Part of this was no doubt due to jealousy, but his betting lines had become less and less reliable as he dabbled in other activities, and contrary to public perception, his Sunday predictions were often wrong. He himself had come to recognize that he could make much more money *talking* about gambling than doing it himself and had ʻapparently stopped betting on his own account—with some notable lapses for major prizefights—by the early 1970s. His lines were often so far off the number that he became somewhat of an inside joke among the wise guys in Las Vegas. As the *Las Vegas Sun* sardonically noted in a farewell obituary-editorial, by the time Snyder reached his pinnacle of fame, those "in need of a big win would tune into CBS's Sunday football pregame show, get Snyder's hottest pick, and then bet the other side."[19]

Whether or not he was a great oddsmaker, however, is irrelevant. At the time he was the most important figure in American sports gambling. Art Manteris is correct when he says The Greek's real significance was that he "brought our business out of the closet . . . by getting on network TV, [by] talking about point spreads in front of the American public." Jimmy the Greek provided, Manteris suggests, "a major breakthrough."[20]

Even as Snyder's star was falling in Las Vegas, another talented handicapper's was rising. In 1967 Bob Martin decided to follow the crowd from the East Coast to Las Vegas. In 1967 he began working as a lines maker at the Churchill Downs Race and Sports Book. Until he "retired" to a minimum security prison in 1983 for illegally transmitting betting information across state lines, Bob Martin was unquestionably "The Man" in Las Vegas.

Bob Martin was a gregarious and engaging professional gambler with an interesting past. A native of Brooklyn, he had learned to bet parlay cards during the 1930s in dingy storefront bookie joints and to gamble on baseball with the regulars sitting in the bleachers at Ebbetts Field. He paid his way as a student for two years at New York University by earning a 25 percent commission on each football parlay card he booked on campus. He majored in journalism because it enabled him to work as a stringer for midwestern newspapers and gain free admission to the press row at Madison Square Garden basketball games. He recalled, "I wasn't interested in writing so much as I was in getting a seat in the press box. I was betting on those games and I had the best seat in the house. Ned Irish didn't like it, but I'd show him my telegram from a midwestern newspaper and he'd reluctantly give me a press pass."[21]

Martin watched lots of basketball, and he also hung out at Little Lindy's restaurant, where he met and picked the brains of New York City's best sports gamblers. He became proficient at handicapping boxing, spending countless hours watching fighters work out at the legendary Stillman's Gym and ply their trade at Madison Square Garden. He often gained an edge when a new fighter came to town by having a friend who worked at the bus station collect all the sport pages left behind in Greyhound buses; he learned a great deal about out-of-town fighters this way and felt it gave him an edge. Like most gamblers, he ran into a losing streak in the late 1940s, but he eventually discovered that it was not his betting instincts that had betrayed him, but the fixing of basketball games and fights.

In the early 1950s, he moved to Washington, D.C., where he booked bets in addition to betting heavily and successfully on his own account. He was arrested during the national antigambling campaign launched by Robert Kennedy in 1961, but his conviction was eventually overturned by the Supreme Court. Martin had been "nailed" by an electronic spike driven into the outer wall of his house by capital policemen. By chance the spike lodged in a heating duct and essentially turned most of his house into a hidden microphone. On the basis of the conversations picked up, he and his associates were sentenced to fourteen-year jail terms by a hard-nosed visiting federal judge from Montana. A friend convinced the famed Washington attorney Edward Bennett Williams to appeal Martin's conviction as a test case on invasion of privacy. The case was ultimately reviewed by the Supreme Court, and his conviction overturned. True to form, Martin placed a $1,000 bet with a friend on the final vote of the nine justices (he won, having taken to heart his attorney's prediction that it would be a unanimous 9–0 decision).[22]

Like many of his East Coast gambling peers, Martin headed for Las Vegas, where the police were more friendly and sports gambling legal. As the lines maker for the Churchill Downs Race and Sports Book, he quickly became a popular figure in town—a hulking, jowly man given to wearing gaudy checkered pants with striped jackets and chain-smoking cigarettes, with a Scotch on the rocks in his hand and a humorous comment on his lips. Martin proved to be the last of the old-style lines makers, reading at least a dozen sports pages every day, chatting by telephone with a network of friends around the country, ultimately relying on his intuition to decipher the way bettors would react to his line. His line was most assuredly a qualitative one, not one generated upon a mountain of data and refined by computerized regression analysis. Readily accessible to friends and newcomers alike, he was a good listener, always ready to assimilate new information. Within a short time after he arrived in 1967 his line was recognized as being the most reliable. His fame grew rapidly, and he became known as "The Man" and "The Head Linesman" by the city's wise guys.[23]

In 1975 Martin moved to the downtown Union Plaza Hotel and Casino as sports book manager. His reputation for "rare judgment and ability" ensured that when his new lines went up, they were quickly reported along the Strip and telephoned across the nation by an amazingly effective informal network. When he wrote his numbers on the big white board, a bevy of observers, who were reportedly paid ten dollars for their efforts by grateful bookies from Miami to Seattle, would rush to the bank of telephones on the wall to report his numbers. Martin loved to tell stories, one being that following Joe Namath and the New York Jets' famous upset win of the Super Bowl in 1969, he received a sarcastic letter from a Columbia University journalism student who snorted, "Don't you feel ashamed of yourself for putting out such a bad line?" But as Martin liked to tell friends with a twinkle in his eye, "On the contrary, I think it's one of the best lines we ever put up." And indeed his initial 17-point spread neatly split the money between the Jets and the Colts, although many books had to raise the line to 18 and 19 points as bettors climbed on the ill-fated Colts bandwagon.

The final line across the country was 18. Much to the joy of bookies, Martin had once again put up a "splitter" of a number on a big game.[24]

In 1983 Martin was sentenced to a thirteen-month prison term by a federal judge, having been caught by wiretap discussing wagering information across state lines. His argument that he was merely using his First Amendment right of free speech did not impress the court. Sixty-four years old when he was released from federal prison, Martin dabbled for a time at his old profession, eventually moving back to New York City in the mid-1990s to retire.[25]

Bob Martin's departure from the scene in 1983 produced a major changing of the guard. The new "Man" who emerged as the unchallenged lines maker for the nation (and in some respects the world) was in reality a corporation headed by an ex-rebel of the 1960s, Michael Roxborough. His Las Vegas Sports Consultants, Inc., has its computerized headquarters on the top floor of a Las Vegas bank building located off the Strip. A native of Hanover, New Hampshire, "Roxy" dropped out of American University after one semester. He spent time in Vancouver, British Columbia, managing two Roy Rogers fast-food franchises owned by his father, but he found that he preferred his frequent gambling visits to Reno and Las Vegas. In 1975 at the age of twenty-four, "with long hair and jeans," he left the humdrum world of restaurant management and moved to Las Vegas, where he paid the rent by playing poker and betting on sports. "The only thing I found out was I had to work 60 hours a week at gambling to escape the conventional work of 40 hours a week," he later recalled.[26] In 1981 Roxborough took a position as an assistant sports book manager at the Club Cal-Neva in Reno. Within a few years he had demonstrated a special facility at handicapping, and he began earning substantial fees for setting money lines on baseball. He then moved back to Las Vegas to establish his handicapping business.[27]

By 1990 Roxborough dominated the world of sports gambling. In contrast to men like Bob Martin, who loved to bet against their own line whenever the "suckers" moved it in the wrong direction, Roxborough opted to create an image of absolute integrity by quitting his own sports wagering. The public image he projects is that of a conservative business executive. The sports journalist Frank Deford reported that Roxborough greeted him for an interview in his suite of offices on the twelfth floor of the Valley Bank Building in a "button down Oxford, rep tie, tweed-bag coat . . . mousey spectacles." Another writer, Richard Zacks, reported that he "wears dark, conservative suits, carries a beeper, and depends upon computers and sophisticated data bases." Roxborough emphasizes to inquiring journalists that he always files "well-documented income-tax forms" and that he consciously seeks to dress and act as a successful, honest businessman: "I want to project a certain image that everything is on the up and up," he says.[28]

Also unlike Jimmy the Greek and Bob Martin, from the time he opened his business Roxborough has relied heavily on modern technology. He uses computers to dig important data out of enormous databases, some going back over twenty years. In his offices computers steadily crank out information indicating long-term trends that incorporate an almost endless number of variables. By the late 1980s he had built a list of subscribers worldwide, and his line had become the industry's standard. When a visitor once asked how his office arrives at a particular line, he casually pointed to a stack of computer printouts generated by one of his dozen staff members. Consistency and reliability are the hallmarks of his work, and his business continues to grow. In the year 2000 he had no serious competition.[29]

And so it has come to this. A privately held corporation with a president who is seldom seen in public in anything but a conservative business suit, who carries a pager and cell phone, whose corporate offices are wired electronically to the world by fax, telephone, Internet, e-mail, satellite, and news services. His subscribers circle the globe, and his numbers are treated like gold. He is deeply aware that his line can be affected by a myriad of variables and that a bad initial line can, in a few minutes, produce a financial disaster for his subscribers. But all of the technology and massaging of esoteric data notwithstanding, Roxborough acknowledges that, like those who came before him, ultimately he and his associates have to translate computer printouts into a very human decision based on their own experience and instincts.[30]

The "Las Vegas Line," as Roxborough's product is often known, is the target of millions of bettors across the land. It is also the target of the descendants of Leo Hirschfield, the so-called touts. Although many tout services are fly-by-night operations that seem to come and go with the wind, others have been in existence for years. During the 1990s it was estimated by close observers that at any time approximately 750 tout services operate across the country, making their money by selling advice to clients on which games to bet. The impact of these services is difficult to judge because they are unlicensed and unmonitored. One journalist estimates that during football season the number of customers seeking help in making their picks exceeds two million persons.[31]

These services apparently obtain clients from the ranks of unsuccessful gamblers eager to get even, or from uncertain neophyte gamblers seeking professional guidance. Tout services use aggressive advertising techniques, including direct mailings, the Internet, telephone solicitations, and advertisements in newspapers and magazines. The more famous of these persons — or at least the more aggressive — finagle appearances on cable television and radio talk shows where the moderators permit them to give out their toll-free telephone numbers.

They avoid federal prosecution by claiming to be providing information for the purpose of entertainment under the First Amendment free-speech clause. The great percentage of touts are viewed by professional sports gamblers as out-and-out frauds. Many make outrageous claims of past success by reporting only a carefully selected sampling of their records; some simply lie. Their rates vary, but a football season of normal service via a 1–900 telephone number averages between $1,000 and $2,500 a year. Charges of $100 or more are often made on special games, which are hyped as "steams" or "locks" to indicate that they are sure things. Many times, of course, they are not. Lem Banker is not far from the truth when he describes the great majority of touts as "guys who went broke gambling their own money, and now are trying it with yours."[32]

Sport Magazine investigated touts in 1981 and concluded that "for every good service there are 10 impostors, cheats, and pirates." The author of this investigation quoted a veteran bookmaker who, shaking his head at advertisements proclaiming over 80 percent correct predictions, observed that in Las Vegas each year several handicapping contests are entered by the best of professional sports gamblers. It is rare when any of these professionals wins much above 60 percent of their bets over a full season. Looking at the inflated claims of unscrupulous touts, he commented, "The field is filled with charlatans and frauds."[33]

Many tout services routinely share information about their clients with each other, and once a person establishes a relationship with one, he can be certain to see his mailbox overflowing with junk mail from a host of others. Many are boiler-room operations that will have a cold caller inquire, "How did you do last season with [Such and Such Sports Service]?" The honest answer in all likelihood is not very well. The caller will then say a few derogatory words about that service and suggest that the client switch to the one he is offering, which of course has a much better won-lost record. What the caller does not say is that the same person owns both services, because some businessmen operate several tout services simultaneously, or merely change the name of their service when their terrible record makes it expeditious to do so.[34]

Early in the 1990s Torrance, California, businessman David James set out to demonstrate the craziness of the tout business. Although he knew very little about football, he was intrigued by the advertisements for services he read in *The National* (a short-lived national daily sports newspaper). For two years he offered his picks via a toll-free telephone number (1–800-WIN-BIG3), advertising himself as "Harv Edwards: America's Best Sports Analyst." He and a friend made the picks "off the tops of our heads," raking in about $4,000 a week on 1–900 toll calls from eager clients. In his third year he dropped "Harv Edwards" and remade himself into the "Whiz Kid: Bookies hate him. You will love him!" He published advertisements in sports magazines using an old high school reunion photograph that made him look "like a bespectacled Big 6 CPA at best and a hopelessly bookish nerd at worst." Business increased. His secret picking system? This self-proclaimed "Whiz-Kid" had his four-year-old son simply point to one team or another in the newspaper. Before taking phone calls, James made up a few plausible reasons why his son's selections were correct—inclement weather forecasts, injuries, a team's poor record on AstroTurf, its great record playing in domed stadiums, long-range trends between the teams, a team's history of covering as a "road dog," a coach's desire for revenge, and so on. As James said, "stuff that was totally un-checkable." Like most touts he even used the standard magic words that seem to appeal to desperate gamblers, such as "Lock of the Month," "Guaranteed Winner," "Steam Game," and "Game of the Year."[35]

In 1993 James made $60,000 but then quit his service when he came to realize he was becoming emotionally tied to his son's picks! Besides, he had made his point, and he soon thereafter told his story to *Forbes Magazine*. One thing James had learned was why bookmakers make money: the clients he talked to on his 1–900 line were terrible money managers: they often upped their bets when they were on a losing streak, grasping for any angle to make up previous losses. This was most evident when they would try to get even with a large bet on Monday Night Football after losing big over a weekend. "I got more calls for the Monday night game than all the other games combined," he chuckled. He also learned that it paid to charge high prices: "The more you charge the better they think you are."[36]

Tout services come and go, but technology is definitely changing the way the modern bookmaker does business. Like other businessmen, the modern bookie might be equipped with computer databases, spreadsheets of client files, fax machines, e-mail, access to the Internet, portable computers, credit card machines, hand-held electronic data storage devices, satellite dishes, voice mail, call forwarding (to avoid law enforcement phone taps), and cellular telephones. Except at Nevada's books, where bookmakers still greet their customers face-to-face and real currency changes hands, most bets with street bookies are made over the phone using previously established credit lines. Just as technology has greatly shaped the world of the modern bookmaker, it seems likely to produce a seismic change in the landscape of sports gambling itself. Although Nevada's books are now permitted to accept telephone bets on established accounts from Nevada residents, they are still forbidden to accept bets by electronic means from out of state, nor are casino-based sports books permitted to accept bets brought across state lines by courier. In 1999 one northern Nevada casino was hit with a quarter of a million dollar fine by the Nevada Gaming Board for working too closely with couriers bringing satchels full of money on football weekends from Sacramento and Bay Area bettors.

One of the most intriguing developments has been the explosive growth of Internet-based sports books. Internet betting has the definite potential of severely undercutting many illegal bookmakers and even poses a modest threat to Nevada's sports books. Bettors can establish via the Internet an account for as little as $500 with offshore sports books, most of which are in the Caribbean. Although many of these books are reportedly less than stable, others have established themselves as trustworthy and capable of providing the same services as a neighborhood bookmaker. One of the most popular and trusted of these new electronic bookies is actually located in Australia. So, with a click of a computer mouse the bettor can get a bet down on a local college game by communicating electronically with a faceless bookie halfway around the world. Of course, that cyber bettor could be just fourteen years of age, or a compulsive gambler who is using his maxed-out credit cards as his source of betting capital. Without effective controls, Internet betting poses major questions. As it grew rapidly in the late 1990s, it was targeted by a few concerned senators for scrutiny. Whether effective controls can be placed upon these offshore books, given constitutional constraints and the lack of effective technology, remained in serious doubt as the new century dawned. In July of 2000 the Congress failed to pass legislation designed to curb all forms of Internet wagering.[37]

The accelerating rate of technological change in American society has thus affected the ways in which sports wagering takes place. The bookie who kept wagers in his head or wrote them on the back of an envelope has given way to the digital age.

12

Sports Wagering under Siege

As sports wagering became ever more entrenched in American popular culture, the more outspoken became its critics. In 1973 *U.S. News and World Report* featured a story on sports wagering that was headlined "Now, An 'Epidemic' of Legalized Gambling." In 1975 Senator John L. McClellan of Arkansas launched his second senatorial investigation into gambling, this time hauling Jimmy the Greek before his panel for intensive, albeit relatively friendly, grilling.[1] Critics warned about the dangers of compulsive sports gambling and repeatedly trotted out the sorry case of former Ohio State and Indianapolis Colts quarterback Art Schlichter as their primary case in point. In 1985 Tulane University was racked by a point-shaving scandal that took on a new twist—players were accused of dumping games in return for illegal drugs. This case came only a few years after a Boston College player admitted in 1979 to shaving points at the behest of a notorious eastern gambler, Richie "The Fixer" Perry, a noxious figure who in 1991 resurfaced all too close to the high-profile University of Nevada Las Vegas basketball team.[2] Finally, the banishment of Pete Rose from professional baseball in 1989 for allegedly gambling on baseball games, including possibly those he played in or managed, shocked the nation and added to the concern over the influence of gambling on organized sports.

In 1986 *Sports Illustrated* weighed in with a lengthy examination of the impact of sports gambling. It was at the time the most detailed treatment of the topic by a popular medium. Although they presented arguments for and against the practice, the magazine's editors made it clear that they saw gambling as a major threat to the integrity of American sports. "Most Americans tend to view such wagering as a naughty-but-nice diversion," they wrote. "Yet, from the Black Sox scandal of 1919 to the Tulane basketball fixes of last season, nothing has done more to despoil the games Americans play and watch than widespread gambling on them. As fans cheer their bets rather than their favorite teams, dark clouds of cynicism and suspicion hang over games, and the possibility of fixes is always in the air."[3]

The lead article focused on two major trends, the shift away from horse races to football and basketball, and the incredible growth of betting across the country. One Chicago bookie, who estimated his total handle at $1 million a year, suggested that television was the major factor in changing betting preferences: "It used to be that about 85 percent of my customers made bets on horses. Now it's just the opposite—90 percent of their bets are on team sports, with football way ahead, then basketball and baseball." Television, the appreciative bookie said, "has done wonderful things for gambling in America." But in *Sports Illustrated's* view, the enormous level of betting was indicative of the potential for future mischief. "Sports gambling in America is this big: No one knows how big it is." Noting that in 1975 the McClellan committee had estimated the total betting handle at about $20 to $25 billion annually, the magazine cited the FBI's organized crime investigations head as placing it in 1984 at $70 billion. The article cited another study offering the NFL's estimation that betting on professional football alone exceeded $50 billion. Estimating the profit derived by bookmakers for 1985 at $5 billion, *Sports Illustrated* claimed that such a figure was "roughly equivalent" to the amount earned by the Exxon Corporation.[4]

Although the series of articles presented accurate data on how the new gambling world operated—including a humorous essay on the colorful if not goofy Las Vegas handicapper "Harry the Hat"—the major thrust of the reporting was that gambling posed the biggest threat to American collegiate and profes-sional sports in history. The tenor was ominous. Gambling had "taken a grip on American life that is more powerful and more pervasive than ever before. It has become, by every reliable indication, a gigantic industry." Although the magazine noted that this was a national phenomenon, it honed in on legalized sports gambling in Nevada, a state it described as "singularly eccentric." As the heart of the national sports gambling network, it was made clear, Nevada had to shoulder the responsibility for the national craze.[5] The magazine's electronic media competitors, CBS and NBC television, were sharply criticized for putting Jimmy Snyder and Pete Axthelm (a *Newsweek* sports columnist) on the air to tout betting picks; Axthelm was quoted, in a sharply negative context, for readily agreeing that his NBC-TV Sunday pregame commentary was supportive of betting on NFL games: "Oh, definitely. I think gambling is great fun."[6]

Buried within this special issue was a half-page box that discussed the positive aspects of gambling. It was based on two interviews, one with University of Nevada Las Vegas sociologist James Frey, the other with psychologist Robert

Custer. Frey emphasized that gambling was a natural part of human nature: "Risk is a very significant part of our lives. Fathers don't mind if their sons play poker at an early age because poker is a way of learning to deal with money, risk, challenge, and competition. People don't want to admit it, but a great part of gambling is consistent with the American way. We admire people who take risks, and we have ever treated the very colorful historical gamblers, such as Doc Holiday, in a positive way." To this academic, whose campus was located two blocks off the Las Vegas Strip, betting in an office pool or on a football game "can be a positive form of recreation." Custer, a leading researcher on compulsive gambling, echoed Frey. Although noting that out-of-control gambling can create havoc for some individuals, Custer suggested that the propensity of Americans to put their money down on a prizefight or basketball game was deeply embedded in American history: "The Americans came in as the pioneers, the risk takers. They don't mind taking the risk, and they will take the consequences. Risk is part of our pioneer spirit." Properly controlled, he said, gambling was a "positive form of recreation. There is an excitement to it, a sense of action that people may or may not get in other ways. Social gambling is a tremendous amount of fun, and that is therapeutic. Sure, there's always a chance of winning some money, but mostly it offers relaxation, real pleasure, and a fairly inexpensive form of escape."[7]

That said, the nation's most prestigious sports journal came down hard on gambling. It excoriated the NFL for officially opposing gambling while tacitly supporting it, for example, by releasing official injury reports each Monday for the benefit of gamblers. But more important, the NFL had long tolerated within its ownership a group of well-known high rollers, including Carroll Rosenbloom (Colts and Rams), Tim Mara (Giants), Charles Bidwell (Cardinals), Mickey McBride (Browns), Leonard Tose (Eagles), and Art Rooney (Steelers). Newspapers that carried the Las Vegas Line or other odds services were chastised for not having the courage to withstand their readers' wrath by refusing to publish them. (It quoted Indiana University basketball coach Bobby Knight's colorful comment that publishing the betting line "was the equivalent of printing prostitutes' telephone numbers as a public service"). And CBS and NBC were denounced for permitting Axthelm and Snyder to hype gambling on their pregame programs; the magazine noted that television ratings often relied on the outcome of the point spread to keep viewers glued to their television sets long after a game's outcome had been decided.

The issue was comprehensive and powerful. But it had one glaring omission: it made not a single recommendation on how to curb the "epidemic" so vividly described.

At the time the *Sports Illustrated* issue appeared, both Art Schlichter and Pete Rose had been engulfed by their own gambling problems. Schlichter was a star football player who candidly and repeatedly admitted that he had a compulsive gambling problem, but despite the intervention of many well-meaning persons, he could never shake the gambling demons that overwhelmed him. Conversely, Pete Rose never admitted that he had bet on baseball and adamantly refused to accept the possibility that he had a serious gambling problem, extensive circumstantial evidence notwithstanding.

The story of All-American quarterback Art Schlichter was, as *Sports Illustrated* reported, "a textbook case of a man's promise destroyed by gambling."[8] After a sensational career as an Ohio schoolboy quarterback, in 1978 he accepted a scholarship at Ohio State, where his sparkling play more than lived up to expectations. Possessed of a powerful and accurate arm, he impressively led the Buckeyes to winning seasons and three postseason bowl appearances. Before his senior year he was featured on the cover of the college football preview issue of *Sports Illustrated*, and at the end of the season he was a consensus first-team All-American. The Baltimore Colts made him their first-round draft pick the following spring. However, by this time Schlichter had already become a compulsive gambler. As a teenager he had become fascinated with gambling on card games, and when he arrived in Columbus he became a regular at the local Scioto Downs racetrack, betting (and usually losing) fifty dollars a visit. He soon escalated his betting levels, making increasingly larger wagers on baseball and football with Columbus bookies. By the middle of his rookie season with the Colts he had already lost his $350,000 signing bonus and his $140,000 salary. He became so obsessed that, during a game, when he went to the line to call a play he often found himself distracted by the scoreboard, showing the running scores of other NFL games he had bet on. His gambling habit led to a year's suspension from the NFL, but he was reinstated in 1984. Unable to stop his gambling, he was permanently barred from the league in 1986.

Schlichter continued his uncontrollable behavior. Faced with enormous gambling debts, he stole credit cards, money, and checks from friends and employers, even his father, wife, and sister-in-law. He often used his personal charisma to bilk funds from the gullible, who were apparently mesmerized by his charming personality. In one notable instance he conned $100,000 out of an Indianapolis widow in an elaborate sports ticket–money laundering scheme. Committed by an Indiana judge to the Center for Compulsive Gambling in Baltimore, seven weeks into his therapy program he was caught betting and kicked out of the program. He spent two stints in jail for theft and bank fraud, but even confinement in prison did not deter this dedicated gambler: prison officials discovered that he had used a prison pay telephone to place large bets on games through an acquaintance in Las Vegas. In the spring of 2000 he eluded police after a routine traffic stop, but a few days later he was arrested, after having stolen money and credit cards from a onetime friend in Grove City, Ohio, who had given him a place to stay. During this twenty-year period Schlichter had committed several felonies, all in search of money to gamble with or to pay off his huge losses. Faced with the possibility of a twenty-year jail sentence, his wife having long since divorced him, Schlichter seemed resigned to his fate. He told *Sports Illustrated*, "When you start stealing from your family and friends, it is only a matter of time before you're in jail or you put a gun to your head."[9]

But no episode better demonstrated the complex problems that gambling presents for an established professional sport than the saga of baseball star Pete Rose. Organized baseball had been shaken to its foundation by the Black Sox scandal of 1919, and in its wake had put in place stringent antigambling policies for anyone associated with a team or league. It was only a few months after *Sports Illustrated* published its gambling issue in 1986 that organized baseball secretly began its investigation into allegations that Rose had violated its ironclad ban prohibiting gambling on baseball. When news of the investigation was first revealed in the Cincinnati press in early 1989, the residents of the Queen City rallied to Rose's defense, angrily denouncing the commissioner of baseball for impugning the integrity of their hometown hero.

Rose was a Cincinnati native who had grown up in a working-class neighborhood on the west side of town near the Ohio River, just a few miles from the future site of Riverfront Stadium. He was a star football and baseball player at Western Hills High School, and when he made the starting lineup of the Cincinnati Reds in 1963, he was readily embraced by the baseball-happy residents of the Queen City. He had a great rookie season, batting .273 and scoring 101 runs, and he never looked back. He was popular not simply because of his on-the-field accomplishments but because his intense desire, incredible hustle, and never ending effort enabled him to succeed despite only modest natural ability. Pete Rose was the epitome of the "blue-collar" player.

Between 1965 and 1980 he batted over .300 in all but one season, and in the 1970 All-Star Game he stunned fans everywhere by bowling over catcher Ray Fosse of the Cleveland Indians with a brutal body block, the likes of which are not seen in an exhibition game. Rose's exuberant, enthusiastic style of play—he always ran full speed to first base after a base on balls—earned him the popular nickname first pinned on him by a bemused Mickey Mantle during spring training in 1963: "Charlie Hustle." His hard-driving play made him the favorite among many stars on the powerful Big Red Machine teams of the mid-1970s.

As teammate Hall of Fame player Joe Morgan said, "Pete doesn't have a lot of great physical abilities. He made himself into a ballplayer."[10]

And indeed he did, pushing his 5'10", 175-pound frame to its limits, giving no quarter to rival players, always going full bore. He left the Reds in 1978 after a salary dispute, but after spending six years in Philadelphia and Montreal, he returned to Cincinnati as player-manager in 1984. He was welcomed back as a conquering hero, the local boy made good. Now forty-three years old and still in great physical condition, he was nearing a record that most baseball fans had long assumed would never be broken — Ty Cobb's career base hit total of 4,191. The following September Rose got hit number 4,192, a soft line-drive single into left center field. True to form he did not leave the game to revel in his accomplishment; instead, he later stretched a double into a triple with a magnificent head-first slide, and ended the game by making an improbable diving catch of a line drive as the Reds beat the San Diego Padres 2–0.

Four years later Rose's many accomplishments were overshadowed by rumors that he had a serious gambling problem and that he was under investigation by Commissioner Peter Ueberroth for violating baseball's cardinal rule. Rose's penchant for making large bets at local racetracks had long been common knowledge in the Queen City: he would often be seen at nearby River Downs placing bets at the big-dollar windows, and reporters knew that Rose loved to talk about his love of betting on the horses, a practice not encouraged but not prohibited by baseball. By the mid-1970s he was apparently also betting heavily on football and basketball with several bookies in several American cities and even in Canada. Like most compulsive gamblers, Rose was not an intelligent bettor, plunging heavily and losing far more often than he won. Despite a rapidly escalating income he was continually in debt. When he maxed out on one bookie he moved onto another, becoming well known within gambling circles as unreliable when it came to settling his accounts. In the late 1970s his gambling problem was quietly reviewed by baseball's hierarchy, but the commissioner's office decided to do nothing, a decision that, according to journalist Michael Sokolove, emboldened Rose to gamble even more: "It wasn't that baseball couldn't touch Rose, but that it didn't seem to want to."[11]

In 1986, however, the rumors and allegations about heavy gambling and serious cash flow problems could no longer be overlooked, and Commissioner Ueberroth quietly ordered a thorough investigation. In February of 1989 Ueberroth hired a former FBI agent now operating a Washington, D.C., detective agency to follow up on several serious allegations uncovered by the initial investigation. Within a few months John Dowd had obtained, through a series of interviews with Cincinnati-area gamblers and narcotics dealers, substantial evidence that convinced him not only that Rose had been betting on major league baseball almost daily and very heavily—up to $5,000 or more on a single game—but also that he had begun betting on the team that he was managing.

On May 9, 1989, Dowd submitted a 225-page report to Ueberroth, along with 2,000 pages of supporting documents and interview transcripts. Dowd's report was based primarily on the information he had elicited from many of Rose's off-field associates, a surprising number of whom were known drug dealers and gamblers—not exactly the type of individuals one would want to build a court case around.[12] But Ueberroth, and incoming commissioner A. Bartlett Giamatti, were not going to court. They merely had to deal with Rose under the policies of organized baseball. Giamatti brought to his new position extraordinary credentials for a baseball executive. A prominent scholar of early modern literature, an academic dean, and for five years president of Yale University, Giamatti was determined to uphold the essential myths upon which baseball had long prospered. He was appalled by the damaging record Dowd set before him and soon became convinced that Rose had bet for years not only on major league baseball games but also on the Reds while he was their manager. Dowd's report was sloppily constructed, and he had no specific evidence to prove absolutely that Rose had broken baseball's cardinal rule. But he did have many betting sheets a handwriting expert said were in Rose's hand, he had ample testimony that he had squeezed from Rose's alleged bookies and gambling associates, he had a long list of telephone calls made from Rose's home and office to known bookies, calls made during the baseball season. But he did not have a "smoking gun."[13]

Giamatti was morally outraged by what he viewed as an affront to the integrity of baseball. Over the years he had taken a romantic, even lyrical, view of baseball as an apt metaphor for the competitive cycles of American society; it was much more than a game, it was the unique "national game," knowledge of which could give important insights into the American character. Unfortunately, Giamatti handled the investigation poorly, at one point writing a letter to a Cincinnati judge sitting on a case involving one of Rose's accusers, informing the judge that the individual had been very helpful in the Rose investigation. The judge was appalled by what he considered Giamatti's effort to influence the judicial process. Convinced of Rose's guilt, Giamatti had even edited Dowd's report to correct grammatical errors and to make it more readable and therefore more plausible. Rose's attorneys learned of this and concluded that Giamatti was doing everything he could to railroad their client.

Rose's attorneys went on the offensive. They effectively grilled Giamatti in a lengthy deposition, deeply shaking him and exposing his predisposition on the matter. They had established, at least to their satisfaction, that their client would not receive a fair hearing from the new commissioner. A public civil trial, however, held dangers for both sides. For several weeks in the summer of 1989, Giamatti and Rose and their advisers maneuvered for advantage as the case dominated the sports news.

Ultimately, they came to an agreement before Giamatti convened a formal hearing, reaching a technical legal settlement in which Rose did not admit to gambling on baseball but nonetheless accepted a "lifetime ban" from the game. Apparently, Rose and his attorneys had been led to believe by Giamatti and his associates that he could apply for — and would most likely receive — readmission in a year. Not so, as it turned out. The former English professor was at his eloquent best as he informed a packed press conference of the settlement. He used such words as "stain," "a sorry end of a sorry episode," and "disgrace to the game." Most significant, after his highly emotional, moralistic formal statement, Giamatti responded to a reporter's question by saying: "In the absence of a formal hearing and therefore in the absence of evidence to the contrary, I am confronted by the factual record of Mr. Dowd. On the basis of that, yes, I have concluded he bet on baseball."[14]

Pete Rose was thus out of baseball, having agreed to be placed on the "permanently ineligible list." Giamatti was overnight turned into a national hero, controlling the moral high ground. Rose had lost a public relations battle to a master of the English language. "I will be told that I am an idealist," Giamatti said. "I hope so. I will continue to locate ideals I hold for myself and for my country in the national game, as well as in other of our national institutions."[15] Rose felt betrayed by Giamatti — he and his attorneys had withdrawn their lawsuit against the commissioner and had agreed to a settlement in which Rose did not admit to betting on baseball and would, they thought, be eligible to apply for reinstatement in one year. Now, outside of that agreement, Giamatti had found a clever way to establish in the public's mind that Rose was guilty of betraying the national game. His crime was as great, it was implied, as that of the Chicago Black Sox in 1919. It was now apparent that Rose would not be reinstated in one year.

A furious Pete Rose, afraid that his dream of being elected to the Hall of Fame was now in danger, immediately called a press conference to proclaim his innocence. But skeptical reporters, who had many times caught Rose dissembling on questions about his gambling activities, were not satisfied with his ambiguous answer when asked why, if he had not bet on baseball, he had agreed to a "lifetime" banishment. At the end of the press conference, Rose said defiantly, "I don't think I have a gambling problem. Consequently, I will not seek any help of any kind."[16] There were relatively few knowledgeable baseball fans — even the many true believers in Cincinnati — who still believed in his innocence.

The saga of Pete Rose and Bart Giamatti had all of the tragic twists that the
eminent Yale Shakespearean scholar would have appreciated—had he lived to
witness them. Just ten days after his shocking announcement over Labor Day
weekend, an exhausted Giamatti died suddenly at age fifty-two of a massive
coronary at his summer vacation home on Martha's Vineyard. Although the
attack was most likely brought on by the stress produced by the Rose controversy,
Giamatti had also contributed to his early death, having ballooned in recent
years to more than eighty pounds above his normal weight and having spent his
adulthood as a multi-pack-a-day smoker. But many of organized baseball's future
leaders apparently placed the blame for Giamatti's death on Pete Rose.

Now banned from the game he loved, his dream of entering the Hall of Fame
in limbo, Rose's problems had only begun. Many years earlier the FBI had turned
over to the IRS information about Rose's heavy gambling and his failure to report
his profits from the sale of his baseball memorabilia—to pay gambling debts he
even had sold the black Muzino bat with which he broke Ty Cobb's record.
The IRS had an unbeatable case: Rose had not reported major gambling wins at
racetracks, and between 1984 and 1987 he had not reported at least $350,000 of
profits made at autograph signings and from sales of his memorabilia, including
World Series rings and assorted gloves, balls, and uniforms. In July 1990 Rose
agreed to a plea bargain in federal court and was sentenced to five months in
federal prison. Although he admitted his sorrow to the judge, he still refused to
admit ever having bet on baseball. As James Reston Jr. writes in his detached
study of this unhappy event, Pete Rose "continued to deny the undeniable."[17]

More than a decade later, Pete Rose remains on the "permanently ineligible
list," and consequently his name cannot be placed on the annual Hall of Fame
ballot. Most observers believe that he could get widespread support for his Hall
of Fame bid by publicly admitting his baseball gambling and apologizing. This
he has refused to do, steadfastly clinging to his earlier denials. It is apparent,
however, that until he does make such a public statement, his name will not
make the ballot. The closest Rose has ever come to making a confession occurred
only a few months after Giamatti banned him from baseball. On a Phil Donahue
television show in November of 1989 Rose said, "After I was banned from baseball . . . I decided to see a psychiatrist. Since then I have come to learn and accept
the fact that I have a problem related to gambling. . . . and I am getting help."[18]

⛏

As the twentieth century drew to a close, publicity surrounding several highly
publicized allegations about efforts by gamblers to get college athletes to dump

games or shave points stimulated the NCAA to abandon its benign neglect stance toward gambling and become the leading advocate on behalf of federal antigambling legislation. At stake, of course, was the multibillion dollar cartel that big-time college athletics had become. Since its emergence as an important force in intercollegiate athletics after the Second World War, the NCAA had done little more than offer lip-service opposition to gambling. But the highly publicized basketball scandals at Boston College in 1979 and at Tulane University in 1985 sounded a tocsin: if lightly compensated college athletes decided to cash in on opportunities afforded them by would-be fixers, the entire enterprise could be jeopardized.

During the 1990s sports pages increasingly took note of the heavy increase in college campus betting; student bookies were reported to be active on most campuses, and in 1998 the University of Michigan Department of Athletics released a stunning report that concluded that 45 percent of college athletes had placed at least one bet on a college athletic contest during the previous year. Even such supposedly pristine athletic operations as the Ivy League's were stunned by revelations of extensive gambling by athletes on games other than those in which they participated. In 1994 an effort by some amateur gamblers to fix a basketball game between Arizona State and the University of Washington resulted in arrests by the FBI. In 1997 a Northwestern running back fumbled late in the game near the goal line; subsequent investigations revealed he had bet $400 with a campus bookie that the Wildcats would not cover the point spread. In 1996–97 rumors flew in Fresno over allegations that members of the Fresno State Bulldog basketball team had shaved points (after a detailed investigation the FBI did not file any charges). In retrospect, these events were relatively minor and isolated and did not give the appearance of systematic wrongdoing, in contrast to the scandals of the 1950s and 1960s.

But the perception was growing that a serious problem did exist. NCAA Executive Director Cedric Dempsey took the initiative and launched an extensive antigambling program. He was convinced that "we are seeing an increase in the involvement of organized crime in sports wagering."[19] Informative antigambling brochures were sent to coaches and athletic directors, stern new policies were announced that contained draconian punishment for coaches or players who gambled on any college sports contest, posters were put up in locker rooms, and an executive position was created within the organization to combat campus gambling. That position was filled by former Defiance College track coach William Saum. A veteran NCAA career executive whose major experiences had been in enforcement of recruiting and eligibility policies, Saum launched an aggressive campaign. In 1997, when social conservatives with strong ties to the well-organized Christian Coalition were able to secure a congressional resolution establishing a federal commission, the National Gambling Impact Study Commission, to examine the impact of gambling on American life, Saum and Dempsey saw a unique opportunity.

Between 1997 and 2000 Saum led the NCAA charge. He believed that college sports existed for the enjoyment of spectators and the experience obtained by athletes. Fans, he said, should "go to games to watch the spontaneous action and reaction on the field, to watch the coaches' decisions, the officials' decisions, the athletes' decisions. And certainly we're not there to hope that an athlete runs up the score just for the point spread." Saum was sufficiently realistic to recognize that he was fighting a rearguard action: "Gambling will continue but we will create enough barriers on our college campuses to have a significant effect. We are naive to think we can remove the problem, but we believe programs will affect the rate at which it occurs."[20]

Saum got a friendly reception from the conservative members of the federal commission. But although gaming officials were initially fearful of the apparently strong antigambling views of five of the nine commission members, those fears proved to be largely unfounded. After conducting hearings around the country, the commission released a surprisingly benign document that failed to recommend the severe measures that many commercial gaming leaders had initially feared, such as new federal taxes or the establishment of a federal regulatory agency. The commission had heard from a host of concerned governors, congressmen, state legislators, mayors, chambers of commerce executives, as well as gaming spokesmen who warned against any major changes in the national gaming structure. As it gathered its evidence, the commission was confronted by a powerful phalanx of community and political leaders who did not want to have to pass new taxes to make up for possible loss of gaming tax or state lottery revenues, or who feared a negative economic impact on communities and states in which various forms of gambling had taken root. Thus the commission had to content itself with raising questions and suggesting the importance of future studies and careful monitoring of such widely discussed issues as Indian casino gaming, compulsive gambling, and the negative social consequences of gambling.

But gambling on college sports, legal in just one small state, presented a target of convenience for the commission's five conservatives. Commission member Rev. James Dobson of Colorado Springs, head of the organization Focus on the Family, summarized the majority thinking: "This infection [of sports gambling] threatens to undermine college sports, disillusion fans, and damage the careers and the integrity of some of our most promising young people. . . . We must not simply accept the unseemly spectacle of Nevada casino operators raking in millions of dollars a year from what used to be wholesome competition of 18 and 19 year olds." Hence the majority voted to include a policy recommendation that wagering on high school, Olympic, and college sports be made illegal in all states. The reference to high schools and the Olympics was irrelevant, of course, since Nevada books do not deal in those venues. The target was the estimated $1.2 billion bet in Nevada's 100 legal sports books on college basketball and football. The commission based its recommendation upon the curious contention that wagering on college sports did not meet its test of providing the "positive impacts" of other forms of gambling. "In particular, sports wagering does not contribute to local economies or produce many jobs. Unlike casinos or other destination resorts, sports wagering does not create other economic sectors."[21]

Ironically, by singling out college sports betting in Nevada for special consideration, the commission put itself in the embarrassing position of restricting the one form of gambling in which the bettor has an opportunity to win on a sustained basis—although available evidence suggests that few do. Under the pari-mutuel system, the management of a horse or dog track is guaranteed a hefty percentage take of about 15 percent on each race. Unlike the situation with table games or slot machines, where probability tables guarantee the house a long-term favorable return, the sports book manager does not know what his profit or loss will be on a particular game or even over a complete season. The sports bettor at least has a chance to win, and the sports books most definitely have a chance to lose. None other than Jimmy the Greek outraged his casino executive friends when he wrote in defense of sports wagering that casino gambling was "a killer," "a disease," "a non-profit sport," in which "the percentages are always against you." Snyder bluntly concluded, "Nobody makes a living betting in casinos."[22] At least sports betting provided the intelligent and persistent player the opportunity to win. Whether he did or not depended on his skill—with a modicum of luck tossed in for good measure.

Noting that the commission had singled out the fixing of college games, Russ Culver, an analyst for a major Internet sports betting site, Vegas Insider, remarked, "If there's going to be a fix, they're not going to go through Las Vegas bookmakers." One of sports journalism's gambling experts, Stephen Nover, denounced the recommendation as "stupid, the product of an old-in-thought, out-of-whack group of reactionaries."[23]

The commission majority, however, had hit on the one facet of the burgeoning gambling industry that continued to disturb many thoughtful Americans. It was one thing to permit a state lottery to operate or to permit adults to risk their paychecks at the casino tables, but the idea of betting on games played by teenagers seemed to many to go too far. One of the leading Democratic candidates for the 2000 presidential nomination, former New Jersey senator, onetime Princeton All-American basketball player, and New York Knicks professional star Bill Bradley, had a typical reaction. His 1994 statement presented on the Senate floor was quoted effectively in the commission's final *Report:*

> I am not prepared to risk the values that sports instill in youth just to add a few more dollars to state coffers. . . . State-sanctioned sports betting conveys the message that sports are more about money than personal achievement and sportsmanship. In these days of scandal and disillusionment, it is important that our youngsters not receive this message. . . . [S]ports betting threatens the integrity of and public confidence in professional and amateur team sports, converting sports from wholesome athletic entertainment into a vehicle for gambling. Sports gambling raises people's suspicions about point-shaving and game fixing.[24]

Buttressed with such influential support, in the spring of 2000 the NCAA convinced Democratic senator Patrick Leahy (Vt.) and Republican senator Sam Brownback (Kans.) to introduce legislation embracing the commission's recommendation. Initial interest seemed tepid, but then in May Arizona Republican John McCain, freshly returned to the Senate from his failed presidential bid, joined in the sponsorship and quickly moved it to the top of the Senate's agenda. The NCAA turned out high- profile college coaches Tubby Smith, Dean Smith, and Lou Holtz to testify on behalf of the bill, and Nevada casino lobbyists recognized that this was the type of "feel-good" issue that many congressmen would support because it had no impact on their own states and they did not want to risk being portrayed by rivals in the November elections as having voted against a ban on college sports gambling. The casino industry's lobby arm, the American Gaming Association, found itself in a tenacious dogfight. Its lobbyists discovered that their well-reasoned arguments were ineffective in the face of the moral issues raised by the bill's supporters. The lobby contended that the bill would not touch the estimated 250,000 illegal bookies operating across the country and that the Nevada books actually provided the only meaningful line of defense against a fix because of their ability to spot the flow of "unusual" money on a game, but their words fell on deaf ears. Ultimately, only parliamentary tactics by Senator Harry Reid of Nevada, the Democratic Whip, prevented the bill from coming to a vote where passage seemed probable. Whether or not the legislation would resurface when a new president and Congress took office in January of 2001 was anyone's guess, but the strong support the McCain-Leahy-Brownback bill received in Congress indicated that the future of Nevada's sports books was now in play. It also echoed earlier fervent antigambling crusades extending back to the colonial era.

Epilogue

The last Sunday in January has become the biggest day of the year for American bookmakers. Super Bowl Sunday has also become the nation's most popular unofficial holiday, a day for friends, football, food, and drink—and a time for placing a bet. During the last decade of the twentieth century, Americans wagered an estimated $3 billion on this one game alone. About $75 million was wagered per game in Nevada's sports books, enabling them to squeeze out profits ranging from $400,000 to $7.5 million, although they lost $500,000 on the 1995 game between San Diego and San Francisco when heavy money poured in on the 49ers in the hours before kickoff.[1] But although the national media inevitably focuses on Nevada's Super Bowl betting, at least 95 percent of the money wagered on the game is handled by illegal bookies in the other forty-nine states; offshore "virtual" sports books available on the Internet are grabbing an increasing share of the action. Many of the estimated thirty million gamblers who bet on the game play for modest stakes; during the two weeks before the game, amateur gamblers are busily buying squares on the boards at their local taverns or investing five or ten dollars in the office pool.

For regular sports gamblers, on the other hand, Super Bowl Sunday is a time to work overtime on their handicapping. Many gamblers, in debt with the season coming to an end, look to the Super Bowl as their last chance to get even for the season. They will make a large play, often using their credit line with their bookie, in hopes of getting out of the hole. It is these regulars to whom the bookies look for their livelihood. "Jerry," a veteran of twenty-five years booking bets in Cleveland, told *U.S. News and World Report* in 1997 that he clears between $250,000 and $300,000 annually from his business and looks forward to the Super Bowl as one of his biggest paydays. "If there is one thing I've learned in all of these years of booking bets," he said with a grin, "it is that the public is always wrong."[2]

The gullible suckers who provide "Jerry" a comfortable suburban lifestyle are easy pickings, of course. But what about the professional gambler, the so-called wise guy? To these careful practitioners of the art, the Super Bowl is simply another game, another potential money-making opportunity. If the right numbers aren't present, the wise guys will more than likely take a pass on the game, or perhaps make a modest bet merely to share in the excitement.

Take, for instance, the 1999 Super Bowl pitting the upstart Atlanta Falcons against the favored defending champions, the Denver Broncos. "There's always another game, and you can win or lose just as easily. The Super Bowl is just another game to me," says Louie, a studious Reno gambler, as he surveys the electronic board high above the cavernous Reno Hilton Race and Sports Book. Because the stakes for this game are so high, he knows that the initial line set by Roxy Roxborough will be a good one, and that the various Nevada sports book managers will watch the flow of monies on the two teams carefully to make any necessary adjustments. In this instance, Louie decides that Roxborough's initial line, released twelve days before the game, of Denver −7 (meaning that a bet on Denver will require the Broncos to win by 8 points or more) is very close to his own calculations—Louie uses his own complex power rating system that he keeps on his home computer—and so he decides to wait and watch the movement of the line. Roxborough's initial line was another professional triumph; for five days the line did not move, but an upsurge in Denver money forced most books to push the line to +7½ points. There it stayed until kickoff on January 31.

Ultimately, Louie decides to pass on the game, leaving the field to the less sophisticated, the thrill seekers, or those who have evaluated the game differently. A popular bartender at a local bistro, Louie does in fact make a bet the morning of Super Bowl Sunday, but it's on a lackluster Monday night college basketball game between two teams with losing records. His system tells him that this is a "high value" game, and so he puts four units on the underdog. (Like most savvy bettors, Louie manages his money by assigning to each game a potential "value" that his handicapping system reveals. His betting unit is $100, and his bets normally fluctuate between one and four units; occasionally he might wager up to six units when he spots an unusually attractive opportunity.) A source in Kansas City has reported to him that the favorite's number two scorer severely sprained an ankle in a game Saturday night, and as occasionally happens in low-profile games, the line has not yet reflected that important development.

In the days immediately before the Super Bowl the money pours into the extravagant sports book at the Reno Hilton like a tide rising in anticipation of a tsunami. When the Las Vegas Sports Consultants established the early line at Denver −7, many experienced bettors got their money down early on Atlanta, reasoning that the stout Atlanta defense, which had stifled the potent attack of the favored Minnesota Vikings in the NFC championship game, would be equal to the task of containing the one-two Bronco punch of quarterback John Elway and running back Tyrell Davis. That money, however, was being balanced by the casual bettors, who were going heavily for the favorite, as they usually do. The line also reflected the anticipation that a large amount of Denver money will pour into the books when the several thousand Denver fans who have booked airline flights to Reno and Las Vegas arrive on Saturday.

The hotels in Reno and Las Vegas begin to fill up with high rollers intent on making large wagers and watching the game in one of many hotel rooms equipped with large-screen television sets and bars overflowing with drink and food. Several retired NFL players have been hired by the hotels to greet the gamblers at the door and to mingle with the crowd, shaking hands, slapping backs, telling war stories, and dispensing information heavily laced with football jargon. One enterprising hotel has even announced that it's booked the Oakland Raider cheerleaders for its Super Bowl party. At the Hilton, a more sedate assemblage of a few hundred "invited guests," known to the casino management as individuals who will bet heavily on the game, repair to a smaller room where the food and drink are free and a special window is set up where the minimum bet is $1,000.

While the serious bettors study the possibilities of betting into the point spread, others contemplate the odds on the straight money line, where a bet on the Broncos will require a bet of $2.70 to win $1.00. The over/under proposition attracts the attention of most bettors as they survey the board, but the figure of 53 seems to Louie and other wise guys to be about right; it's a given that the Falcons will not score more than three touchdowns, but their tenacious defense has the potential to hold the Bronco offense in check enough to keep the final score below 53 points. However, they also know that if Elway gets a hot hand and if Davis can break a few long runs from scrimmage, the Broncos could easily push the number over 53. The over/under strikes most sophisticated bettors as too risky for their taste, and the exuberant Denver fans push it to 54 a few days before the game.

Louie and his peers look with absolute disdain on one of the major money-makers for the books—the proposition bets. These "props" are based on factors that are not readily susceptible to rational handicapping: Which running back will score the first touchdown? the last touchdown? Which receiver will catch the first touchdown pass? Will any kick returner take a punt back for a touchdown? Which team will be penalized the most yardage? Which team will win the coin toss? Will Michael Jordan score more points in the Chicago Bulls game on Sunday than Denver'll score against the Falcons? Louie dismisses the props as "sucker bets" but understands that they provide enjoyment for the amateur bettors and a bonanza for the house. Many who play the props compound their vulnerability by doing so on a parlay card for which they have to successfully pick three or more propositions in order to win a ridiculously low 4–1 payoff. But for the amateur enjoying the excitement of the game, putting twenty dollars or so on a few props intensifies the pleasure of the moment.

While Louie has opted to not play the game, he confides that if he were forced to make a bet, he would "take the points" because of the increasingly strong defense that the Falcons have put on the field during the last weeks of the season and the playoffs. Mark agrees. A Reno sales representative, he has developed a relatively sophisticated approach to football wagering over the past eight years. His personal library contains several well-thumbed books on how to get an edge on the professional lines makers, a prospect that he understands—but is reluctant to concede—is unlikely, given the databases available to experienced lines makers. Nonetheless, Mark feels he's up to the challenge, and each fall he invests several hundred dollars in a subscription to a sports service he has come to regard as honest; unlike many tout services that merely provide a verbal recommendation over an 800 telephone line, his also publishes a detailed weekly newsletter with timely information, including an updated statistical breakdown of each professional and Division 1-A college team.

Mark enjoys the challenge of trying to outsmart the lines makers, and as a former high school football player he thinks he has a special feel for the factors that contribute to a game's outcome. An enthusiastic fan, he bets primarily because he enjoys being part of the "action"; if he makes money so much the better, but greed is not his primary motivation. His football gambling is one of his primary recreational activities, and he estimates that he devotes about fifteen hours a week during the season to his hobby, reading the statistic-laden U.S.A. Today sports pages plus two other daily newspapers and spending an hour or more most evenings in front of his television set watching ESPN's saturation coverage of college and professional football. He keeps careful records and notes on his wagers but is unwilling to share those with an interviewer. He says he is more inclined to bet on college games during the regular season because the line on professional games can be set with much more precision owing to the small number of teams in the NFL and the enormous amount of information on them available to lines makers and gamblers alike. He believes that on any Saturday, however, there are several college games which afford him a definite edge, often games between lesser known mid-level teams in the West. He faithfully uses his tout service—the newsletter, which arrives on Wednesday, a "late-breaking" FAX communication on Friday evening, and verbal picks that he gets on Saturday morning via the 800 number—to help him identify a small number of games, usually five, on which he will bet between one and five units. Unlike Louie's, Mark's units are $50. On a given Saturday he will have between $500 and $1,200 in play. His goal is to win 60 percent of his bets, but he admits that at season's end he is happy to break even. Mark is reluctant to reveal the current season's record but concedes that he is only a few hundred dollars ahead as the Super Bowl looms.

Mark's sport service has recommended the Falcons at +7½, explaining that its breakdown of the personal match-ups of key personnel points toward a low scoring game that should give a slight edge to the underdog. Mark tends to agree, and on his way home from the office on Friday night he stopped by a sports book in a neighborhood casino and "took the points," playing five units—$250—on the Falcons. On Sunday morning Mark is looking forward to watching the game with several friends and their spouses. Clicking on the television set at 11 a.m. he is stunned to learn that one of the key Atlanta defenders, identified by Mark's sports service as providing a main line of defense against Elway's aerial attack, has been arrested late Saturday night by an undercover Tampa policewoman for soliciting sex. Safety Eugene Robinson was not only humiliated by the arrest but was held in custody until after midnight. Mark is grateful that Robinson will not miss the game, but will he be mentally ready to play in the game? Will he be able to play well with only a few hours sleep? How will his flaunting of team rules affect the Falcons?

Robinson's arrest is a last-minute variable that no handicapper could have anticipated. Yet veteran bettors have learned to accept the unexpected. Mark's worst fears are borne out early in the second quarter. With the ball on the Denver twenty-yard line, Bronco quarterback John Elway rolls to his right and fakes a short pass that freezes Robinson for a crucial moment; that is enough, as wide receiver Rod Smith sprints past him, takes in Elway's forty-yard pass in full stride, and coasts into the end zone for a touchdown that breaks the game open. It was later revealed that Falcon team members angrily criticized Robinson in the locker room before the game. The sharp focus that coach Dan Reeves had sought for his team had been disrupted by Robinson's lack of judgment, and on that one play that found Robinson wanting, the tide of the game turned against Mark and his $250 wager.

The so-called smart money that had been put on the Falcons was kept by the books as the Broncos controlled the game and easily covered the spread with a 34–19 score. The less sophisticated betters who had gone with the favorite and the team with the more famous quarterback collected their bets—minus, of course, the books' 9 percent vigorish. Interesting enough, the total score of

the game came down right on Michael Roxborough's initial 53 points, before
Denver enthusiasts pushed the over/under to 54, thereby denying the gamblers
who took the under, on the assumption that Atlanta's defense was ready to make
a good showing, an opportunity to stand in the payoff line at the casino.

As he watched the game from behind his bar, Louie quietly congratulated
himself for showing discipline when the social pressure was to get involved with
the game. Mark, on the other hand, consoled himself that he had handicapped
the game correctly but had been done in by the unanticipated misbehavior of a
key player. And so it went across the country: winners congratulated themselves
on their betting acumen, and losers found a way to rationalize their losses.
Bookies in New York, Chicago, Seattle, and all points in between, along with
their legal brethren in Reno and Las Vegas, were content to add up their profits.
Nevada's books took in $77.4 million and enjoyed a profit of $5 million. Not bad
for one day's work.

⚑

Super Bowl Sunday is proof that, as *U.S. News and World Report* commented in
1997, "laying an illegal wager on a sports game has never been easier, and more
Americans are doing it than ever."[3] What is the reason for this phenomenon?
Why do increasing numbers of Americans bet on athletic contests? As identified
in the preceding pages, sports wagering is deeply rooted in the American past,
but during recent decades the convergence of two major factors has provided
the impetus for the enormous upsurge in gambling activity. Beyond question,
the impact of modern communications has been a fundamental factor. Thanks
to the explosion of cable networks, including several channels devoted strictly
or primarily to sports, the American public has been increasingly bombarded
with more news about more teams. Radio talk shows have proliferated, and the
conversation between hosts and callers often revolves around point spreads and
odds. Both radio and television shows during the autumn are devoted to providing
betting information. The Internet has literally thousands of sites devoted to sports
coverage, many of them focused on sports wagering. As sports became an ever
increasing part of American popular culture, it was only logical that increased
levels of gambling would ensue.

Second, gambling has also become part of mainstream American popular
culture. With forty-eight state governments sanctioning some form of gambling,
the onetime powerful moral arguments against gambling have crumbled. With
millions of Americans each week playing state-operated lotteries, the act of
putting $100 down on the Browns to cover the spread against the Redskins is no

longer seen as aberrant behavior. Americans have come to equate gambling with other forms of entertainment, such as going to the movies, watching television, or playing golf. "This huge phenomenon has blossomed in the economy, and turning back the clock to keep it from happening is not going to happen," Eugene Christiansen, a national gambling consultant, concluded in 1999.[4] Newer studies of the number of compulsive gamblers, once pegged at 10 percent of the public, have shown that the overwhelming percentage of gamblers do so for entertainment and with the full understanding that there is a high possibility that they will lose money. The great majority of American gamblers are prudent, able to exercise control over their betting and the money they budget for it. Current estimates place compulsive gambling at no more than 2 percent of the adult population, and researchers have found that compulsive gambling is not a stand-alone illness but rather one that is coupled with other compulsive forms of behavior, including alcoholism and nicotine addiction.[5]

The great percentage of Americans who do gamble, though, do not bet on sports. Casino marketing experts know that women are the major clientele for their slot machines, and that men and women tend to play blackjack or other table games about equally. Men make up the overwhelming percentage of poker players. Both sexes are apt to buy lottery tickets in equal numbers; significantly, the lower the educational and income levels, the higher the likelihood of participation. Although the lack of hard data makes any generalizations some-what suspect, our observations of Nevada casinos and interviews with bookies elsewhere enable us to make several generalizations about the demographics of sports wagering in contemporary American society.

Sports gambling is definitely sex specific: at least 98 percent of all sports gamblers are male; we have been hard pressed to find any regular female gam-blers at Nevada sports books, and conversations with bookies indicate that this pattern holds in other states. Regular sports gamblers are also overwhelmingly Caucasian, although our observations indicate that younger Asian and black males participate at substantial levels. Sports gambling is not class specific, although the majority of participants come from blue-collar groups; professional men, many with college degrees, are also steady customers for the book makers. There is a clear age factor at work: The younger the gambler, the more likely he is to be involved in team sports. The older the gambler, the more likely he is to be content with playing the horses. If that trend remains, the slow decline in horse race betting handles will inevitably accelerate in the years to come. One outcome of that development could easily be increased pressure on state governments to legalize sports betting to make up for falling tax revenues. Although race and class are identifiable factors among participating males, the unifying factor seems to be that the regular sports bettor has grown up with sports, often playing more than one team sport as a youth, and more important, having early on had a strong interest in being a fan of professional or college teams. For many men, placing a bet on an upcoming game is merely a natural and logical progression of behavior patterns begun in childhood.

The sociologist Garry Smith concludes that there are essentially four motivations behind most sports gamblers: challenging their intellectual and reasoning capacities, deriving pleasure out of beating the system, wanting to make money, and sharing a feeling of camaraderie with like-minded friends. Smith echoed many an observer of the sports gambling environment when he wrote, "For many bettors, the challenge of making the right choice is more important than the money; the money just represents a convenient way of keeping score."[6] The close relationship between the underlying values of sports handicapping and the American economic system is something that critics seek to dismiss, but that nexus is of considerable symbolic importance. As the journalist Roger Dionne wrote in 1980, "Sports betting is the same in principle as anything in private enterprise, it's a risk, and the guy who works the hardest and is the brightest is going to come out ahead."[7] Ultimately, except for the compulsive gambler, the appeal of sports wagering is that it provides a high level of satisfaction to the participants. In 1975 the sociologist Otto Newman noted that gambling was often listed as a social problem by academics, journalists, and public policy makers, but his data led him to conclude that "within all accepted standards of definition, gambling cannot validly be said to constitute a social problem in objective terms."[8]

The NCAA's efforts to get betting on college sports declared illegal and the 1999 recommendation of the National Gambling Impact Study Commission prove that such ideas have not persuaded the majority of Americans. Yet the incongruity of the persistence of resistance to one particular form of gambling while governments and society have embraced so many others cannot be overlooked. While the issue of sports betting remains a lively one, it is instructive to remind ourselves that in the year 2000—when thirty-seven states conducted multimillion dollar lotteries, forty-four states offered some form of horse or dog racing, forty-seven states licensed bingo games, and twenty-five states were home to full-scale casinos—only Nevada offered full legal sports betting services. The American public and its policy makers should also understand that law enforcement has increasingly looked upon sports betting as a harmless victimless crime, and the number of arrests has declined to almost nil. Illegal bookies, such as the prosperous bookie Jerry from Cleveland, who skates away tax free with his quarter-of-a-million-dollar annual income have thus been permitted to operate an enormous untaxed and unregulated business. Nationwide that business is believed to exceed $100 billion annually. As the journalist William Johnson noted in 1991, "It isn't a question of whether we should legalize sports gambling in the U.S. It is a question of why we have been so stupid as to leave this lucrative and hugely popular segment of sport to the Mob and the office pool for so long. The great American gambling pot should be tapped—now—to help bail out our debt-ridden governments."[9]

Academics who study the gaming industry agree that in the area of sports wagering, three basic options regarding sports gambling are available to state and federal law makers: (1) In emulation of the "war on drugs," they can legislate harshly against the practice and appropriate huge sums of money in what will most certainly be a futile effort to enforce the law. (2) Continuing a century-long practice, they can permit existing prohibitive legislation to remain on the books but not make a concerted effort to enforce those laws. (3) Or they can legalize the activity, regulate it effectively as the state of Nevada does, and in the process create a new and substantial source of tax revenue.[10] If the position taken by the Gambling Impact Study Commission is any indication of the way the winds of politics are blowing, it would seem that option number two will remain the preferred public policy.

The odds on option number three being adopted within the first decade of the new millennium have been set by the authors of this book at 15–1.

Appendix

Essential Facts about
Nevada Sports Books, Bookies,
and the Vig

Merriam Webster's Collegiate Dictionary, tenth edition, defines a bookmaker as "one who determines odds and receives and pays off bets." The place where a record of his business activity is registered is known as his "book," thereby causing his customers to use the informal term "bookie." Legal sports books now operating in Nevada can hardly be called bookies, however. They are an elaborate and integral part of enormous casinos, offering many amenities and providing the atmosphere of a sophisticated entertainment business. As in all businesses, the sports books in Nevada are always alert to new ways of improving their bottom line.

Since about 1985 these sports books have relied on Las Vegas Sports Consultants, Inc., headed by Michael "Roxy" Roxborough, to set their odds and betting lines. The Las Vegas sports books have thus displaced the local bookies as the nation's premier line setters on any given sporting event. Illegal bookies across the nation normally accept the "Las Vegas Line" as their starting point, but many will "shade" that line to reflect local trends and popular local teams. For example, Reno's sports books normally adjust the line on San Francisco 49er games by moving the spread one point against the team that most northern Nevada bettors consider their favorite team. Similarly, bookies in Pittsburgh will shade the line against the Steelers, knowing full well that many fans simply love to bet on their favorite team.

What is the typical bettor up against when he or she places a bet at a Nevada sports book? These highly sophisticated operations rely heavily on both quantitative and qualitative information. Their managers bring many years of experience to their craft. Essentially, the manager is seeking to evenly "split" the monies bet on an event to guarantee that he will make a profit no matter the outcome of the contest. Book managers do not like to have money "in play." If truth be known, book managers would love to operate on the pari-mutuel system that is used at all of the nation's racetracks. Under this system the state government mandates that a certain percentage of all monies wagered go directly to the track operators before the final odds are computed and the payouts made to winners. The same state government also mandates that another percentage of the total betting handle on each race be paid to the state treasurer before payouts are calculated.

Unfortunately, the only attempt in Nevada to organize sports books on a pari-mutuel basis met with strong opposition from customers. The pari-mutuel system is based upon the final amounts of monies wagered on an event, and so the bettor never knows the odds he has received on his bet until after the event occurs; he only knows what the odds were at the time he placed his wager. Those odds may and often do change, sometimes drastically, after a bet has been registered. Hence the sports bettor does not like the pari-mutuel system because he cannot be guaranteed that the odds or point spread posted at the time he made his bet will still be in play when the event begins. Thus two of the central features of the pari-mutuel system are anathema to the modern sports bettor: (1) the total amount of monies paid out are based upon the amount bet on the event, minus the track's and the government's guaranteed takeout (which is about 20 percent of the betting handle), and (2) the bettor cannot control the odds or point spread of the bet he makes. Interest in pari-mutuel horse race betting has been on a steady decline among knowledgeable bettors for the last half-century.

In contrast to the pari-mutuel system, the contemporary bettor making a wager on a football game knows exactly the conditions of his bet. They are locked in when his bet is registered. The odds or point spread may change later, but the terms of that wager will not change; his bet is secured. This means that for every event on which bets are accepted, the sports book is at risk if it does not equally balance the monies bet. It can, and often does, lose money on an event.

So how does the sports book manager keep his bottom line in the black? He does it by adjusting two factors under his control. First, the book charges a fee for handling the bet. This fee is commonly referred to in the business as the "vigorish," or simply "the vig." It is also known in certain gambling circles as "the juice." The second option available to the book manager is to adjust the odds or point spread in such a way as to encourage bettors to place wagers in equal amounts on both sides. This is called "moving the line."

Straight Bets

The backbone of the sports book trade is the "straight" or "flat" bet, which is always booked at odds of 11 to 10. Odds of 11–10 require the bettor to put up $11 to win $10. An $11 wager returns to the winner $21. The loser receives nothing. The vigorish, or house percentage, in this case amounts to 9.09 percent on all winning bets. It should be noted that most bettors completely misunderstand the nature of the bookmaking system, thinking that it is the *losers* who are paying a 10 percent vigorish on their losing bets. Losers don't actually pay the vigorish, they just lose their bet. Rather, it is the *winners* who pay the vigorish. To understand this, consider what happens in a situation of offsetting wagers. The loser puts up $11, chooses unwisely, and loses his $11. The vigorish on this transaction is zero. He just lost an $11 bet. The winner puts up his $11, chooses wisely, and reaps a return of $21 (his $11 bet plus his winnings of $10). So the actual vigorish is 9.09 percent, since the winner would have received $22 if no vigorish were charged ($11 bet plus an $11 payoff). So, contrary to what is written in many a guide to sports betting, it is the winner who actually pays the vigorish that enables the sports book to make a profit. Successful sports bettors recognize this fact of life: reduced payouts on winning bets are the cost of doing business with a sports book.

If one assumes that all wagers are placed on events for which the probability of the outcome is 50/50, like tossing a coin and predicting "heads" or "tails," then a sports book that handles ten bets of $10 each, with the coins landing five times on heads and five times on tails, would collect $110 dollars and pay out $105 to winning bettors (5 × 21). The book thus retains $5 as its vigorish for conducting the coin tosses. The $5 profit on bets of $110 represents approximately 4.545 percent of the total handle on this event.

Of course, football and basketball games are not coin tosses. The likelihood of each team winning being precisely 50 percent is not great. But in fact the sports book does operate on the slim favorable margin of just 4.545 percent. This means that the sports book manager must carefully establish point spreads to ensure that, as much as possible, 50 percent of the money comes in on each side of the contest. If a preponderance of the monies bet is on one side, the book is at risk if the majority of bettors are correct in their estimation of the winner. Unlike in the pari-mutuel system, the sports book is at risk for a loss—sometimes major—if the books are not balanced at kickoff time. The fact that legal sports books continue to operate at a profit demonstrates just how accurate the art of establishing point spreads has become, especially on big-game days when as many as a hundred separate contests are on the board for bettors to select from. (Baseball betting is a distinctly different phenomenon and will be addressed later in this appendix.)

What this house advantage of 4.545 percent means to the bettor should not be underestimated. The bettor who makes only "straight" bets in the same amount on a succession of games must be correct on his bets 52.27 percent of the time to break even. (If he is correct on 52.27 percent of his bets and incorrect on 47.73 percent, he will nullify the house's natural advantage of 4.545 percent.) The fact that sports books prosper and most bettors end up net losers in the long run is due to three essential factors: (1) the skill of the sports book manager in establishing an accurate point spread; (2) the inability of bettors to have the discipline to make straight bets of the same amount over a succession of bets, since winners tend to increase the size of their bets because they think they are "hot," while losers tend to increase the size of their bets to "get even"; and (3) the seemingly irresistible lure to bettors of higher payouts on smaller but more difficult wagers that in fact carry built-in higher percentage advantages for the sports book. These wagers are offered by enterprising sports books to more easily separate the bettor from his money.

These numbers expose as fraudulent the outlandish claims made by many tout services, or "sports services," that their selections routinely win at rates of 70 percent or even 80 percent or higher. If 52.27 percent is the break-even point for straight bettors, those touts who can select winners 70 percent of the time would not need to work so hard to attract new customers to their services. They could simply live the good life by betting on their own selections. But they obviously don't predict winners 70 percent of the time, and they prefer to collect their service fees from naive customers who believe their selectively reported won-lost history. Touts reporting high win percentages are indeed louts.

Totals

An increasingly popular form of wagering in Nevada sports books is estimating whether the total number of points scored in a contest will go over or under a number posted by the sports book manager. This concept evolved from bettors wagering on whether a runner, human or equine, would complete a race in a specified time. The late Bill Dark of the Del Mar Sports and Race Book in Las Vegas extended this concept to scoring on team sports.

In April of 1964 Dark accepted a wager from a customer who wanted to bet that a game between the Cincinnati Reds and the Los Angeles Dodgers would result in a shutout (the game matched ace pitchers Sandy Koufax and Jim Maloney, who had combined for seventeen shutouts in the 1963 season). Dark reframed the bet by offering to accept a wager on whether the total runs scored in the game would be over or under 3½. He lost the initial over/under bet when the game ended 3–0 in favor of the Dodgers. Before long, Dark began offering "totals" wagering on other baseball games and the concept soon spread to other sports. By the 1980s football totals were being offered on parlay cards.

Totals wagering is generally offered on a straight 11–10 system. The sports book's natural 4.545 percent house advantage on 11–10 wagers will be maintained if the sports book manager can post accurate over/under totals that will split the action without creating major moves in the posted number. Totals wagering is now offered on most team sporting events.

Parlays and Parlay Cards

The attraction of larger returns on smaller wagers is illustrated by the widespread popularity among casual sports bettors of parlays and parlay cards. A parlay is a series of two or more bets set up in advance so that the original bet plus its winnings are risked on successive bets. The parlay relies on its potential of increased winnings to lure the bettor.

There are two ways bettors can bet parlays in sports books. These are "off-the-board" or on preprinted parlay cards. Off-the-board means that the bettor can choose games on which to bet by selecting them from all the games posted on the large overhead boards in the sports books. The boards contain all the games on which the sports book is accepting action. The other method of playing parlays, and by far the most popular in Nevada, is by using preprinted parlay cards. These cards list only a portion of the games on the overhead board, but the point spread is locked in as printed—it will not change even if the point spread is changed on the board. The parlay card is the most popular form of betting on football games. The card is printed early in the week and available usually on Monday afternoons. It reflects the point spread as it was initially set by the book, so the bettor has the advantage of comparing the original parlay card point spread with the current spread off-the-board before making his wagers. In rare instances—for example, when a key player is injured or suspended after a card is printed—the sports book may not accept betting on that particular game on the card.

It seems that all but dedicated professional gamblers do not understand exactly what the house percentages are on parlays. Currently, sports books pay winners on a two-game off-the-board parlay at odds of 13–5 (a wager of $5 returns a total of $13 plus the original $5 dollars). Paying off two-team parlays at odds of 13–5 is not a number picked randomly or arbitrarily. The number represents the approximate payoff on two successive 11–10 bets. (An $11 bet at 11–10 returns $21, which is then re-bet at 11–10, returning $19.09 plus the $21 wagered, or a total of $40.09. An $11 bet at 13–5 returns $39.60. Note that rounding down the parlay odds to the nearest manageable whole number, the sports book has clipped another 49 cents or 1.22 percent from the 11–10 payoff.) The true odds on a two-team parlay winning, however, are 3–1, since there are four possible outcomes in two even-money propositions. (In terms of the heads and tails example, the possible outcomes are head and head, head and tail, tail and head, tail and tail, or expressed mathematically it is $\frac{1}{2} \times \frac{1}{2} = \frac{1}{4}$, or one chance in four.) By paying off at 13–5, the house percentage is 10.00 percent (consider four bets of $5 each or $20 on the four possible outcomes in the example, which would yield one winner paid off at $18, house percentage to the book = 2/20th or 10 percent). This house percentage is more than double the advantage to the house on straight bets. Is it any wonder that parlay players are always welcomed warmly by sports book managers?

Successive off-the-board parlays can be computed in the same manner. Three-team parlays off-the-board return 6–1 to successful bettors on a proposition that has eight possible outcomes yielding true odds of 7–1. The house percentage in this case is 1/8 or 12.5 percent. Four-team off-the-board parlays pay off at odds of 10–1 on a proposition that has sixteen possible outcomes or 15–1 odds. The house percentage in this case rises to 5/16, or 31.25 percent. Five-team off-the-board parlays, which pay off at 20–1, result in a house percentage of 11/32, or 34.37 percent. Finally, six-team off-the-board parlays (which are the largest such bets sports books will accept) pay off at 40–1, yielding a house percentage of 25/64 or 39.06 percent. Bettors attempting to overcome a house's natural advantage of almost 40 percent need Hall of Fame handicapping skills, plenty of luck for good measure, and a large capacity to absorb losses.

Prospects for parlay card players is equally bleak. Parlay cards vary in the odds offered to the bettor because each sports book publishes its own cards, so the shrewd bettor should compare cards of several sports books before making a bet. The odds generally fall within fairly narrow limits, however, and for the purposes of our analysis the most common odds will be used to calculate the house percentages.

Parlay cards generally differ in four ways from parlays off-the-board. First, most cards express point spreads by using half points, to avoid the problem of tie games. (Tie games on off-the-board parlays are handled by disregarding the tie game and thereby reducing the parlay to the next lower number of teams.) Second, the minimum number of teams that can be bet on a parlay card is three, as opposed to two for off-the-board parlays. Third, the maximum number of teams that can be played on a parlay card is increased to ten and sometimes more. Finally, and very subtly, parlay cards list their payoffs using the form "3 for 3 teams pays . . . 6.5 *for* 1." The key word here is "for" instead of "to," which means that a bettor wagering $1 on the parlay card would receive $6.50 for a winning three-team card. If, however, the bettor wagered $1 at odds of 6.5 *to* 1, a winning bet would be paid off at $7.50 (the winning $6.50 plus the $1 bet returned). Thanks to this carefully contrived wording, the real odds of a three-team parlay are 5.5 to 1, a substantial reduction. Off-the-board parlays, paying 6 to 1 on three teams, result in a house advantage of 12.5 percent; paying 5.5 to 1 (or 6.5 for 1) on parlay cards increases the house advantage to 18.75 percent.

On the other hand, parlay card odds are slightly better than off-the-board parlay odds when playing four-, five-, or six-team parlays. At the ten-team parlay level, cards paying 850 for 1 would be yielding a house advantage of approximately 36.5 percent on the true odds of 1,023 to 1. About the only good thing that can be said for such high-risk parlay bets is that they offer better odds than a state lottery.

Teasers, Pleasers, and Other Exotica

Fully aware that the betting public enjoys product diversity and new forms of wagering, Nevada's sports books have increasingly offered their customers a veritable smorgasbord of wagering gimmicks.

Teasers are one increasingly popular item on the menu. Teasers are parlays on which the bettor is permitted to "tease" or move the point spread in either direction to enhance his chances of winning. For example, if the Dallas Cowboys are −10 against the Washington Redskins, which would be −10/+10, the bettor on a standard 6-point teaser (the smallest teaser offered in football wagering) may move the point spread 6 points in either direction. For example, the bettor may move (or "tease") the line so that the Cowboys are −4 and the Redskins are moved to +16. Obviously, the bettor must pay for this luxury in the form of reduced payoffs. On a two-team teaser parlay, the bettor must lay 11–10, which are the odds on a single game flat bet. Three-team teasers return 9–5 as opposed to 6–1 on straight three-team parlays. These bets, where the bettor can move the point spread, look tantalizing—hence the term *teaser*—but serious handicappers know that in many games the point spread is actually immaterial: either the favorite wins by enough points to cover the original spread or the underdog wins the game outright without needing the original point spread to cover the bet. Handicappers must seriously weigh the benefits of a 6-point teaser against the reduced payoff.

Off-the-board teasers are also available, in which the bettor can raise the spread in increments of a half point by paying an increased vigorish. In our teaser example, a two-team, 6-point teaser may be bet at 11–10 odds. To increase the teaser to 6½ points the bettor must lay odds of 12–10 (or 6–5). Seven-point teasers require laying odds of 13–10, and 7½-point teasers cost the bettor 14–10 (7–5). Some major sports books offer 10- and 14-point teasers by raising the minimum number of teams which must be played while lowering the payoffs ever further.

Teasers can also be played on special teaser parlay cards in the same way that off-the-board straight bets can be played on regular parlay cards. Teaser parlay cards come in two forms: the regular teaser, with the point spread moved 6 points from the original point spread on the regular parlay cards; and the Big Teaser, with 10-point moves in the spread.

An anomaly created by the use of teasers is that a bettor can "middle" a game. Middling is when the bettor takes both sides in a game using different point spreads. Suppose, in our initial teaser example, the bettor played a two-team, 6-point teaser selecting both the Dallas Cowboys at −4 and the Washington Redskins at +16 in the same game. The bettor has created a 12-point middle between the teams. The parlay would win if the Cowboys won the game by at least 5 points but less than 16. Sophisticated handicappers often use teasers in conjunction with parlays on games played at different times or on different days to create middles and no-lose situations where the bettor must win some money regardless of which team wins the game. This concept of middling games by betting on both sides of the same game at different point spreads is known by the far more respectable names of hedging and arbitrage when done in the investment world of stocks and bonds.

Teasers are less popular in basketball wagering because they are limited to moving the point spread 4 points in either direction. Since higher scoring in basketball reduces the premium placed on moving the point spread, many bettors are unwilling to sacrifice larger payoffs in exchange for moving the spread 4 points.

Pleasers are another form of exotic wagering which use parlay cards but move the point spread against the bettor and in favor of the house instead of vice versa. Called "pleasers" because of the incredible odds offered on winning parlays, these cards are currently available only in a limited number of sports books and only for professional football games played in the NFL.

The pleaser is a parlay in which the point spread is moved 7 points against the bettor. In the teaser example with the Cowboys at −4 and the Redskins at +16, the spread was moved from −10/+10. In a pleaser parlay using the same example of a −10/+10 game, the point spread would be moved to a −17/+3. Bettors wanting to bet on the favorite would have to take the Cowboys at −17 rather than −10; those choosing the Redskins would get them at +3 rather than at +10. The house has, in effect, created its own 14-point middle against the bettor. In return for this extremely unfavorable and difficult to overcome move in the point spread, a winning wager receives huge payouts. Three-team pleasers come in at 240–1. Pleaser odds run up to ten teams (50,000–1). Unfortunately for those willing to jump into the pleaser pool, there are few weeks during an NFL season in which more than three or four games fall outside the house's favorable middle created by the reverse move in the point spread.

"Buying the hook" is still another form of point spread manipulation on straight off-the-board wagering. "Buying the hook" allows the bettor to move the point spread off a "bad" number. To move the point spread to get off certain commonly recurring numbers, the bettor must lay 12–10 odds on a straight bet rather than the normal 11–10. The handicapper must decide whether the extra vigorish is worth moving a game from +7 to +7½, thus avoiding the number 7 and requiring the underdog to lose by at least 8 points, or by more than one touchdown. On the other hand, buying the hook to bring the point spread down to 6½ allows the favorite to cover the spread with one touchdown. Key numbers that skilled football bettors often want to avoid and which generate the most action in buying and selling the hook are 3, 6, 7, and 10. Some books place limits on situations in which this gambit is permitted.

The odds on teasers, pleasers, and buying hooks do not lend themselves to precise mathematical calculation, since two variables—the number of games in which the original point spread is a factor and the number of times scores fall on certain numbers—vary from season to season.

"Proposition bets" are wagers that are best expressed in the form of a question. They occur irregularly during a season in major team sports but enjoy their greatest popularity during the Super Bowl. There are literally hundreds of proposition bets that are made around the Super Bowl—from those that reflect the evaluation of playing skills (will John Elway of the Denver Broncos complete more passes than Chris Chandler of the Atlanta Falcons?), to the unique or unusual (will there be a safety scored in the game?), to the ludicrous (will the total points scored by both teams plus 16 points equal the number of strokes Tiger Woods takes in a golf tournament played the same day?). These "props" carry odds in the form of a money line spread (explained below) with steep built-in house percentages. They are immune to rational handicapping processes.

In recent years proposition wagering has popped up in unusual places. Will Sammy Sosa hit sixty or more home runs this season? Yes: at −$1.60. No: at +$1.20. Will Tony Gwynn bat .360 or higher this season? Yes: at −$1.40. No: at even money. Suffice it to say, the sports books managers leave as big a middle as possible in setting the money odds.

Following the Money Line

The advent and widespread acceptance of the point spread, coupled with increased expertise on the part of line makers, has made betting sports as close as possible to a 50–50 proposition. Some bettors, however, still prefer the old-fashioned method of betting on the actual outcome of games, that is, without the interference of the concept of the point spread. For those traditionalists, the sports books offer money line wagers. This form of betting is based not upon point spread but upon the odds on each team as determined by the bookmaker which are offered on a plus and minus dollar figure in proportion to the teams' estimated chances of winning the contest. For example, if the Cowboys are favored by 3 points over the Redskins and the bettor wishes to bet the game on the money line without the use of the point spread, the odds offered might be listed as −1.60/+1.40 (this is known in the bookies' jargon as a "twenty-cent line"). Bettors choosing the Cowboys, the favorite team, will have to wager $1.60 to win $1.00. Bettors who opt for the Redskins, the underdog, without the benefit of a point spread are rewarded by having to wager just $1.00 to win $1.40. The favorable house percentages in this example are 4.0 percent when the book lays the $1.40 odds and 3.5 percent when the book takes the odds at $1.60.

By attracting a proportional amount of wagering on both sides of the game, the house advantage is a function of the difference in the posted odds. Obviously, the heavier the favorite, the more the house percentage would be reduced. To compensate for this shrinkage, the gap between the posted odds must be widened to maintain profitability. With a 7-point spread the odds offered might be widened to −2.40/+2.00, creating a forty-cent line. The favorable house percentages in this case are 6.15 percent and 2.57 percent. Just as point spreads are adjusted to take into account the amount of money being bet on each team, the money line will be moved in the same direction that the point spread moves.

Money line wagering is the main method of wagering on baseball, for two reasons: the importance of the starting pitcher to a team's chance for victory; and the fact that no major league baseball team could survive posting a seasonal record proportionally similar to a 1–15 or 2–14 NFL team. Major league baseball is much more competitive than professional football—despite the NFL's constant hype, especially when a mismatch is in the offing, that "on any given Sunday, any team . . ." The New York Jets' 1–15 record for the 1996 season would translate into a 10–150 major league baseball season. Even one of the worst teams in baseball history, Casey Stengel's lovable losers, the 1962 New York Mets, managed a 40–122 season.

In any event, sports books now use what is known as a ten-cent line, or "dime line," in posting odds for baseball games. All games are posted with a ten-cent gap between the favorite and underdog. A game may start out as −1.40/+1.30 and move whenever too much money comes in on one side. A game in which neither team is favored would be posted as −1.05/−1.05, indicating that the bettor puts up $1.05 to win $1.00 no matter which team he selects. This dime line offers the bettor more attractive odds than straight bets on football or basketball using the 11–10 system, where each bettor is putting up $1.10 to win $1.00. The house advantage using baseball's −1.05/−1.05 dime line is 2.38 percent, approximately one-half the 4.54 percent on 11–10 bets. If one team is a prohibitive favorite in a game, the dime line gap is widened to maintain profitability, as in any other money line bet.

As an added inducement to attract bettors to baseball, the bettor is offered the option of canceling the bet if one or both of the listed starting pitchers does not open the game. This is especially important in games in which the bettor is laying big odds because of the dominance of one of the starting pitchers.

Modern baseball wagering does employ one form of point spread betting. In every game a separate money line is offered with the favorite at −1½ runs and the underdog at +1½ runs. This bet is known as the "baseball run line" and generates unusual money lines where the favorite to win the game will occasionally be the underdog, giving up one and a half runs. However, bettors must factor into their handicapping the ability of each team to win close one-run games over the course of the season before venturing into these treacherous wagering waters.

This dual system of having a run line combined with a money line is in fact more common in betting on National Hockey League games. Until recently, hockey was the poor stepchild of the sports betting world. The spread of the NHL across the United States plus the exposure given hockey on sports television networks has led to increased interest in betting on hockey.

Hockey uses a combination of money line odds coupled with a goal point spread to encourage action on both sides of a game. It is not unusual for a hockey team to be listed as −1/-$1.20, meaning the bettor must lay 6–5 odds (-$1.20) and give up one goal. Even half goal point spreads are extremely important because of the number of tie games that take place in hockey.

The Future Is Now

Sports books also offer long-term "futures bets." Futures betting is offered on most team sports and some individual sporting events. Odds are posted before the beginning of a new season on each team's estimated chances of winning the championship. In larger sports books, odds may also be offered on lesser championships as well; for example, in football bettors can accept odds on the Super Bowl or on the league's conference championships. In baseball, wagers can be placed on divisions, leagues, or World Series results for any given team.

In order to understand house percentages on futures bets (or bets on individual sports such as golf, tennis, and auto racing), the bettor must be able to convert odds, established by evaluating the chances of winning, into booking percentages. For example, if the Dallas Cowboys are listed at 3–1 odds to win the Super Bowl, the line maker is estimating that the Cowboys have a one in four (¼) chance of winning the Super Bowl, which converts into a booking percentage of 25 percent. If the Denver Broncos are the next choice by the line maker at 4–1, their booking percentage is 20 percent (1/5). The total percentages of all NFL teams should equal 100 percent before any wagering starts, and the percentages should then be adjusted as money is wagered on each team. Unfortunately for the bettor, the booking percentages on futures bets and individual events usually reach 200 percent or higher. Notwithstanding the house's favorable percentage of 50 percent or higher in some cases, futures wagering has some value in hedging and arbitrage betting techniques.[1]

Although modern sports books now offer a far greater range of betting opportunities than at any time in history, the difficulty in overcoming the house's natural advantage remains a constant. For the serious sports handicapper, the game remains the same as the one encountered more than a half-century ago by Sidney "Shoebox" Brodson. It requires long hours of hard work to assimilate and evaluate the amount of information available to today's bettor. It is important for the bettor who wants to make money to understand the house's natural advantage and how to overcome it with skill, patience, and sound money management techniques that are every bit as challenging as those facing investors in the stock, bond, commodities, and real estate markets.

Notes

Introduction

1. Findlay, *People of Chance*, p. 4.
2. Fabian, *Card Sharps and Bucket Shops*, p. 7.
3. *Final Report, The National Gambling Impact Study Commission*, p. 1-1.
4. The minor exception is a marginal football parlay game offered each autumn by the Oregon Lottery based on National Football League games.
5. The best study of the impact of television on American sports is Benjamin Rader, *In Its Own Image*. However, Rader does not discuss the relationship of television and sports betting.
6. Interview with Lem Banker.
7. Quoted in Looney, "The Line Pulled Out of a Hat," p. 61.
8. Quoted in Deford, "Laying It All on the Line," p. 54.

Chapter 1

1. Findlay, *People of Chance*, pp. 11–35.
2. Ibid., pp. 11–38.
3. Gorn and Goldstein, *Brief History of American Sports*, pp. 3–17; Rader, *American Sports*, pp. 2–6.
4. Gorn and Goldstein, *Brief History of American Sports*, pp. 6–9.
5. Ibid., pp. 9–17.
6. Rader, *American Sports*, pp. 5–9.
7. Gorn and Goldstein, *Brief History of American Sports*, pp. 9–17.
8. Rader, *American Sports*, pp. 7–9.
9. Chafetz, *Play the Devil*, pp. 13–19; Gorn and Goldstein, *Brief History of American Sports*, pp. 9–17.
10. Gorn and Goldstein, *Brief History of American Sports*, pp. 17–30, quotation on p. 25; Rader, *American Sports*, pp. 10–11.
11. Breen, "Horses and Gentlemen," pp. 329–47; Findlay, *People of Chance*, pp. 22–30.
12. Longstreet, *Win or Lose*, pp. 34–35; Gorn and Goldstein, *Brief History of American Sports*, p. 22.
13. James, *Life of Andrew Jackson*, pp. 107–18; Findlay, *People of Chance*, pp. 38–39; Chafetz, *Play the Devil*, pp. 45, 178–80.
14. Quoted in Levine, *American Sport*, pp. 18–26.
15. Chafetz, *Play the Devil*, pp. 171–85; Gorn and Goldstein, *Brief History of American Sports*, pp. 71–73.

16. Chafetz, *Play the Devil*, pp. 285–97; Longstreet, *Win or Lose*, pp. 57–87; Sasuly, *Bookies and Bettors*, pp. 58–64, quotation on p. 61.

17. Sasuly, *Bookies and Bettors*, pp. 65–90; Rader, *American Sports*, pp. 83–84.

18. Sasuly, *Bookies and Bettors*, pp. 69–105.

19. Ibid., pp. 76–105.

20. Ibid., pp. 94–105.

21. Flynt, "The Pool-Room Spider and the Gambling Fly," pp. 513–21.

22. Quoted in Longstreet, *Win or Lose*, p. 143.

23. Ibid., pp. 144–55.

24. Riess, "Professional Sports and New York's Tammany Machine," p. 163.

Chapter 2

1. Asinof, *Eight Men Out*, p. 10

2. Alexander, *Our Game*, pp. 1–58; Rader, *American Sports*, pp. 64–73; Gorn and Goldstein, *Brief History of American Sports*, pp. 78–81; interview with Sonny Reizner.

3. Asinof, *Eight Men Out*, pp. 10–15.

4. Ibid., pp. 10–11.

5. Quoted in "For Honest Baseball," p. 120.

6. Alexander, *Our Game*, pp. 29–30.

7. Quoted in Asinof, *Eight Men Out*, p. 11.

8. Alexander, *Our Game*, pp. 115–20.

9. Seymour, *Baseball*, p. 293.

10. The problem of detecting a fix remains true a century later; as Las Vegas handicapping guru Michael Roxborough explains, "Just based on results, you can never assume a game is fixed. Results are so random in sports that you can never look at a result and say it must be fixed." Quoted in Stern, "The Man Who Makes the Odds," p. 21.

11. Alexander, *Our Game*, pp. 115–20; Asinof, *Eight Men Out*, pp. 10–15.

12. Alexander, *Our Game*, p. 118; Asinof, *Eight Men Out*, p. 14; Alexander, *Our Game*, p. 119.

13. Fullerton, "Baseball on Trial," pp. 183–84.

14. Murdock, *Ban Johnson*, pp. 184–85.

15. Alexander, *Our Game*, pp. 122–29; Longstreet, *Win or Lose*, pp. 166–72; Asinof, *Eight Men Out*, pp. 15–38; Katcher, *The Big Bankroll*, p. 140.

16. Quoted in Katcher, *The Big Bankroll*, pp. 144–45.

17. *New York Times*, November 6, 1928, p. 22; Longstreet, *Win or Lose*, pp. 171–72; Chafetz, *Play the Devil*, pp. 422–32; Katcher, *The Big Bankroll*, esp. pp. 326–35.

18. Sasuly, *Bookies and Bettors*, p. 91; Asinof, *Eight Men Out*, p. 1; Katcher, *The Big Bankroll*, p. 148; *New York Times*, November 6, 1928, p. 22; see also "There's a Straight Man Born Every Minute" for an insightful retrospective examination of Rothstein's shrewd gambling instincts and his close association with the owner of the New York Giants, Charles Stoneham.

19. Alexander, *Our Game*, p. 124. Lardner, "Remember the Black Sox?" provides an insightful, authoritative summary of the case.

20. Asinof, *Eight Men Out*, pp. 123–234.

21. Ibid., pp. 123–74.

22. Lardner, "Remember the Black Sox?"

23. Katcher, *The Big Bankroll*, p. 144; Asinof, *Eight Men Out*, pp. 236–73.

24. Asinof, *Eight Men Out*, p. 273; Alexander, *Our Game*, pp. 130–35; for an understanding of the American people's attitude and the hope they placed in Landis, see "Judge Landis, the New Czar of Baseballdom."

25. Asinof, *Eight Men Out*, pp. 273, 279–83, Landis quoted on p. 280.

26. Ibid., pp. 288–93; Lardner, "Remember the Black Sox?"

27. Quoted in Longstreet, *Win or Lose*, p. 171; for a slightly different wording of the same episode, which was reported that day by four separate observers, see Lardner, "Remember the Black Sox?" p. 84.

28. James, *The Bill James Historical Baseball Abstract*, pp. 138–39. Serious students of the national pastime have long debated, with considerable but often inconclusive evidence at their command, the actual extent of gambling in organized baseball before 1921. James lists thirty-eight players whose careers were shadowed by serious allegations of fixing games, failing to report fixed games, or consorting with known big-time gamblers. His list includes such prominent players as Ty Cobb, Tris Speaker, Heine Zimmerman, Smokey Joe Wood, and Frankie Frisch. In 1926 Landis permitted Cobb and Speaker to retire rather than defend themselves from charges by pitcher Dutch Leonard that in 1919 they had conspired, along with Wood, to have the Cleveland Indians lose to Detroit on the final day of the season so that the Tigers could claim third-place money and they could reap a harvest from personal bets placed with a bookie. Cobb and Wood apparently did not get their bets down in time and lost out on a payday as the Tigers defeated Cleveland 9–5. Both later denied any wrongdoing, but incriminating letters were found, and as Wood said in 1975, "Things were so different then" (ibid.). See also, "The Cobb Gambling Scandal," p. 20.

29. *The Nation*, October 18, 1920, pp. 395–96.

Chapter 3

1. Scarne, *Scarne's New Complete Guide to Gambling*, p. 34.

2. Rader, *American Sports*, pp. 83–84; Scarne, *Scarne's New Complete Guide to Gambling*, pp. 32–35; Chafetz, *Playing the Devil*, pp. 375–87.

3. Scarne, *Scarne's New Complete Guide to Gambling*, pp. 36–38.

4. Ibid., pp. 35–38; Sasuly, *Bookies and Bettors*, pp. 106–12.

5. Ogden, *Legacy*, pp. 97–99; Sasuly, *Bookies and Bettors*, pp. 108–10.

6. Ogden, *Legacy*, pp. 7–56; Cooney, *The Annenbergs*, pp. 27–54.

7. Cooney, *The Annenbergs*, pp. 31–35.

8. Ogden, *Legacy*, pp. 57–88; Cooney, *The Annenbergs*, pp. 40–55.

9. Cooney, *The Annenbergs*, pp. 54–55; Ogden, *Legacy*, pp. 87–90.

10. Cooney, *The Annenbergs*, pp. 56–59, quotation on p. 59; Sasuly, *Bookies and Bettors*, pp. 112–14.

11. Cooney, *The Annenbergs*, pp. 63–64; Sasuly, *Bookies and Bettors*, pp. 112–22.

12. Quoted in Ogden, *Legacy*, p. 99.

13. Cooney, *The Annenbergs*, p. 59.

14. Ogden, *Legacy*, pp. 98–100, quotation on p. 100; Cooney, *The Annenbergs*, pp. 56–130.

15. Quoted in Cooney, *The Annenbergs*, pp. 64–65.

16. Ibid., pp. 70–71, 74–80.

17. Ibid., pp. 101–37.

18. Ibid., pp. 138–67, quotation on p. 149.

19. Ogden, *Legacy*, pp. 517–19; Cooney, *The Annenbergs*, p. 311.

20. "Bookies and Bosses," p. 15.

21. Scarne, *Scarne's New Complete Guide to Gambling*, pp. 38–39.

22. Ibid., p. 39.

23. Ibid., pp. 24–25.

24. Ibid., p. 38.

Chapter 4

1. Balboni, "Moe Dalitz: Controversial Founding Father of Las Vegas," pp. 26–27. The historian Mark Haller too writes that although all ethnic groups were represented among urban gambling figures, if any one group stood out, it was second- and third-generation eastern European Jewish immigrants. Haller, "The Changing Structure of American Gambling in the Twentieth Century," pp. 93–97.

2. Haller, "Changing Structure of American Gambling," pp. 91–92.

3. The literature on this subject is enormous, but see Reuter, *Disorganized Crime*, pp. 14–43, and King, *Gambling and Crime*, p. 27; see also Martin, "The Pig-Skin Game."

4. See three sympathetic biographies: Hoyt, *A Gentleman of Broadway*; Breslin, *Damon Runyon*; and Clark, *The World of Damon Runyon*.

5. Clark, *The World of Damon Runyon*, pp. 198–99.

6. In 1999 the winner of the Belmont Stakes was named after Runyon's lovable but inept boxer, The Lemon Drop Kid.

7. For a generous exposure to Runyon's breezy style, see the collections of his short stories: *More Guys and Dolls*, and *The Best of Damon Runyon*. For a perceptive analysis of his fascination with sports betting, see Clark, *The World of Damon Runyon*, pp. 194–206.

8. Quoted in Clark, *The World of Damon Runyon*, p. 200.

9. Quoted in ibid., p. 202.

10. Strine and Isaacs, *Covering the Spread*, p. 12.

11. For a concise examination of the crucial role played by the new media of the 1920s, see Sperber, *Onward to Victory*, pp. 30–31.

12. For an overview of this media phenomenon, see Rader, *American Sports*, pp. 116–18, 149; Sperber, *Onward to Victory*, pp. 29–40, 78–88; Inabinett, *Grantland Rice and His Heroes*; and Fountain, *Sportswriter*.

13. Lardner, "Money to Burn," p. 78; and Martin, "The Pig-Skin Game," p. 9.

14. Martin, "The Pig-Skin Game." The modern version of the old football pool cards, the parlay cards offered by all Nevada sports books and some urban bookies, continue this tradition, offering the bettor lowered returns while usually requiring a minimum of three bets based on the established point spread.

15. Martin, "The Pig-Skin Game," pp. 8–9; Frank, "Easy Pickings?" p. 44; "The Press and the Gambling Craze," p. 1142.

16. Martin, "The Pig-Skin Game," pp. 8–9.

17. Bigelow, "Inside the Gambling Industry," pp. 214–15.

18. Martin, "The Pig-Skin Game"; "Spoiling a Sport"; Frank, "Easy Pickings?"; Lardner, "Money to Burn."

19. Lardner, "Money to Burn."

20. Sperber, *Onward to Victory*, pp. 82–83.

21. Frank, "Easy Pickings?" pp. 44–45.

22. Ibid.; Sperber, *Onward to Victory*, pp. 161–65, Hoover quoted on p. 161.

Chapter 5

1. *Newsweek*, December 18, 1944, p. 84; Roberts and Olsen, *Winning Is the Only Thing*, pp. 80–81; Rader, *American Sports*, pp. 284–85; O'Brien, *Bad Bet*, pp. 241–42; and Rosen, *The Scandals of '51*, pp. 20–21.

2. Roberts and Olsen, *Winning Is the Only Thing*, p. 81; Boyle, "The Brain That Gave Us the Point Spread."

3. Gambler quoted in Sheridan, "The Spread's the Point," p. 75; Boyle, "The Brain That Gave Us the Point Spread."

4. Boyle, "The Brain That Gave Us the Point Spread"; Moore, *The Complete Book of Sports Betting*, pp. 10–12; Roberts and Olsen, *Winning Is the Only Thing*, p. 81; O'Brien, *Bad Bet*, p. 240; Sperber, *Onward to Victory*, pp. 286–87.

5. Sheridan, "The Spread's the Point." For an instructive exploration of the gambling career of Ed Curd, see an extended interview with him conducted by Mort Olshan, *The Gold Sheet*, October 10 and 17, 1987.

6. Sheridan, "The Spread's the Point."

7. Strine and Isaacs, *Covering the Spread*, pp. 11–16; Olshan, *Winning Theories of Sports Betting*, pp. 30–34.

8. Rosen, *Barney Polan's Game*, pp. 181–83; telephone interview with Charles Rosen.

9. Roberts and Olsen, *Winning Is the Only Thing*, p. 81.

10. Scores of books have been published over the years that explain the point spread system and how to outthink the line maker. For some higher quality examples of this dubious genre, see Banker and Klein, *Lem Banker's Book of Sports Betting*; Lang, *Sports Betting 101*; Olshan, *Winning Theories of Sports Betting*; Moore, *The Complete Book of Sports Betting*; Grossman, *You Can Bet On It!*; Cardoza, *The Basics of Winning Sports Betting*; and Patrick, *Sports Betting*.

11. Rosen, *Scandals of '51*, p. 26.

12. Gardner and Gould, "The Brain of the Bookies," p. 106. See also O'Brien, *Bad Bet*, p. 240; Strine and Isaacs, *Covering the Spread*, pp. 12–14. Mort Olshan describes how he and three other handicappers would meet on Monday mornings with Leo Hirschfield to arrive at the final line in *Winning Theories of Sports Betting*, p. 31.

13. Gardner and Gould, "The Brain of the Bookies," pp. 106–9; Lardner, "Touchdown by the Slide Rule," p. 52.

14. Olshan, *Winning Theories of Sports Betting*, pp. 30–31.

15. *New York Times*, January 31, 1945, p. 24.

16. Gardner and Gould, "The Brain of the Bookies," pp. 106–9. In 1957 Mort Olshan moved to Los Angeles to set up his own operation and introduced *The Gold Sheet*, which in 1999 remained one of the most respected sports gambling publications.

17. *New York Times*, January 31, 1945, p. 24; *Saturday Evening Post*, editorial, December 23, 1944. See also Sperber, *Onward to Victory*, p. 287.

18. *New York Times*, January 31, 1945, p. 1; April 3, 1945, p. 21.

19. *New York Times*, April 3, 1945, p. 21.

20. *New York Times*, January 30, 1945, p. 1; February 1, 1945, p. 26; April 3, 1945, p. 29.

21. *New York Times*, March 6, 1945, p. 23.

22. *Time*, October 30, 1944; *New York Times*, January 31, 1945, p. 45; "Dribble Time"; Allen quoted in Sperber, *Onward to Victory*, p. 288.

23. *New York Times*, March 5, 1945, p. 26; Olsen quoted in Sperber, *Onward to Victory*, p. 288.

24. *Newsweek*, February 12, 1945, pp. 78–79.

Chapter 6

1. Rosen, *Barney Polan's Game: A Novel of the 1951 Basketball Scandals*, pp. 181, 181–82.

2. Ibid., pp. 182, 183–84.

3. Ibid., pp. 333–34.

4. For a vivid example of the righteous indignation that resounded across America, see the veteran *New York Times* sports columnist Arthur Daley's sharp attack on the fixers and culpable athletes, which is encased in a ringing defense of the values and virtues of major college athletics. "Sports Are Honest: A Defense."

5. Roberts and Olsen, *Winning Is the Only Thing*, pp. 80–86; Davies, *America's Obsession*, pp. 23–25; Rosen, *The Scandals of '51*, pp. 240–48.

6. Rosen, *The Scandals of '51*, p. 215.

7. Ibid., p. 123; Roberts and Olsen, *Winning Is the Only Thing*, p. 84.

8. For example, see two of Clair Bee's best-selling Chip Hilton novels: *Championship Ball* and *Strike Three*.

9. Sperber, *Onward to Victory*, pp. 316–26.

10. Bee, "I Know Why They Sold Out to the Gamblers."

11. Sperber, *Onward to Victory*, pp. 310–15.

12. Ibid.; Rosen, *Scandals of '51*, pp. 241–42.

13. Rosen, *Scandals of '51*, pp. 147–90.

14. Moldea, *Interference*, pp. 151–52, 440; Sperber, *Onward to Victory*, pp. 330–40.

15. Rosen, *Scandals of '51*, pp. 147–98; Sperber, *Onward to Victory*, pp. 327–43.

16. Rosen, *Scandals of '51*, pp. 41–44; Rosen, *Barney Polan's Game*, pp. 13–71; Sperber, *Onward to Victory*, pp. 293–97.

17. Quoted in Sperber, *Onward to Victory*, p. 297.

18. "Let's Not Duck the Real Issue in Sports Mess."

19. Sperber, *Onward to Victory*, p. 298.

20. "Throwing It All Away," p. 32.

21. Rosen, *Scandals of '51*, pp. 68–69; Sperber, *Onward to Victory*, p. 304.

22. Frank, "Basketball's Big Wheel."

23. Sperber, *Onward to Victory*, pp. 309–26.

24. Rosen, *Scandals of '51*, p. 6; Sperber, *Onward to Victory*, p. 229.

25. Rosen, *Scandals of '51*, pp. 123–34, 159.

26. Ibid., pp. 39, 195–97.

27. Ibid., pp. 152–53, 191.

28. Ibid., p. 196. Streit seems to have revealed his racial bias when he sentenced Sherman White, the black center from LIU, to Rikers Island for a year but treated three white players from Bradley with surprising leniency.

Chapter 7

1. William Moore, *The Kefauver Committee*, pp. 16–41.

2. Ibid., pp. 25–41; Smith, *The Mafia Mystique*.

3. Sasuly, *Bookies and Bettors*, pp. 138–43; Smith, *The Mafia Mystique*, p. 301; Gorman, *Kefauver*, p. 80; Rosecrance, *Gambling without Guilt*, pp. 42, 88.

4. Sasuly, *Bookies and Bettors*, pp. 140–41.

5. Ibid., p. 101; Sasuly, *Bookies and Bettors*, pp. 167–80.

6. Gorman, *Kefauver*, p. 75; Fontenay, *Estes Kefauver*, p. 161.

7. Moore, *The Kefauver Committee*, pp. 42–73.

8. Halberstam, *The Fifties*, pp. 191–94.

9. Moore, *The Kefauver Committee*, pp. 60–66.

10. Ibid., pp. 42–73; Gorman, *Kefauver*, pp. 3–79; Fontenay, *Estes Kefauver*, pp. 3–168.

11. Moore, *The Kefauver Committee*, pp. 74–171; Sasuly, *Bookies and Bettors*, pp. 166–80.

12. For example, see Moore's sharp analysis of the myth and reality surrounding the committee and the issue of organized crime, in his trenchant chapter "The Mafia as Myth," in *The Kefauver Committee*, pp. 114–34; see also Smith, *The Mafia Mystique*, esp. pp. 62–89; and Reuter, *Disorganized Crime*, pp. 1–44.

13. For a summary of Brodson's testimony and its cool reception by the Kefauver committee, see "College-Trained Bets."

14. Moore, *The Kefauver Committee*, pp. 135–234; Smith, *The Mafia Mystique*, pp. 121–22; Sasuly, *Bookies and Bettors*, pp. 166–80; Gorman, *Kefauver*, pp. 74–102; Fontenay, *Estes Kefauver*, pp. 164–86.

15. Moore, *The Kefauver Committee*, pp. 206–42; Gorman, *Kefauver*, pp. 126–27; Fontenay, *Estes Kefauver*, pp. 174–82.

16. Moore, *The Kefauver Committee*, p. 25.

17. Ibid., pp. 235–42; Smith, *The Mafia Mystique*, pp. 121-88; quotation from *Third Interim Report of the Committee to Investigate Organized Crime in Interstate Commerce*, p. 2. See also Balboni, *Beyond the Mafia*.

18. Sasuly, *Bookies and Bettors*, p. 172.

19. *Third Interim Report of the Committee*; Moore, *The Kefauver Committee*, pp. 74–113, provides an extensive and penetrating examination of the committee's emphasis on the horse wire as the network providing the interstate connection for organized crime. Reuter provides sound analysis of the committee's overemphasis on the horse wire in *Disorganized Crime*, pp. 14–17. See also, Sasuly, *Bookies and Bettors*, pp. 166–80, for an insider's perspective of the committee's lack of understanding of the nature of horse race gambling and sports gambling in general.

20. Lardner, "The Substance of Man's Daydreams," p. 79.

21. Sasuly, *Bookies and Bettors*, pp. 166–95.

22. Watson, *Defining Visions*, pp. 7–21; Halberstam, *The Fifties*, p, 195; Patterson, *Grand Expectations*, pp. 348–52.

Chapter 8

1. Halberstam, *The Fifties*, pp. 190–94; see also Moore, *The Kefauver Committee*; Gorman, *Kefauver*, pp. 75–102; Fontenay, *Estes Kefauver*, pp. 164–86; *Life* magazine quoted in Halberstam, p. 192.

2. Brodson's electric testimony made the front page of the *New York Times*, March 25, 1951. Unless noted otherwise, all further citations of Brodson's testimony are from this front-page article.

3. See also Getter, "How to Bet on Sports—and Win," an article about Brodson's testimony.

4. Snyder, *Jimmy the Greek*, p. 91; Getter, "How to Bet on Sports—and Win."

5. Rader, *In Its Own Image*, p. 56; Davies, *America's Obsession*, pp. 70–85; Rader, *American Sports*, pp. 228–29, 242–44, 254–56; Roberts and Olsen, *Winning Is the Only Thing*, pp. 60–63, 108–11.

6. Sasuly, *Bookies and Bettors*, pp. 177–80.

7. Jacoby, "The Forms of Gambling," p. 40. Jacoby was a nationally recognized card expert and an acute observer of the games Americans liked to play.

8. Reuter, *Disorganized Crime*, pp. 14–44; Sasuly, *Bookies and Bettors*, pp. 196–218.

9. Quoted in Friedman, "Portrait of a New York Bookie," pp. 18, 47–48.

10. Interview with Lem Banker. The essential thrust of Banker's candid comments, made in 1999, is merely an update of his views of the precarious nature of sports betting presented in his interesting and enlightening betting manual, *Lem Banker's Book of Sports Betting*, pp. 113–16. The idea that most bettors lose over a full season of football or basketball is also the oft-expressed view of Mort Olshan; for example, see *The Gold Sheet*, January 24, 1997.

11. For an excellent description of such an operation, see Alson, *Confessions of an Ivy League Bookie*.

12. Interview with Norm Francis (pseudonym). Francis worked for his uncle in a medium-sized eastern industrial city from the mid-1980s into the early 1990s, and he had the opportunity to observe his uncle's many competitors operating in the city in a similar fashion.

13. Friedman, "Portrait of a New York Bookie," p. 47.

14. Ibid., p. 18; Sasuly, *Bookies and Bettors*, p. 208.

15. Interview with Norm Francis; see also the recruitment techniques and on-the-job training as described by Alson in his vivid *Confessions of an Ivy League Bookie*, pp. 3–75. For an impressionistic account of the life of a Baltimore bookie written by his son, see Offit, *Memoir of the Bookie's Son*. Offit's compassionate memoir of his relationship with his father from childhood through early adulthood, the 1930s to the 1950s, provides an intimate look at the ambiguity of the moral code under which professional bookies operate.

16. Bartlett, *The Direct Option*, pp. 80–81; see also DeVos and DeVos, "The Power Couple."

17. *Jimmy the Greek*, pp. 25–33; Wadsworth, *Farewell Jimmy the Greek*, pp. 1–31. In a lengthy and informative interview, Sonny Reizner, retired Las Vegas sports book manager and one of the business's most respected practitioners, related how he and his associates in the world of Boston sports gambling from the 1940s to the 1960s began making small wagers as youngsters, many in their early teens. In Reizner's case, he learned his craft sitting in the bleachers at Fenway Park, observing and then participating in the betting that occurred on each and every pitch. For a brief description of Reizner's early entry into a lifetime of sports wagering, see Grossman, *You Can Bet On It!*, pp. 167–68. See also Reizner's *The Best of Sonny Reizner* for the thinking of a professional gambler in his mid-seventies reflecting on a lifetime devoted to beating the spread.

18. Banker, *Lem Banker's Book of Sports Betting*, pp. 1–7.

19. Interview with Scotty Schettler; interview with Norm Francis.

20. Quoted in Konik, *The Man with the $100,000 Breasts*, p. 151.

21. Sasuly, *Bookies and Bettors*, pp. 196–218; Reuter, in *Disorganized Crime*, pp. 14–

44, presents a useful summary of his several interviews with bookies made during the early 1980s.

22. Konik, *The Man With the $100,000 Breasts*, p. 150; "Smiley Joe" quoted in Friedman, "Portrait of a New York Bookie," p. 47.

23. Konik, *The Man With the $100,000 Breasts*, pp. 150–51.

24. This is the underlying theme presented by Reuter in *Disorganized Crime*, and these generalizations are echoed in Sasuly, *Bookies and Bettors*, pp. 196–214, and in the interviews we conducted with veteran handicappers for this study.

25. Friedman, "Portrait of a New York Bookie," p. 48.

26. Sasuly, *Bookies and Bettors*, p. 216. Interviews conducted for this book reinforced the sense that violence is an extraordinarily rare occurrence in the world of sports gambling.

27. Friedman, "Portrait of a New York Bookie," pp. 47–48.

28. If the Kefauver committee proved one point in its sixteen-city extravaganza, it was that local gamblers could not operate without the consent of local officials, including the police and sheriff departments. See Moore, *The Kefauver Committee*, p. 113. See also "Big-Time Rackets Spread Out," pp. 18–19.

29. The leniency with which the arrested neophyte bookie is eventually treated in Alson's *Confessions of an Ivy League Bookie*, pp. 203–28, is illustrative of the attitude of the criminal justice system toward bookies.

30. Ibid., pp. 158–70.

Chapter 9

1. Roberts and Olsen, *Winning Is the Only Thing*, p. 111.

2. *New York Times*, December 29, 1958, pp. 1ff.; "The Best Football Game Ever Played."

3. Roberts and Olsen, *Winning Is the Only Thing*, p. 111; *Sports Illustrated*, January 5, 1959, pp. 12ff.; *New York Times*, December 29, 1958, pp. 1ff.

4. For a detailed, if hypercritical, history of the National Football League, see Harris, *The League*.

5. Ibid., pp. 45–46.

6. Moldea, *Interference*, pp. 89–91.

7. Ibid., pp. 39–41.

8. O'Brien, *Bad Bet*, p. 239; Moldea, *Interference*, pp. 45–50, Rooney quoted on p. 48.

9. Moldea, *Interference*, pp. 46, 68–71. McBride was determined to give his new team an advantage over its competition. With league rules limiting each squad to forty players, he authorized Coach Brown to hire an additional dozen or so backup players who practiced with the team and were prepared to step in quickly if a regular player was injured. To get around league rules prohibiting the payment of salaries to such individuals, McBride hired them as taxi cab drivers and paid them lucrative wages. From this practice was derived the term *taxi squad* for the eight players now permitted to be employed by each NFL team beyond the current game limit of forty-five players.

10. Ibid., pp. 68–69.

11. Ibid., pp. 51–56, Baugh quoted on p. 56.

12. Ibid., pp. 57–60.

13. Ibid., p. 65.

14. Ibid., pp. 63–65.

15. Ibid., p. 63.

16. O'Brien, *Bad Bet,* pp. 233–38; Roberts and Olsen, *Winning Is the Only Thing,* pp. 103–10.

17. O'Brien, *Bad Bet,* pp. 234–35.

18. Rosen, *Scandals of '51,* p. 226.

19. Tax, "The Facts about the Fixes"; "League Scandal"; *New York Times,* March 18, 1961, p. 1.

20. *New York Times,* June 20, 1961, p. 1; Rosen, *Scandals of '51,* pp. 234–35; "Gamblers' Game."

21. Rosen, *Scandals of '51,* pp. 234–35.

22. *New York Times,* January 11, 1954, p. 1; January 12, 1954, p. 24; March 25, 1954, p. 36; June 25, 1954, p. 34.

23. Rosen, *Scandals of '51,* p. 235; Wolf, *Foul!,* pp. 68–70.

24. Molinas was admitted to the New York State Bar in 1958, but not before a thorough review of his banishment from the NBA. The Bar concluded that he had not been found guilty of a crime—a grand jury had refused to indict him—and therefore could not be denied admission to the Bar.

25. Wolf, *Foul!,* pp. 52–57. Wolf's book describes in detail the agonizing story of Hawkins, who was eventually exonerated and became a star player with the NBA Phoenix Suns. See Davies, *America's Obsession,* pp. 184–94, for a concise summary of the story. In 1992 Hawkins was inducted into the Basketball Hall of Fame.

26. *New York Times,* January 3, 1961, p. 35; January 12, 1961, p. 33.

27. *New York Times,* January 12, 1961, p. 33.

28. *New York Times,* February 12, 1963, p. 4; August 6, 1975, p. 18.

29. *New York Times,* August 5, 1975, p. 34; August 6, 1975, p. 18; Wolf, *Foul!,* pp. 70–71.

30. Editorial, *Sports Illustrated,* March 27, 1961, p. 19.

31. Kirby, *Fumble,* pp. 17–30.

32. Quoted in Jenkins, "A Debatable Football Scandal," p. 19.

33. Kirby, *Fumble,* pp. 61–82.

34. Graham, "The Story of a College Football Fix."

35. Kirby, *Fumble,* pp. 83–134.

36. Jenkins, "A Debatable Football Scandal."

37. Kirby, *Fumble,* pp. 170–205.

38. Harris, *The League,* pp. 22–27; Moldea, *Interference,* pp. 109–27.

39. Maule, "Players Are Not Just People," pp. 22–23; "Judgment Day"; Moldea, *Interference,* pp. 109–27.

40. Maraniss, *When Pride Still Mattered,* pp. 336–42, Hornung quoted on p. 337.

41. *New York Times,* April 18, 1963, p. 1.

42. Ibid., p. 41; Maraniss, *When Pride Still Mattered,* p. 340.

43. *New York Times,* April 18, 1963, p. 41; April 19, 1963, p. 32.

44. Cohane, "Why Pro Football Must Live with Sin," p. 70.

45. Hornung quoted in Maraniss, *When Pride Still Mattered,* p. 338.

46. Moldea, *Interference,* pp. 206–17.

47. Ibid., pp. 215–16.

48. Ibid., p. 216.

49. Wadsworth, *Farewell Jimmy the Greek,* p. 146.

50. Betting a middle is roughly comparable to what arbitragers attempt to do on the stock or bond markets—make money when the price of a security fluctuates. The classic case of such a "middle" was the 1978 Super Bowl between the Dallas Cowboys and the Pittsburgh Steelers. The Steelers opened as a 3-point favorite, and their popularity with bettors forced the line to 5. Many savvy bettors who had taken the Steelers as a 3-point underdog then bet on the Cowboys when it reached 4 1/2. The final score, much to the dismay of the bookmakers, was 35–31, which meant that these bright bettors collected on both bets. The final score had landed in the happy middle.

51. Wadsworth, *Farewell Jimmy the Greek*, p. 149.

Chapter 10

1. Elliott, *History of Nevada*, pp. 84–89; Davies, *The Maverick Spirit*, pp. 3–11.

2. Elliott, *History of Nevada*, pp. 273–306.

3. Ibid., pp. 170–209; Raymond, *George Wingfield*, p. 46.

4. Moody, "Early Years of Casino Gambling in Nevada," pp. 49–63.

5. Turner, *Gamblers' Money*, pp. 31–38; Moody, "Early History of Casino Gambling in Nevada," pp. 54–56; Elliott, *History of Nevada*, pp. 278–82.

6. Raymond, *George Wingfield*, pp. 192–99.

7. *Las Vegas Review Journal*, December 10, 1930, p. 3.

8. Moody, "Early Years of Casino Gambling in Nevada," pp. 56–61.

9. Elliott, *History of Nevada*, p. 278.

10. The best summary of this outrage can be found in the critical treatment of gambling and divorce by Ostrander, *Nevada, the Great Rotten Borough*; see also Turner, *Gamblers' Money*, pp. 36–38; and Lewis, *Sagebrush Casinos*, pp. 55–60.

11. For a perceptive analysis of these factors, see William A. Douglass, "Musings of a Native Son."

12. Elliott, *History of Nevada*, pp. 200, 220.

13. Raymond, *George Wingfield*, p. 195.

14. Davies, *The Maverick Spirit*; Elliott, *History of Nevada*, pp. 326–38.

15. Moody, "Early Years of Casino Gambling in Nevada," pp. 98–291.

16. Ibid., pp. 323–72; Elliott, *History of Nevada*, pp. 307–24; Davies, *Maverick Spirit*, pp. 5–6.

17. Jennings, *We Only Kill Each Other*, pp. 148–64; Moehring, *Resort City in the Sunbelt*, pp. 47–49; Reid and Demaris, *Green Felt Jungle*, pp. 14–34; Moody, "Early Years of Casino Gambling in Nevada," pp. 295–300.

18. Siegel quoted in Reid and Demaris, *Green Felt Jungle*, p. 23.

19. Lacy, *Little Man*, pp. 150–58; Reid and Demaris, *Green Felt Jungle*, pp. 23–34.

20. Lacy, *Little Man*, pp. 150–58; Jennings, *We Only Kill Each Other*, pp. 165–207; Lewis, *Sagebrush Casinos*, pp. 197–99.

21. Lang, *Sports Betting 101*, p. 34; Scarne, *Scarne's New Complete Guide to Gambling*, pp. 37–38.

22. Lang, *Sports Betting 101*, p. 35.

23. Ibid., pp. 34–35; interview with Sonny Reizner; interview with Scotty Schettler.

24. Vacaro quoted in Manteris, *Super Bookie*, pp. 33–35.

25. Hannifin quoted in Pileggi, *Casino*, p. 191.

26. Lang, *Sports Betting 101*, p. 34.

27. Ibid.

28. For concise summaries of the impact of television upon sports, see Roberts and Olsen, *Winning Is the Only Thing*, pp. 113–31; or Davies, *America's Obsession*, pp. 63–99. Rader's *In Its Own Image* is the authoritative book-length study of the subject.

29. Banker, *Banker's Book of Sports Betting*, pp. 1–18; Manteris, *Super Bookie*, pp. 98–99; Plummer, "On the Job," pp. 31–33; interview with Lem Banker.

30. Banker, *Banker's Book of Sports Betting*, pp. 11–14.

31. Professional sports gamblers tend to dismiss Jimmy the Greek as a self-serving promoter with only average handicapping skills. Not surprisingly, that is not the view that appears in his autobiography, *Jimmy the Greek*. For an even more idolatrous view, see Wadsworth, *Farewell Jimmy the Greek*; for a more balanced view, see Manteris, *Super Bookie*, pp. 99–100. Quotation from Rogin, "The Greek Who Makes the Odds," p. 64.

32. Quoted in *Jimmy the Greek*, p. 100.

33. Ibid.

34. Rogin, "The Greek Who Makes the Odds," pp. 56–58.

35. Pileggi, *Casino*, pp. 11–32.

36. Quoted in ibid., pp. 190–92.

37. Quoted in ibid., p. 192.

38. Ibid., p. 12.

39. Quoted in ibid., p. 192.

40. Manteris, "Nostalgia for the Good Ol' Days," p. 8.

41. O'Brien, *Bad Bet*, pp. 186–211, 248–54.

42. "The Biggest Game in Town," p. 30.

Chapter 11

1. Olshan, *Winning Theories of Sports Handicapping*, pp. 30–34; see also Moldea, *Interference*, pp. 60–63.

2. Martin is quoted in Sasuly, *Bookies and Bettors*, p. 199; see also Lang, *Sports Betting 101*, p. 37; and Manteris, *Super Bookie*, pp. 95–97, for a discussion of Martin's contribution to the arcane craft of odds making.

3. Rogin, "The Greek Who Makes the Odds."

4. *Jimmy the Greek*, pp. 108–13.

5. Ibid., p. 111. Quotation from Boyle, "The Bookies Close Up Shop," p. 20.

6. Interview with Lem Banker.

7. Manteris, *Super Bookie*, pp. 99–100.

8. Wadsworth, *Farewell Jimmy the Greek*, pp. 116–282.

9. *Jimmy the Greek*, pp. 145–56.

10. In 1980 the sports book director at the Castaways in Las Vegas, Sonny Reizner, attracted worldwide attention when he posted odds on "who shot J.R.?" The popular television series *Dallas* ended its season in May 1980 with the devious "hero" J. R. Ewing (played by Larry Hagman) being shot by an unknown assailant. This left the television audience to wait until November to find out who from a large cast of possibilities had plugged the television villain Americans loved to hate. Reizner posted his odds (with a $300 maximum bet limit) in a whimsical fashion—he even listed Dallas Cowboy coach Tom Landry at 500–1. Reizner was astounded by the attention his stunt drew. Bettors attempted to call in bets from as far away as Australia (they were rejected under Nevada law forbidding telephone wagers). As Reizner

recalls, "Never did I dream that the impact of this little scheme would reach such huge proportions. Newspapers from all parts of the country posted the line. . . . The telephones never stopped ringing. . . . Some people actually flew to Las Vegas to bet. Little old ladies from Iowa wanted to bet. Baptist ministers wanted to bet. Rabbis wanted to bet. . . ." As a result of this curious episode, the Nevada Board of Gaming Control changed its policies to restrict sports books to accepting bets only on sports contests and horse races. So books could no longer post odds on the outcome of elections and, of course, the outcome of television dramas. *The Best of Sonny Reizner*, pp. 167–69; "Now It Can Be Told: Shedunit." By the time CBS finally aired the shows revealing the culprit to be Kristin Sheppard, J.R.'s sister-in-law, with whom he had been having an affair, she had emerged on Reizner's board as the favorite at 2–1. Who says Nevada gamblers are poor handicappers?

11. *Jimmy the Greek*, p. 151.

12. Quoted in Kahn, "Sports," p. 16.

13. Ibid., pp. 12–22. For a sampling of Snyder's column, see the *Las Vegas Sun*, February 3, 1965; August 16, 1969; September 7, 1969; October 1, 1970; March 1, 1973; and May 6, 1977. The quality of the writing—often using one- and two-sentence paragraphs complete with the inevitable three dots—is consistently mediocre. The only attraction for even a halfway intelligent sports fan would be the betting recommendations.

14. Wadsworth, *Farewell Jimmy the Greek*, p. 172, and see the pictorial section for a reprint of the cartoon.

15. Ibid., pp. 226–36.

16. Ibid., pp. 231–32.

17. Ibid., pp. 237–55, provides Snyder's spin on things, including his claim that he was a "victim of a network conspiracy." Among the things Snyder was quoted as saying, and which he did not deny, were: "They've [African American athletes] got everything, if they take over coaching like everybody wants them to there's not going to be anything left for the whites. I mean all the players are black. . . . The black talent is beautiful. It's great. It's out there. The only thing left for the whites is a couple of coaching jobs." This was because of selective breeding of slaves: "I'm telling you that the black is the better athlete, and he is bred to be the better athlete, because this goes back all the way to the Civil War when during the slave trading . . . the slave owner would breed his big black to his big woman so that he could have a big black kid, you see. I mean that's where it all started." For a sampling of the commentary on this event, see Rowe, "The Greek Chorus"; Berkow, "The Greek and the Preacher"; Wicker, "The Greatest Tragedy"; Anderson, "Greek Loses an Out Bet"; "An Oddsmaker's Odd Views"; and "Sound Bite Sidelines Jimmy the Greek."

18. *Las Vegas Sun*, April 22, 1996, p. 1B.

19. Ibid.

20. Manteris, *Super Bookie*, p. 99.

21. Quoted in Strine and Isaacs, *Covering the Spread*, p. 22.

22. Ibid., p. 245.

23. Ziegel, "He Draws the Super Bowl Line"; Zacks, "The Linemakers"; Maas, "Coffin Corner: Half a Billion Dollars on the Super Bowl."

24. Strine and Isaacs, *Covering the Spread*, pp. 21–22; Zacks, "The Linemakers," pp. 89–90.

25. Zacks, "The Linemakers," p. 89; interview with Lem Banker.

26. Quoted in Deford, "Laying It All on the Line."

27. Cook, "If Roxborough Says the Spread Is 7, It's 7," pp. 356–57.

28. Deford, "Laying It All on the Line," p. 54; Zacks, "The Linemakers," p. 89. See also Nover, "Michael 'Roxy' Roxborough: Superstar of the Industry," in *Las Vegas Sportsbeat*, pp. 61–64.

29. Zacks, "The Linemakers," p. 92; Cook, "If Roxborough Says the Spread Is 7, It's 7," pp. 356–58.

30. Sippl, "How the Line Is Set."

31. Nover, "Touts," in *Las Vegas Sportsbeat*, pp. 72–79.

32. Ibid; Banker, *Banker's Book of Sports Betting*, p. 28. See also "Touts or Louts," a 1987 *Sports Illustrated* essay that estimated that various tout services had a minimum of 100,000 customers. The best single study on this subject is a lengthy investigative report by Rick Reilly, "Ripoffs."

33. Kirsch, "Bettors Beware," quotation on p. 80.

34. One of the most prominent touts during the 1990s was Mike Warren, who operated a large national service out of Baltimore. For an analysis of his methods and his less-than-spectacular success level during the short span of time he advertised as his November "Turkey Shoot," see "Plucked Turkey."

35. Konik, "1-900-N-F-L-S-C-A-M," p. 119.

36. Ibid., p. 121.

37. "Super Sunday, Super Bets: Offshore Sports-Betting Services Boom."

Chapter 12

1. *Commission on the Review of the National Policy Toward Gambling, Hearings on Sports Betting.*

2. Davies, "Nevada's Special Rebel: Jerry Tarkanian," pp. 267–68.

3. "The Biggest Game in Town," pp. 30–31.

4. Ibid., p. 31.

5. Ibid., pp. 31–51.

6. Ibid., pp. 40–41.

7. Putnam, "Another View of Gambling: It's Good For You," p. 56.

8. "Unartful Dodger," p. 28.

9. MacGreger, "Downward Spiral"; Schlichter quoted in "Unartful Dodger," p. 28.

10. Sokolove, *Hustle*, pp. 83–99, Morgan quoted on p. 64; Rose, *Pete Rose: My Story*, p. 178.

11. Sokolove, *Hustle*, p. 196.

12. Ibid., pp. 252–53.

13. Ibid., pp. 253–54; Reston, *Collision at Home Plate*, pp. 259–312.

14. Reston, *Collision at Home Plate*, pp. 306–8.

15. Ibid., p. 308.

16. Ibid., p. 310.

17. Ibid., p. 313.

18. Ibid., pp. 311–12; Davies, *America's Obsession*, pp. 249–50; Rose quoted in Sokolove, *Hustle*, p. 283.

19. *Final Report, The National Gambling Impact Study Commission*, pp. 3-8–3-11.

20. See *St. Louis Post-Dispatch*, March 31, 1999, for an extensive article summarizing the NCAA position on college sports gambling. See also Saum, "Sports Wagering Information

Packet"; and Saum's testimony before the National Gambling Impact Study Commission, November 10, 1998, Las Vegas. Quotations from *NCAA News*, July 5, 1999, p. 5.

21. Dobson quoted in *New York Times*, May 5, 2000; *Final Report, The National Gambling Impact Study Commission*, p. 3-10.

22. Snyder, *Jimmy the Greek*, p. 216; see pp. 216–22 for his negative views on regular casino games.

23. Both commentaries were found on the Internet site for *Vegas Insider*, June 30, 1999, <www.vegasinsider.com>.

24. *Final Report, The National Gambling Impact Study Commission*, pp. 3-8–3-99.

Epilogue

1. *Reno Gazette-Journal*, January 18, 1998, p. 1.
2. McGraw, "The National Bet," p. 55.
3. Ibid., p. 51.
4. Quoted in "Don't Bet on Gambling Reform Anytime Soon."
5. The literature on compulsive gambling is enormous, but it is accurately summarized in O'Brien, *Bad Bet*; and *Final Report, The National Gambling Impact Study Commission*, pp. 4-1–4-20.
6. Smith, "The 'To Do' over What to Do about Sports Gambling," p. 18.
7. Dionne, "'He's Just a Workin' Stiff," p. 40.
8. Newman, "The Ideology of Social Problems: Gambling, a Case Study," p. 549.
9. Johnson, "A Sure Bet to Lower Debt."
10. Eadington, "Comments before National Association of Athletic Directors."

Appendix

1. Critics of sports gambling often refuse to admit that any analogies exist between legitimate investment strategies and gambling strategies. Sports bettors, however, use strategies such as hedging for the same reason that stock market investors use put and call options in their portfolios: to insure profits against future uncertainties. For example, a sports bettor may play a three-team parlay on NFL teams. He chooses Teams A, B, and C on Sunday morning to defeat their respective opponents AX, BX, and CX. He wagers $100 on the three-team parlay and will win $600 if all three teams win. The first two games are afternoon games, but the last game is the NFL's Sunday Night Game of the Week. Teams A and B win, finishing their games about an hour before Team C takes the field. The bettor now has options: he can hedge his bet, or "lay off" in gambling terms. His options are, first, do nothing. If Team C wins he is +$600; if Team C loses to Team CX, he is −$100, losing his original wager. He is at risk because of the uncertainty of Team C. His second option is to hedge the bet by betting $300 straight up on Team CX. If Team C wins now, he wins $600 on his original parlay, loses $300 on his hedge bet, and is +$300 for the day. If Team CX wins, he loses his parlay for −$100, but wins the straight up bet on Team CX for +$300 and is +$200 for the day. The bettor has completed a successful simple hedge. No matter which team wins the Sunday night game, he has assured himself of a profit by using the different starting times for the games to create a no-lose situation.

The sports bettor may also use a form of arbitrage (buying and selling the same commodity at the same time for different prices to create a profit), which in gambling parlance is "creating a middle." This is usually done with teaser parlays. Successfully creating middles is the best of all worlds for the sports bettor, although middles are far more complex than basic hedges. The bettor still cannot lose whether Team C or CX wins the third game, but the added attraction is that if the winning point spread falls within the middle he has created, he will win both sides of the bet. The techniques available in the sports betting market are as numerous and esoteric as those available to the Wall Street broker—and equally legitimate in Nevada's legal sports books.

Bibliography

Books

Albanese, Jay. *Organized Crime in America*. 2nd ed. Cincinnati: Anderson Publishing Company, 1989.

————, ed. *Contemporary Issues in Organized Crime*. Monsey, N.Y.: Criminal Justice Press, 1995.

Alexander, Charles C. *Our Game: An American Baseball History*. New York: Henry Holt, 1991.

Alson, Peter. *Confessions of an Ivy League Bookie: A True Tale of Love and the Vig*. New York: Crown Publishers, 1996.

Asinof, Eliot. *Eight Men Out: The Black Sox and the 1919 World Series*. 2nd ed. New York: Henry Holt, 1987.

Asinof, Eliot, and Jim Bouton. *Strike Zone*. New York: Viking Press, 1994.

Balboni, Alan R. *Beyond the Mafia: Italian Americans and the Development of Las Vegas*. Reno and Las Vegas: University of Nevada Press, 1996.

Banker, Lem, and Frederick C. Klein. *Lem Banker's Book of Sports Betting*. New York: E. F. Dutton, 1986.

Bartlett, Richard C. *The Direct Option*. College Station: Texas A & M University Press, 1994.

Bee, Clair. *Championship Ball*. New York: Grossett and Dunlap, 1948.

————. *Strike Three*. New York: Grossett and Dunlap, 1949.

Breslin, Jimmy. *Damon Runyon*. New York: Ticknor and Fields, 1991.

Cardoza, Avery. *The Basics of Winning Sports Betting*. Cooper Station, N.Y.: Cardoza Publishing Company, 1998.

Chafetz, Henry. *Play the Devil: A History of Gambling in the United States from 1492 to 1955*. New York: Clarkson N. Potter, 1960.

Clark, Tom. *The World of Damon Runyon*. New York: Harper and Row, 1978.

Cooney, John. *The Annenbergs*. New York: Simon and Schuster, 1982.

Daniels, Tony. *The Wise Guy's Bible*. Las Vegas: Tony Daniels Enterprises, 1993.

Davies, Richard O. *America's Obsession: Sports and Society since 1945*. Fort Worth, Tex.: Harcourt Brace, 1994.

————, ed. *The Maverick Spirit: Building the New Nevada*. Reno and Las Vegas: University of Nevada Press, 1999.

Dickerson, Mark G. *Compulsive Gamers*. London and New York: Longman's, 1984.

D'Itri, Patricia Ward. *Damon Runyon*. Boston: Twayne Publishers, 1982.

Elliott, Russell R., with William D. Rowley. *History of Nevada*. 2nd ed. Lincoln: University of Nebraska Press, 1987.

Fabian, Ann. *Card Sharps and Bucket Shops: Gambling in Nineteenth-Century America.* New York: Routledge, 1999.

Findlay, John M. *People of Chance: Gambling in American Society from Jamestown to Las Vegas.* New York: Oxford University Press, 1986.

Fontenay, Charles L. *Estes Kefauver: A Biography.* Knoxville: University of Tennessee Press, 1980.

Fountain, Charles. *Sportswriter: The Life and Times of Grantland Rice.* New York: Oxford University Press, 1993.

Gage, Nicholas, ed. *Mafia, U.S.A.* Chicago: Playboy Press, 1972.

Gorman, Joseph Bruce. *Kefauver: A Political Biography.* New York: Oxford University Press, 1971.

Gorn, Eliott J., and Warren Goldstein. *A Brief History of American Sports.* New York: Hill and Wang, 1993.

Grossman, Larry. *You Can Bet On It!: How to Get Maximum Value from Your Gambling Dollar!* Las Vegas: Grossman Enterprises, 1994.

Halberstam, David. *The Fifties.* New York: Villard Books, 1993.

Harris, David. *The League: The Rise and Decline of the NFL.* New York: Bantam Books, 1986.

Hoyt, Edwin P. *A Gentleman of Broadway.* Boston: Little, Brown, 1964.

Hutchens, John K., ed. *The Gambler's Bedside Book.* New York: Taplinger, 1977.

Inabinett, Mark. *Grantland Rice and His Heroes: The Sportswriter as Mythmaker of the 1920s.* Knoxville: University of Tennessee Press, 1994.

James, Bill. *The Bill James Historical Baseball Abstract.* New York: Villard Books, 1986.

James, Marquis. *The Life of Andrew Jackson.* New York: Bobbs Merrill, 1938.

Jennings, Dean. *We Only Kill Each Other: The Life and Bad Times of Bugsy Siegel.* Englewood Cliffs, N.J.: Prentice Hall, 1967.

Katcher, Leo. *The Big Bankroll: The Life and Times of Arnold Rothstein.* 1959. New York: Da Capo Press, 1994.

King, Rufus. *Gambling and Organized Crime.* Washington, D.C.: Public Affairs Press, 1969.

Kirby, James. *Fumble: Bear Bryant, Wally Butts, and the Great College Football Scandal.* New York: Dell Books, 1986.

Konik, Michael. *The Man with the $100,000 Breasts.* Las Vegas: Huntington Press, 1999.

Lacy, Robert. *Little Man: Meyer Lansky and the Gangster Life.* Boston: Little, Brown, 1991.

Lang, Arne K. *Sports Betting 101: Making Sense of the Bookie Business and the Business of Beating the Bookie.* Las Vegas: GBC Press, 1992.

Levine, Peter, ed. *American Sport: A Documentary History.* Englewood Cliffs, N.J.: Prentice Hall, 1989.

Lewis, Oscar. *Sagebrush Casinos: The Story of Legal Gambling in Nevada.* New York: Doubleday, 1953.

Longstreet, Stephen. *Win or Lose: A Social History of Gambling in America.* Indianapolis: Bobbs-Merrill, 1977.

Manteris, Art, with Rick Talley. *Super Bookie: Inside Las Vegas Sports Gambling.* Chicago: Contemporary Books, 1991.

Maraniss, David. *When Pride Still Mattered: A Life of Vince Lombardi.* New York: Simon and Schuster, 1999.

Moehring, Eugene P. *Resort City in the Sunbelt: Las Vegas 1930–1970.* Reno and Las Vegas: University of Nevada Press, 1989.

Moldea, Dan E. *Interference: How Organized Crime Influences Professional Football*. New York: William Morrow, 1989.

Moore, Jack. *The Complete Book of Sports Betting: A New No-Nonsense Approach to Sports Gambling*. Secaucus, N.J.: Carol Publishing Group, 1996.

Moore, William Howard. *The Kefauver Committee and the Politics of Crime, 1950–1952*. Columbia: University of Missouri Press, 1974.

Munting, Roger. *An Economic and Social History of Gambling in Britain and the USA*. Manchester: Manchester University Press, 1996.

Murdock, Eugene C. *Ban Johnson: Czar of Baseball*. Westport, Conn.: Greenwood Press, 1982.

Neuman, David., ed. *Esquire's Book of Gambling*. New York: Harper and Row, 1962.

Nover, Stephen. *Las Vegas Sportsbeat: Inside the World of Sports Wagering*. Las Vegas: Stephen Nover Enterprises, 1997.

O'Brien, Timothy L. *Bad Bet: The Inside Story of the Glamour, Glitz, and Danger of America's Gambling Industry*. New York: Random House, 1998.

Offit, Sidney. *Memoir of the Bookie's Son*. New York: St. Martin's Press, 1995.

Ogden, Christopher. *Legacy: A Biography of Moses and Walter Annenberg*. Boston: Little, Brown, 1999.

Olshan, Mort. *Winning Theories of Sports Betting*. New York: Simon and Schuster, 1975.

Ostrander, Gilman. *Nevada, the Great Rotten Borough, 1859–1964*. New York: Knopf, 1966.

Patrick, John. *Sports Betting: Proven Winning Systems for Football, Basketball, and Baseball*. Secaucus, N.J.: Carol Publishing Group, 1996.

Patterson, James T. *Grand Expectations: The United States, 1945–1974*. New York: Oxford University Press, 1996.

Peak, Kenneth J. *Policing America: Methods, Issues, Challenges*. Englewood Cliffs, N.J.: Prentice Hall, 1993.

Pileggi, Nicholas. *Casino*. New York: Simon and Schuster, 1995.

Putnam, Douglas T. *Controversies of the Sports World*. Westport, Conn.: Greenwood Press, 1999.

Rader, Benjamin G. *American Sports: From the Age of Folk Games to the Age of Televised Sports*. 3rd ed. Englewood Cliffs, N.J.: Prentice Hall, 1996.

———. *In Its Own Image: How Television Has Transformed Sports*. New York: Free Press, 1984.

Raymond, C. Elizabeth. *George Wingfield: Owner and Operator of Nevada*. Reno: University of Nevada Press, 1992.

Reid, Ed, and Ovid Demaris. *The Green Felt Jungle: The Truth about Las Vegas Where Organized Crime Controls Gambling—and Everything Else*. New York: Trident Press, 1963.

Reizner, Sonny. *The Best of Sonny Reizner*. Las Vegas: Marty Mendelsohn Associates, 1997.

Reston, James, Jr. *Collison at Home Plate: The Lives of Pete Rose and Bart Giamatti*. Lincoln: University of Nebraska Press, 1991.

Reuter, Peter. *Disorganized Crime: The Economics of the Visible Hand*. Cambridge, Mass.: MIT Press, 1983.

Roberts, Randy, and James S. Olsen. *Winning Is the Only Thing: Sports in America since 1945*. Baltimore: Johns Hopkins Press, 1989.

Rose, Pete, with Roger Kahn. *Pete Rose: My Story*. New York: Macmillan, 1989.

Rosecrance, John D. *Gambling without Guilt: The Legitimation of an American Pastime.* Pacific Grove, Calif.: Brooks/Cole Publishing Company, 1988.

Rosen, Charles. *Barney Polan's Game: A Novel of the 1951 Basketball Scandals.* New York: Seven Stories Press, 1998.

——. *The Scandals of '51: How the Gamblers Almost Killed College Basketball.* 1978. New York: Seven Stories Press, 1999.

Roxborough, Roxy, and Mike Rhoden. *Sports Book Management: A Guide for the Legal Bookmaker.* Las Vegas: Las Vegas Sports Consultants, 1998.

Runyon, Damon. *The Best of Damon Runyon.* Edited by Damon Runyon Jr. New York: Hart Publishing Company, 1966.

——. *More Guys and Dolls.* Introduction by Clark Kinnaird. Garden City, N.Y.: Garden City Books, 1951.

Sasuly, Richard. *Bookies and Bettors: Two Hundred Years of Gambling.* New York: Holt, Rinehart and Winston, 1982.

Savage, Jeff. *A Sure Thing? Sports and Gambling.* Minneapolis: Lerner Publishing Company, 1997.

Scarne, John. *Scarne's New Complete Guide to Gambling.* New York: Simon and Schuster, 1974.

Sellin, Thorsten, ed. *Gambling: The Annals of the American Academy of Political and Social Science.* Philadephia, 1950.

Seymour, Harold. *Baseball: The Golden Age.* New York: Oxford University Press, 1971.

Sheehan, Jack E. *The Players: The Men Who Made Las Vegas.* Reno and Las Vegas: University of Nevada Press, 1997.

Shepperson, Wilbur, ed. *East of Eden and West of Zion: Essays on Nevada.* Reno: Univerity of Nevada Press, 1989.

Silberstang, Edwin. *How to Gamble and Win.* New York: Franklin Watts, 1979.

Smith, Dwight C. *The Mafia Mystique.* New York: Basic Books, 1975.

Snyder, Jimmy. *Jimmy the Greek: By Himself.* Chicago: Playboy Press, 1975.

Sokolove, Michael Y. *Hustle: The Myth, Life, and Lies of Pete Rose.* New York: Simon and Schuster, 1990.

Sperber, Murray. *Onward to Victory: The Crises that Shaped College Sports.* New York: Henry Holt, 1998.

Strine, Gerald, and Neil D. Isaacs. *Covering the Spread: How to Bet Pro Football.* New York: Random House, 1978.

Turner, Wallace. *Gamblers' Money: The New Force in American Life.* Boston: Houghton Mifflin, 1965.

Wadsworth, Ginger, with Jimmy Snyder. *Farewell Jimmy the Greek: Wizard of Odds.* Austin, Tex.: Eakin Press, 1996.

Wagner, Hans-Peter. *Puritan Attitudes toward Recreation in Early Seventeenth-Century New England.* New York: Peter Lang, 1982.

Watson, Mary Ann. *Defining Visions: Television and the American Experience since 1945.* Ft. Worth, Tex.: Harcourt Brace, 1998.

Winston, Stuart, and Harriett Harris. *Nation of Gamblers: America's Billion-Dollar-a-Day Habit.* Englewood Cliffs, N.J.: Prentice Hall, 1984.

Wolf, David. *Foul! The Connie Hawkins Story.* New York: Holt, Rinehart and Winston, 1972.

Articles

"Again, the Fix," *Newsweek*, February 26, 1951, p. 74.

Anderson, Dave. "Greek Loses an Out Bet," *New York Times*, January 17, 1988, section IV, pp. 1, 4.

Balboni, Alan. "Moe Dalitz: Controversial Founding Father of Las Vegas," in Richard O. Davies, ed., *The Maverick Spirit: Building the New Nevada*. Reno and Las Vegas: University of Nevada Press, 1999, pp. 24–43.

"Baseball and the Crooks," *The Outlook*, October 13, 1924, pp. 235–36.

"Baseball Scandal," *The Nation*, October 13, 1920, pp. 395–96.

Bee, Clair. "I Know Why They Sold Out to the Gamblers," *Saturday Evening Post*, February 2, 1952, pp. 26–27, 76–80.

Berkow, Ira. "The Greek and the Preacher," column, *New York Times*, January 19, 1988, p. 27.

"Best Football Game Ever Played, The," *Sports Illustrated*, January 5, 1959, pp. 12ff.

Bigelow, Joe. "Inside the Gambling Industry," *American Mercury*, June 1934, pp. 214–18.

"Biggest Game in Town, The," editorial, *Sports Illustrated*, March 10, 1986, pp. 30–83.

"Big-Time Rackets Spread Out," *U.S. News and World Report*, November 10, 1952, pp. 18–19.

"Bookies and Bosses," *Newsweek*, May 15, 1939, pp. 15–16.

Boyle, Robert H. "The Bookies Close Up Shop," *Sports Illustrated*, September 3, 1962.

———. "The Brain That Gave Us the Point Spread," *Sports Illustrated*, March 10, 1986, p. 34.

Breen, Timothy H. "Horses and Gentlemen: The Cultural Significance of Gambling among the Gentry of Virginia," *William and Mary Quarterly*, April 1977, pp. 329–47.

Breslin, Jimmy. "The Fix Was On," *Saturday Evening Post*, February 26, 1963, pp. 15–19.

"Business as Usual," *Newsweek*, April 9, 1951, pp. 75–76.

Cave, Ray. "Portrait of a Fixer," *Sports Illustrated*, May 8, 1961, pp. 20–23.

"Cobb Gambling Scandal, The," *Sports Illustrated*, June 12, 1989, p. 20.

Cohane, Tim. "Behind the Basketball Scandal," *Look*, pp. 85ff.

———. "Why Pro Football Must Live with Sin," *Look*, July 1, 1963, pp. 64–71.

"College-Trained Bets," *Newsweek*, April 2, 1951, pp. 76–77.

Cook, John. "If Roxborough Says the Spread Is 7, It's 7," *Forbes Magazine*, September 14, 1992, pp. 350–63.

Culver, Russ. Commentary, *Vegas Insider*, May 18, 1999, <www.vegasinsider.com>.

Daley, Arthur. "Court Scandal," *New York Times*, January 31, 1945, p. 24.

———. "Menace to All Sports—The 'Fix,'" *New York Times Magazine*, January 5, 1947, pp. 16ff.

———. "Sports Are Honest: A Defense," *New York Times Magazine*, March 24, 1951, pp. 20ff.

Davies, Richard O. "Nevada's Special Rebel: Jerry Tarkanian," in Davies, ed., *The Maverick Spirit: Building the New Nevada*. Reno and Las Vegas: University of Nevada Press, 1999.

Davis, Jerome. "Gambling by Wire," *Christian Century*, April 23, 1930, pp. 525–30.

Deford, Frank. "Laying It All on the Line," *Newsweek*, January 27, 1992, p. 54.

———. "A Long Shot Takes Leave," *Newsweek*, May 6, 1996, p. 74.

DeVos, Richard M., and Helen Devos. "The Power Couple," *Mother Jones*, November 1998, p. 56.

Dionne, Roger. "He's Just a Workin' Stiff," *Sports Illustrated*, February 25, 1980, pp. 38–47.

"Don't Bet on Gambling Reform Anytime Soon," *U.S. News and World Report*, June 14, 1999, p. 26.

Douglass, William A. "Musings of a Native Son," in Wilbur Shepperson, ed., *East of Eden,
     West of Zion: Essays on Nevada*. Reno: University of Nevada Press, 1989, pp. 95–110.
"Dribble Time," *Newsweek*, December 18, 1944, p. 84.
"Fixed Again," *Newsweek*, March 27, 1961, p. 84.
"Flaw in the Diamond," *Literary Digest*, October 9, 1920, pp. 12–13.
Flower, Joe. "A Visit to the Oracle of Las Vegas," *Sport Magazine*, February 1982, p. 21.
Flynt, Josiah. "The Pool-Room Spider and the Gambling Fly," *Cosmopolitan*, March 1907,
     pp. 513–21.
"Football: Payoff or Playoff?" *Newsweek*, December 23, 1946, p. 82.
"For Honest Baseball," *The Outlook*, October 6, 1920, pp. 119–20.
Frank, Stanley. "Basketball's Big Wheel," *Saturday Evening Post*, January 15, 1949, pp. 29,
     132–34.
————. "Easy Pickings?" *American Magazine*, October 1939, pp. 44–45.
Friedman, Charles. "Portrait of a New York Bookie," *New York Times Magazine*, September
     7, 1947, pp. 18ff.
Fullerton, Hugh S. "Baseball on Trial," *The New Republic*, October 20, 1920, pp. 183–84.
"Gamblers' Game," *Newsweek*, June 5, 1961, p. 86.
"Gamblers Move in on College Sports," *Saturday Evening Post*, December 23, 1944, p. 80.
"Gambling in the Garden," *Time*, October 30, 1944, p. 81.
Gardner, Paul, and Allan Gould. "The Brain of the Bookies," *Colliers Magazine*, October 25,
     1947, pp. 106–9.
Getter, Doyle K. "How To Bet on Sports—and Win," *American Mercury*, July 1951, pp. 79–88.
Graham, Frank, Jr. "The Story of a College Football Fix," *Saturday Evening Post*, March 23,
     1963, pp. 80–83.
Haller, Mark H. "Bootleggers as Businessmen: From City Slums to City Builders," in David
     E. Kyvig, ed., *Law, Alcohol, and Order: Perspectives on National Prohibition*. Westport,
     Conn.: Greenwood Press, 1985, pp. 139–57.
————. "The Bruno Family of Philadephia: Organized Crime as a Regulatory Agency," in
     Robert J. Kelly, et al., eds., *Handbook of Organized Crime in the United States*. Westport,
     Conn.: Greenwood Press, 1994, pp. 153–66.
————. "The Changing Structure of American Gambling in the Twentieth Century," *Journal
     of Social Issues* 35 (1979): 87–113.
————. "Policy Gambling, Entertainment, and the Emergence of Black Politics: Chicago
     from 1900 to 1940," *Journal of Social History*, Summer 1991, pp. 719–39.
Jacoby, Oswald. "The Forms of Gambling," *Annals of the American Academy of Political
     Science and Social Science*, Philadelphia, 1950, pp. 39–45.
Jenkins, Dan. "A Debatable Football Scandal in the Southeast," *Sports Illustrated*, March 28,
     1963, pp. 17ff.
Johnson, William. "A Sure Bet to Lower Debt," *Sports Illustrated*, September 12, 1991, p. 144.
"Judge Landis, the New Czar of Baseballdom," *Literary Digest*, December 4, 1920, pp. 47–48.
"Judgment Day," *Newsweek*, April 29, 1963, p. 83.
Kahn, Roger. "Sports," *Esquire Magazine*, September 1971, pp. 12–22.
Kilboorg, Gregory. "What Makes People Gamble," *New York Times Magazine*, September 7,
     1952, pp. 26ff.
Kirsch, Richard. "Bettors Beware," *Sport Magazine*, September 1981, pp. 79–84.

Konik, Michael. "1–900-N-F-L-S-C-A-M," *Forbes Magazine*, supplemental issue, November 21, 1994, pp. 119–21.

Lardner, John. "Money to Burn," *Newsweek*, August 21, 1944, p. 78.

———. "Remember the Black Sox?" *Saturday Evening Post*, April 30, 1938, pp. 14–15, 82–87.

———. "The Substance of a Man's Daydreams," *Newsweek*, April 2, 1951.

———. "Touchdown by the Slide Rule," *Nation's Business*, October 1950, p. 52.

"League Scandal," *Time*, April 24, 1963, p. 45.

"Let's Not Duck the Real Issue in Sports Mess," *Saturday Evening Post*, March 24, 1952, p. 10.

Looney, John. "A Big Loss for a Gambling Quarterback," *Sports Illustrated*, May 30, 1983, pp. 30–31.

———. "The Line Pulled Out of a Hat," *Sports Illustrated*, March 10, 1986, pp. 58–61.

Maas, Peter. "Coffin Corner: Half a Billion Dollars on the Super Bowl," *Esquire*, February 1992, p. 63.

MacGreger, Scott. "Downward Spiral," *Cincinnati Enquirer*, July 2, 2000, pp. 1, 18.

Manteris, Art. "Nostalgia for the Good Ol' Days," *Players Guide to Las Vegas Sports Books*, January 2000, pp. 8–12.

Martin, W. Thorton. "The Pig-Skin Game," *Saturday Evening Post*, February 8, 1936, pp. 8–9ff.

Maule, Tex. "Players Are Not Just People," *Sports Illustrated*, April 29, 1963, pp. 22ff.

McGraw, Dan. "The National Bet," *U.S. News and World Report*, April 7, 1997, pp. 50–55.

Newman, Otto. "The Ideology of Social Problems: Gambling, a Case Study," *Canadian Review of Sociology and Anthropology* 11 (1975): 541–50.

Nover, Stephen. "Commission Proposal Does More Harm Than Good," *Vegas Insider*, May 18, 1999, <www.vegasinsider.com>.

"Now It Can Be Told: Shedunit," *Time*, December 1, 1980, p. 70.

"Oddsmaker's Odd Views, An," *Sports Illustrated*, January 25, 1988, p. 7.

Olshan, Mort. Editorial, *The Gold Sheet*, January 24, 1997.

"Plucked Turkey," *Sports Illustrated*, December 7, 1992, p. 12.

Plummer, William. "On the Job: Lem Banker of Las Vegas," *People Weekly*, December 12, 1983, pp. 31–33.

"Press and the Gambling Craze, The," *Christian Century*, September 24, 1930, pp. 1142–44.

Putnam, Pat. "Another View of Gambling: It's Good For You," *Sports Illustrated*, March 10, 1986, p. 56.

Reilly, Rick. "Ripoffs," *Sports Illustrated*, November 18, 1991, pp. 115–24.

Riess, Steven A. "Professional Sports and New York's Tammany Machine, 1890–1920." In Riess, ed., *Major Problems in American Sport History*. Boston: Houghton Mifflin, 1997, pp. 159–67.

Rogin, Gil. "The Greek Who Makes the Odds," *Sports Illustrated*, December 18, 1961, pp. 56–65.

Rowe, Jonathan. "The Greek Chorus," *Washington Monthly*, April, 1988, pp. 31–34.

"Schlichter Stumbles," *Sports Illustrated*, January 26, 1987, p. 7.

Sheridan, Danny. "The Spread's the Point," *Sport*, July 1991, pp. 75–76.

Sippl, Chuck. "How the Line Is Set," *The Gold Sheet*, October 25, 1986.

Smith, Garry J. "The 'To Do' over What to Do about Sports Gambling: Sanitizing a Tainted Activity." In William R. Eadington and Judy A. Cornelius, *Gambling and Public Policy: International Perspectives*. Reno: University of Nevada Institute for the Study of Gambling and Commerical Gaming, 1991, pp. 13–38.

"Sound Bite Sidelines Jimmy the Greek," *Newsweek*, January 25, 1988, p. 63.

"Spoiling a Sport," *Literary Digest*, March 14, 1934, pp. 48–49.

"Sports Are Honest: A Defense," *New York Times Magazine*, March 4, 1951.

Stern, Hal. "The Man Who Makes the Odds," *Chance*, Winter 1999, pp. 15–21.

"Super Sunday, Super Bets: Offshore Sports-Betting Services Boom," *U.S. News and World Report*, January 26, 1998, pp. 54–55.

Tax, Jeremiah. "The Facts about the Fixes," *Sports Illustrated*, March 27, 1961, pp. 18–19.

"There's a Straight Man Born Every Minute," *Newsweek*, April 10, 1972, p. 48.

"Throwing It All Away," *New York Times*, March 22, 1998, pp. 27ff.

"Touts or Louts," *Sports Illustrated*, December 7, 1987, p. 15.

"Unartful Dodger," *Sports Illustrated*, May 29, 2000, pp. 28–29.

Wicker, Tom. "The Greatest Tragedy," *New York Times*, January 21, 1988, p. 9.

Zacks, Richard. "The Linemakers," *Atlantic Magazine*, October 1986, pp. 89–93.

Ziegel, Vic. "He Draws the Super Bowl Line," *Sport Magazine*, January 1981, p. 50.

Newspapers and Newsletters

Cincinnati Enquirer
The Gold Sheet
Las Vegas Sun
NCAA News
New York Times
St. Louis Post-Dispatch

Documents

Collins, Lynda, and David Reiter. *"I'm Mad as Hell, and I'm Not Going to Take It Anymore."* Scottsdale, Ariz.: American Sports Publishing, 1998.

Commission on the Review of the National Policy toward Gambling, Hearings on Sports Betting. Washington, D.C.: GPO, February 19, 1975.

Extent and Nature of Gambling among College Student Athletes, The. Ann Arbor: University of Michigan, Department of Athletics, 1999.

Mendelsohn, Marty. *The Theory and Practice of Las Vegas Style Sports Betting as Taught at U.N.L.V.* Las Vegas: Marty Mendolsohn Associates, 1996.

Saum, William S. "Sports Wagering Information Packet," NCAA press packet, February 15, 1999.

———. Testimony before the National Gambling Impact Study Commission, November 10, 1998, Las Vagas. Available from NCAA national office.

Summary Document of Casino Gambling in the United States. University of Nevada, Reno: Institute for the Study of Gambling and Commerical Gaming, 1999.

Third Interim Report of the Committee to Investigate Organized Crime in Interstate Commerce. Washington, D.C.: Government Printing Office, 1952.

Interviews

Banker, Lem, April 16, 1999.
Francis, Norm (pseudonym), June 8, 1999.
Reizner, Sonny, April 17, 1999.

Rosen, Charles, March 28, 1998.
Schettler, Scotty, April 18, 1999.

Unpublished Materials

Eadington, William. "Comments before National Association of Athletic Directors," June 15, 1999. Summary available in *NCAA News*, July 5, 1999.
Moody, Eric N. "The Early Years of Casino Gambling in Nevada, 1931–1945." Ph.D. dissertation, University of Nevada, Reno, 1997.

Index